Collectible Television Memorabilia

by Dian Zillner

Photographs by Suzanne Silverthorn

77 Lower Valley Road, Atglen, PA 19310

This book is dedicated to my daughter, Suzanne Silverthorn.
One of my favorite memories is of a very young Suzanne sitting
in front of the television, sailor hat perched on her head, enjoy-
ing hours of "Popeye" cartoons. "Toot-toot."

"Family Affair Puzzle" No. 4558. © 1971
Family Affair Company. Western Publishing
Company. $10-15. ◆ *Buffy and Jody
Coloring Book*. © 1969 Family Affair
Company. Whitman-Western Publishing
Company. $10-15.

Printed in Hong Kong.
ISBN: 0-7643-0162-4

We are interested in hearing from authors with book ideas on related
subjects.

Library of Congress Cataloging-in-Publication Data

Zillner, Dian.
      Collectible television memorabilia/by Dian Zillner.
         p. cm.
      Includes bibliographical references and index.
      ISBN 0-7643-0162-4 (pbk.)
      1. Television broadcasting–United States–Collectibles. I. Title.
PN1992.8.C64Z55 1996
791.45'75'029473-dc20   96-22056
                              CIP

Notice

All of the items in this book are from private collections.
Grateful acknowledgment is made to the original producers of
the materials photographed. The copyright has been identified
for each item whenever possible. If any omission or incorrect
information is found, please notify the author or publisher and it
will be amended in any future edition of the book.

The prices listed in the captions should be used only as a
guide, and should not be used to set prices for television memorabilia. Prices vary from one section of the country to another
and also from dealer to dealer. The prices listed here are the
best estimates the author can give at the time of publication, but
prices in the collectibles field can change quickly. Neither the
author nor the publisher assumes responsibility for any losses
that might be incurred as a result of consulting this price guide.

Published by Schiffer Publishing, Ltd.
77 Lower Valley Road
Atglen, PA 19310
Phone: (610) 593-1777
Fax: (610) 593-2002

Please write for a free catalog.
This book may be purchased from the publisher.
Please include $2.95 for shipping.
Try your bookstore first.

Contents

"I Dream of Jeannie" doll made to represent Barbara Eden. The doll is 20" tall and was made by Libby in 1966. The doll has a vinyl head and hard vinyl body, rooted hair, and sleep eyes. Head is marked "c 1966/Libby." $175-225.

Gene Autry Coloring Book (#1256). © 1955 by Gene Autry. Published by Whitman Publishing Company. $25-40. ✦ Billfold © Gene Autry. $30-40.

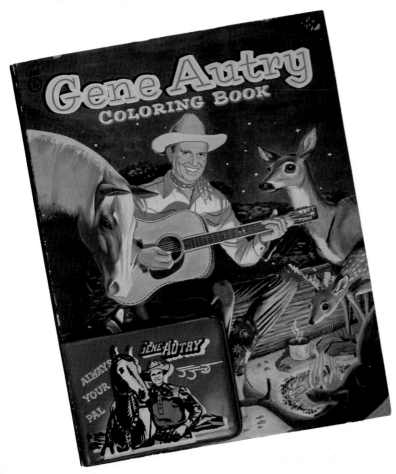

Acknowledgments

I want to express my thanks to the collectors who shared material and pictures in order to make this book possible. Special acknowledgment goes to "repeat" helpers: Elaine Price, Mary and Werner Stuecher, James Werts, Jackie Robertson, and Dora and Al Pitts. New contributors include Cindy Sabulis, Edith and James Wise, and "52 Girls."

A special "thank you" goes to the members of my family who were, once again, so helpful during the writing of this book. To my daughter, Suzanne Silverthorn, who took most of the photographs, and to my son-in-law, Mark Silverthorn, who baby-sat so she could, an extra vote of appreciation.

Acknowledgment and extra recognition is also extended to Schiffer Publishing Ltd. and its excellent staff, particularly to Sue Taylor, layout editor, and editor Leslie Bockol, who helped with this publication. Without their support and extra effort, this book would not have been possible. I would also like to thank Peter Schiffer who has yet to say "no" to one of my developed projects and who continues to offer encouragement and support and even an extension when it is needed.

"Wagon Train" trading card. © Revue Studios. © TCG Topps cards. $2-3.

Hopalong Cassidy Sticker Fun Stencil (#2191). Whitman Publishing Company. © 1951 by Hopalong Cassidy, Inc. $30-35. ◆ *Hopalong Cassidy* comic book published by Fawcett Publications, dated Sept. 1953. © Wm Boyd. $15-18.

Introduction

Collecting television memorabilia is a hobby that just keeps growing. Perhaps it is because the character collectibles, especially, bring back memories of a less stressful time in our lives; or perhaps it is because this hobby can be pursued in so many different ways. Whole collections can be built on just one character or program like "Howdy Doody," "Hopalong Cassidy," "Charlie's Angels" or "Roy Rogers." In 1959 alone, there were more than thirty-two different western programs on the three major networks, making this a substantial collecting field all by itself. Or the collector can emphasize just one era of television programing—perhaps the 1950s or the 1960s—to assemble a collection. Another interesting collection could be made using only one item from as many different programs as could be found; some collectors specialize only in the games from TV programming, or only the coloring books. Still other more mainstream collectors add television items to a larger collection of dolls, paper dolls, or toys. Whatever route is chosen, the pursuit of products made in connection with television programs continues to grow.

When purchasing items for a collection, it is important to remember that book prices are usually for products in near mint condition. A coloring book that has been used, a game that has missing pieces, or a talking toy that no longer talks should have a much lower price than that appearing in the price guide. It is up to the collector to decide if an item fits in his collection, if it is not in excellent condition. Some collectors purchase a piece in order to have the example and then "trade up" when the opportunity arises.

The prices for television memorabilia are influenced not only by condition but also by demand. Although the age of the product is important, the popularity of the series is another factor in the cost of a collectible. Items from shows like "The Addams Family," "The Munsters," "Howdy Doody," and most western programs (including those of Roy Rogers, Gene Autry, and Hopalong Cassidy) are especially desirable right now. Products from other 1960s shows like "I Dream of Jeannie," "Bewitched," "Man From U.N.C.L.E.," "The Andy Griffith Show," "Leave it to Beaver," "The Monkees," and "The Dick Van Dyke Show" are also much in demand by today's collectors. The scarcity of an item also plays a part in the price of a television collectible. That is what makes a game like the one from "The Dick Van Dyke Show" so valuable.

Although a few products are still being made for some new television programs, the issuing of material for nearly every series is a thing of the past. Perhaps that is what makes the collecting of television memorabilia such fun. There are a limited number of those past products still available and in order for a collector to find an elusive treasure, he may have to wait for another collector to sell a collection.

The television memorabilia collector can be as discriminating in his purchases as he desires. A vast variety of material was produced and selecting what area to pursue is part of the fun of collecting. I hope this book will help in the process.

"Howdy Doody's TV Game" made by Milton Bradley. © Kagran Corp. circa 1953. $45-55.

Television
Memorabilia

A

The A-Team

Mr. T. became a star on the series "The A-Team" on NBC in 1983. The adventure series was about a soldier-of-fortune organization. George Peppard portrayed John "Hannibal" Smith. Mr. T. (Lawrence Tero) was B. B. Baracus; Templeton and Murdock were played by Dirk Benedict and Dwight Schultz.

Related products include the following: action figures by Galoob (1983); 12"-tall Mr. T., also by Galoob; Mr. T. rubber stamps, and lunch box also from 1983. These items are copyrighted by Stephen J. Cannell productions.

Mr. T Traveling the USA Coloring Book © 1983 Ruby-Spears Enterprises, Inc. Big T Enterprises, Inc. Published by Harbor House Publishers, Inc. $5-10. ✦ "The A Team" van made by ERTL (#1823). Stephen J. Cannell Productions. $10-15.

Mr. T doll, 12" tall, © 1983 by Stephen J. Cannell Productions. Big Ts Enterprises, Inc. Made by Lewis Galoob, Inc. $8-10. ✦ "The A-Team Ball Darts," © 1983 Stephen J. Cannell Productions. Synergistics Research Corp. $10-15.

"The A-Team: B.A. Lends a Hand in the Race for the Formula" game. Package and contents © 1984 Parker Brothers. The A-Team is a trademark of Stephen J. Cannell Productions. $10-15.

A-Team figures, © 1983 Stephen J. Cannell Productions. Made by Lewis Galoob, Inc. Dolls portray Amy A. Allen, John "Hannibal" Smith, Templeton Peck "The Face," and "Howling Mad" Murdock. Each figure is approximately 5" tall. $15-18 each.

Mr. T fully poseable action figure made by Lewis Galoob, Inc. © 1983 by Stephen J. Cannell Productions. $15-18. ✦ Mr. T lunch box and thermos, © 1984 by Ruby-Speares Enterprises, Inc./Big Ts Enterprises, Inc. Made by Aladdin Industries Inc. $10-15. ✦ Thermos © 1983 by the same companies. $4-6.

Adam-12

The police drama "Adam-12" premiered on the NBC network on September 21, 1968. The two stars of the show were Martin Milner (Officer Pete Malloy) and Kent McCord (Officer Jim Reed). Adam-12 was their patrol car. Other cast members were William Boyett (Sergeant MacDonald), Gary Crosby (Officer Ed Wells), and Fred Stromsoe (Officer Woods). The series came to an end in 1975.

Related program items include an Aladdin lunch box, comic books, and paperback books.

The Addams Family

"The Addams Family" was a popular ABC thirty-minute weekly program that aired from 1964 to 1966. The sixty-four episodes revolved around a very unusual family based on characters created by cartoonist Charles Addams for *The New Yorker* magazine, reflecting Addams' offbeat sense of humor. The ghoulish family lived in a Gothic house that looked like a Halloween haunted house. The head of the household was Gomez, a rich lawyer played by John Astin, and his wife was Morticia, played by Carolyn Jones. Their children were Wednesday (Lisa Loring) and Pugsley (Ken Weatherwax). Another spooky character was Uncle Fester, a role created by former child movie star, Jackie Coogan.

Products based on the show included the following items: *Addams Family Activity Book,* Saalfield (1966); "Addams Family Colorforms Cartoon Kit," (1965); board game by Ideal (1964); Gomez hand puppet, 10" tall (1964); Lurch Remco figure, 5 1/2" tall (1964); "Thing" bank by Poynter (1965); Morticia figure, 4" tall (1964); Milton Bradley puzzle (1965). All these products were copyrighted by Filmways TV Productions, Inc.

A cartoon series with the same title appeared from 1973 to 1975 on NBC. The products from this program carry a copyright from Hanna-Barbera Studios. Both a game by Milton Bradley and a lunch box by King-Seeley Co. were produced based on this series.

"The Addams Family Game" (from cartoon series). Made by Milton Bradley, © 1973 Hanna-Barbera Productions. Inc. $25-30.

"The Addams Family Card Game," produced by the Milton Bradley Company, © 1965 Filmways TV Production Inc. $30-35.

Wednesday doll, 18 1/2" tall. Tagged "Chas. Addams' Character Dolls Wednesday, Pugsley, Morticia, Granny Frump Aboriginals Ltd." Circa 1960s. Although the doll does not mention the television show, it came from around the same time period. The doll is all cloth and wears her original clothing. $125-150.

The Addams Family: An Activity Book (#4331). Published by Saalfield Publishing Company, 1965. $25-30.

The Adventures of Ozzie and Harriet

"The Adventures of Ozzie and Harriet" began on television as a typical family situation comedy in 1952. The television family was a real-life family as well, and each member used his own name in the program. The father and mother were veteran show-business personalities Ozzie and Harriet (Hilliard) Nelson; their sons were David and Ricky. As the boys grew up, Ricky became a teen idol singing star, and the series outlasted other shows of its kind because of his popularity. The program ran on ABC from 1952 to 1966. Other cast members included Don DeFore as Mr. Thornberry, and in later years, the boy's wives, June and Kris Nelson.

Saalfield Publishing Co. produced both a coloring book and a paper doll book featuring the Nelson family. Other products which dealt with Ricky Nelson alone included another paper doll book as well as his numerous records and magazine features.

Ozzie and Harriet with David and Ricky in Paper Dolls (#4319). Saalfield Publishing Company, 1954. © Ozzie Nelson. From the collection of Elaine Price. $75-90.

TV Radio Mirror, July 1958, with Ricky Nelson cover. Published by Macfadden Publications, Inc. $8-10. ✦ Ricky Nelson Cut-Outs (#2081). Whitman Publishing Company, 1959. © Ricky Nelson. $50-75.

Ozzie and Harriet, David and Ricky Coloring Book (#125910), published by The Saalfield Publishing Company. $25-35. ✦ TV Star Parade, January 1967, with extended Nelson family as cover subjects. Published by Ideal Publishing Company. $8-10.

The Adventures of Rin Tin Tin

Rin Tin Tin was the name of a very famous movie dog from the early days of film. The name was reinstated for a television program which began as a half-hour series in 1954. In "The Adventures of Rin Tin Tin," a boy named Rusty and his dog were found by cavalry officer Lieutenant Masters after the two survived an Indian raid. The plots of the series revolved around the 101st Cavalry stationed in California in the 1880s. The dog (owned and trained by Lee Duncan) and the boy Rusty (played by Lee Aaker) helped the Lieutenant (played by James Brown) and the other cavalry members in the action each week. The series was on ABC from 1954 to 1958, and continued another run for the same network from 1959 to 1961. Then the program moved to CBS and played from 1962 to 1964.

Besides a coloring book published by Whitman Publishing Co. (1955), other tie-in products included View-Master reels; a puzzle by Jaymar (1957); a board game by Transogram (1955); several books; a Rin Tin Tin Fort Apache playset made by Marx (late 1950s); a Paint by Numbers set by Transogram (1956); a plush stuffed dog by Smile Novelty Toy Co (1959); and hats, neckties, and other items of children's clothing.

Rin Tin Tin and the Ghost Wagon Train by Cole Fannin. Published by Whitman Publishing Company. © 1958 by Screen Gems, Inc. $4-6. ✦ *The Adventures of Rin Tin Tin Coloring Book* (#1257). Published by Whitman Publishing Company, 1955. © Screen Gems, Inc. $15-20. ✦ *Rin Tin Tin and the Lost Indian*, A Little Golden Book. Published by Simon and Schuster. © 1958 by Screen Gems, Inc. $4-6.

The Adventures of Rin Tin Tin Coloring Book (#1195). Whitman Publishing Company, © 1956 by Screen Gems, Inc. $15-20. ✦ *Rin Tin Tin One of the Family* by Frank Kearns. Published by Whitman Publishing Company. © 1953 by Lee Duncan. $4-6. ✦ *Rin-Tin-Tin and the Outlaw* by Charles Spainverral. Published by Simon and Schuster, Little Golden Book. © 1957 by Screen Gems, Inc. $4-6.

The Adventures of Robin Hood

"The Adventures of Robin Hood" first appeared on the CBS network on September 26, 1955. The show lasted until the fall of 1958 and was later syndicated. The series was based on the familar English stories of Robin Hood, which date from 1191. Most of the action takes place in Sherwood Forest, where Sir Robin of Locksley becomes known as Robin Hood as he and his followers attempt to defeat Prince John and return Richard the Lion-Hearted to the throne. Former movie actor Richard Greene played the part of Robin Hood, and Alexander Gauge was Friar Tuck. Little John was portrayed by Archie Duncan and Bernadette O'Farrell was Maid Marian.

Tie-in merchandise included puzzles produced by Built-Rite, a game by Bettye-Bye Products, and a metal lunchbox by Aladdin Industries.

"The Adventures of Robin Hood" picture puzzle. From the Built-Rite Famous TV Stars Series. © 1956 Off. Films, Inc. $15-18. ✦ TV Guide with Robin Hood cover, May 12, 1956. Published by Triangle Pub., Inc. $4-6.

Alf

"Alf" was a series for kids that ran on NBC from 1986 to 1990. Alf was an alien life form from the planet Melmac. Max Wright and Anne Schedeen played the parts of the parents, Willie and Kate Tanner, in the house where Alf hid from the government.

Alf lunch box and thermos, © 1987 by Alien Productions. Made by Thermos. $10-15. ✦ Puzzle by Milton Bradley, © 1987 by Alien Productions. $5-8.

Alfred Hitchcock Presents, and The Alfred Hitchcock Hour

"Alfred Hitchcock Presents" was an anthology of mystery and suspense dramas which were introduced by the master of suspense himself, Alfred Hitchcock. The program aired on CBS from 1955 to 1960 and on NBC from 1960 to 1962. The program name was then changed to "The Alfred Hitchcock Hour" and it continued on the air until May 10, 1965.

A game and many paperback books were some of the items produced to take advantage of the popularity of the Hitchcock programs.

"Alfred Hitchcock Presents Why" game, © 1958 by Milton Bradley Company. From the collection of Jeff Zillner. $20-25.

All in the Family

"All in the Family" was the first situation comedy to focus on 'forbidden' topics. Instead of portraying the usual television family with story lines involving teens needing extra money or a date for the prom, the Bunker household coped with prejudice in the neighborhood, political issues, and other meaningful topics. The show began on January 12, 1971 on the CBS network. Most of the action took place at the Bunker home in Queens, New York. The head of the household, Archie Bunker (played by Carroll O'Connor), worked as a dock foreman. Also living in the house were Archie's wife Edith (Jean Stapleton), his daughter Gloria (Sally Struthers), and his son-in-law Mike Stivic (Rob Reiner). Archie, a prejudiced, conservative, blue collar worker, was pitted against his liberal college student son-in-law as they try to understand the changes occurring in society during the 1970s. The program was ranked as the most watched show in the United States during the 1971-1972 season, according to the Nielsen ratings. The series held this number one position for five years. In 1979 the format was changed and the show became "Archie Bunker's Place." With the loss of the former cast members, the show also lost its popularity. Its long run came to an end in 1983.

Products representing characters in the program include the following: Archie Bunker's Grandson Joey Stivic doll (14" tall), made by Ideal (1976); Archie Bunker For President Beer Mug; pinback "Vote Archie"; "All in the Family" card game by Milton Bradley (1972); "All in the Family" game by Milton Bradley (1972); paperback books; and a record album made by Atlantic (1971).

"The All in the Family Game," © 1972 by Milton Bradley Company under Berne and Universal Copyright Conventions. $12-18.

"Archie Bunker's Grandson Joey Stivic" doll. Part played by Jason and Justin Draeger on the show. Made of vinyl with a one piece-body. Made by Ideal in 1976. The doll has rooted hair and is anatomically correct. Head is marked "Ideal Toy Corp." Back is marked "© 1976 Tandem Prd's Inc. Ideal 5-58." $35-40.

All My Children

"All My Children," one of the most popular of the daytime serials, premiered on January 5, 1970. The storyline concentrated on the Tyler family from Pine Valley. The first cast members included movie star Ruth Warrick as Phoebe Tyler, Rosemary Prinz (formerly on "As the World Turns") as Amy Tyler, and Diana de Vegh as Ann Tyler.

Although few products were made to tie in with this show, Ruth Warrick promoted a book written about her life during her days as a "soap" star, and an adult game was marketed bearing the program's name.

"How To Host a Murder / All My Children." © 1991 Decipher Inc. © 1991 American Broadcasting Company, Inc. $5-8.

American Bandstand

"American Bandstand," the famous music program for teens, began as a local Philadelphia program in 1952. It premiered on the ABC network in the fall of 1957. The series remained on the air for decades, with several format and name changes. The famous "forever young" host, Dick Clark, remained at the helm as popular music stars changed from Elvis Presley, to the Beatles, to the Supremes, and beyond.

One of the most sought-after products from the early years of "American Bandstand" is the Dick Clark doll. It was made by Juro Novelty Co. in the late 1950s. The doll is 27" tall, with a stuffed body and vinyl head and hands. It was called an autograph doll and was made for older teens so they could collect autographs on the doll's jacket.

The Andy Griffith Show

"The Andy Griffith Show" appeared on CBS from 1960 to 1968. In its 249 episodes, Sheriff Andy Taylor (Andy Griffith) appeared as a concerned single parent raising his son Opie (Ronny Howard). Andy's Aunt Bee (Frances Bavier) provided a woman's touch in the household. The series was based in the rural community of Mayberry, North Carolina. Although the main characters had jobs in law enforcement, the small town had very little crime so the weekly stories usually revolved around the life of the popular Mayberry residents. Comedy highlights were provided by Don Knotts in his role as deputy Barney Fife and by Jim Nabors, who played Gomer Pyle. The Nielsen ratings gave this show the honor of being the most watched series in the United States during the 1967-1968 year.

Products associated with the show included two coloring books (one called *Ronnie Howard of "The Andy Griffith Show"*) and a record produced by Capitol.

Doll portraying Dick Clark, the host of "American Bandstand." Doll was made by Juro (Eegee) in 1958. It is 26" tall, with vinyl head and hands and a cloth body. Head is marked "Juro." The doll cost $7.98 when new. Current value $225-275.

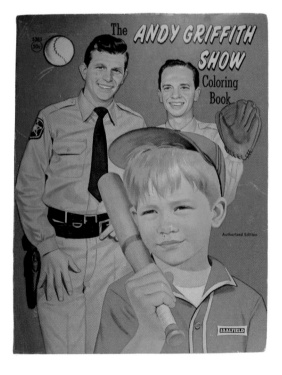

The Andy Griffith Show coloring book, published by Saalfield Publishing Company. © MCMLXIII (1963) by Mayberry Enterprises, Inc. $50-60.

TV Guide from May 11, 1963 published by Triangle Publications. Don Knotts, Ronny Howard, and Andy Griffith are featured on the cover. $4-6.
✦ Autographed picture of Andy Griffith dates from the 1960s. $25-35.

Annie Oakley

"Annie Oakley" aired on ABC from 1953 to 1958. The story took place in the 1860s and centered around Annie Oakley (Gail Davis), who was an expert sharpshooter, and her brother Tagg (Jimmy Hawkins). The program was mainly geared to children, so many toys and other products were produced to tie in with the show.

These included a Milton Bradley board game (1955); Aladdin lunch box (1955); sewing set by Pressman; paper dolls and coloring books by Whitman; children's clothing; Sparkle Picture Craft set by Gabriel Toys; and Magic Erasable Pictures by Transogram (1959).

Annie Oakley with Tagg and Lofty Cut-Out Dolls (#2056). Published by Whitman Publishing Company, 1955. © Annie Oakley Enterprises, Inc. $75-100. ◆ *Annie Oakley Cut-Out Dolls* (#2043). Whitman Publishing Company, 1954. © Annie Oakley Enterprises, Inc. $75-100. Both books from the collection of Elaine Price.

Annie Oakley Cowgirl Outfit manufactured by Leslie-Henry Company, Inc. Mount Vernon, New York. Circa 1955. $75-100.

Annie Oakley Coloring Book (#1756). © Annie Oakley Enterprises, Inc., 1957. Published by Whitman Publishing Company. $45-55. ◆ *Annie Oakley Cut-Out Dolls* (#1960). Published by Whitman Publishing Company, 1956. © Annie Oakley Enterprises, Inc. $75-100. ◆ *Annie Oakley in Danger at Diablo*. Published by Whitman Publishing Company, 1955. © Annie Oakley Enterprises, Inc. $5-8.

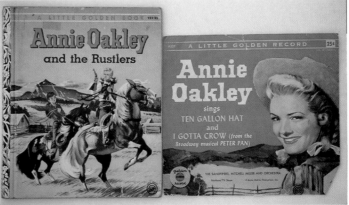

Annie Oakley and the Rustlers by Ann McGovern. A Little Golden Book published by Simon and Schuster. © 1955 by Annie Oakley Enterprises, Inc. $5-8. ◆ Annie Oakley Sings: "Ten Gallon Hat" and "I Gotta Crow," Little Golden Record by Simon and Schuster. © Annie Oakley Enterprises. $9-12.

The Aquanauts

"The Aquanauts" was a short lived television program which aired on CBS from September 1960 until May 1961. The Hawaiian adventure drama starred Keith Larsen as Drake Andrews and Jeremy Slate as Larry Lahr.

The show did inspire a board game made by Transogram in 1961.

The Archie Show

"The Archie Show" was based on the popular comic strip of the same name, which was drawn by Bob Montana. The animated cartoons were by Filmation Studios and featured high school students Archie Andrews, Jughead Jones, Betty Cooper, Veronica Lodge, Reggie Mantle, and Sabrina (the teenage witch). CBS aired several versions of the Archie Show beginning in 1968.

Although many Archie products have been produced, most were made because of the popularity of Archie the comic strip character. The lunch box and thermos, made by Aladdin with 1969 copyright dates, probably were inspired by the successful television production. Jaymar also produced a jigsaw puzzle featuring the Archie characters during the 1960s, and paper dolls and coloring books were manufactured by Whitman (Western Publishing Co.) in the early 1970s.

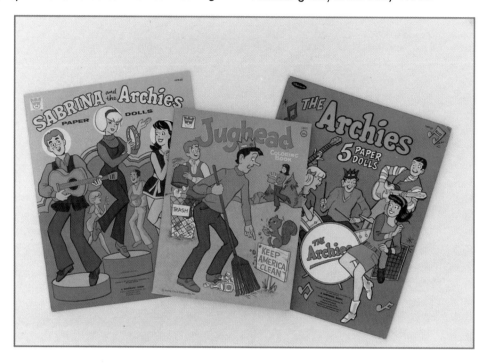

Sabrina and the Archies Paper Dolls (#1978). © 1971 by Archie Music Corp., Inc. Whitman Publishing Company. $15-18. ✦ *Jughead Coloring Book* (#1045). © Archie Comic Publications, Inc., 1972. Published by Western Publishing Company. $8-10. ✦ *The Archies 5 Paper Dolls*. Published by Whitman Publishing Company. © 1969 by Archie Comic Pub., Inc. $15-18.

Arrest and Trial

The "Arrest and Trial" program included two parts: first the arrest of a criminal, and then the trial. The show ran for one year from September 1963 to September 1964. Featured players included Ben Gazzara as Sgt. Nick Anderson amd Chuck Connors as John Egan, the defense counselor.

Transogram produced a board game based on the show in 1963.

Arthur Godfrey and Friends

"Arthur Godfrey and Friends" was one of several television programs hosted by former radio personality Arthur Godfrey. It was on this show that many future stars received their first exposure to the television audience. Regulars included Pat Boone, The McGuire Sisters (Christine, Phyllis, and Dorothy), Marion Marlowe, Janette Davis, Julius Larosa, Lu Ann Simms, Frank Parker, The Chordettes, and Haleloke. Although Godfrey usually portrayed a kind "father figure" on the show, he could also be very cruel-for example, when he fired singer Julius Larosa during a live program. Godfrey was a continuing part of the television scene from 1948 until 1961. For many of these years, he was a host on several different television shows each week. Included were "Arthur Godfrey's Talent Scouts" (CBS 1948-1958), "Arthur Godfrey and His Ukelele" (CBS 1950), "Arthur Godfrey Time" (CBS 1952-1959), "The Arthur Godfrey Show" (CBS 1958-1959) and "Candid Camera" (co-host, CBS 1960-1961). His "Friends" program aired on CBS from 1949 to 1956.

Because of the popularity of Godfrey's many programs, he and his cast members were frequently used as subjects for the various television magazine publications. A toy ukelele was also produced which carried the Godfrey name. Two of the most sought after Godfrey collectibles bear the names of Godfrey's cast members. These are dolls made in the image of singers Lu Ann Simms and Haleloke. The Simms doll was a hard plastic walking doll made by the Roberta Doll Co. The Haleoke doll was made of hard plastic. The doll was dressed in a grass skirt and top and sometimes was available with a suitcase containing other clothing. Neither doll is marked with its name, so they are hard to identify unless they are in original condition with their tags.

Lu Ann Simms walking doll, 16" tall and made of hard plastic. The doll represents a regular singer on "Arthur Godfrey and His Friends." Made by Roberta Doll Company, Inc., circa 1953. Her tag reads "One of Arthur Godfrey's Friends/ Lu Ann Simms Walking Doll/CBS Television Star/ Mfg. by Roberta Doll Company, Inc." The number "170" appears on the back of her head. The doll has a ponytail, wears a red dress trimmed in ric-rac, and carries a purse with her name on it. The doll also came in 18" and 21" sizes. $200+.

Radio-TV Mirror from March 1953. Published by Macfadden Publishing. Cover features Godfrey stars Julius La Rosa and Lu Ann Simms. $8-10 ✦ TV Guide from September 7, 1957 published by Triangle Publications. Cover features Godfrey and another of his stars, Janette Davis. $4-6. ✦ The McGuire Sisters 3 Cut-Out Dolls (#1983). © 1959 by The McGuire Sisters, Whitman Publishing Company. The sisters appeared on the Godfrey television programs also. $60-75.

TV Star Parade featuring Arthur Godfrey on the cover, August 1953. Published by Ideal Publishing Corp. $8-10. ✦ Autographed picture of the late Authur Godfrey. $35-50.

Hard plastic doll representing Haleloke, a singer on the Godfrey show. Made in the USA in 1954 by the Cast Distributing Corp. The doll is 18" tall and is a jointed walker. $175+.

B

B. J. and the Bear

"B. J. and the Bear" was aired on NBC from February 1979 to August 1981. The story line for the show revolved around cross-country truck driver B. J. McCay (Greg Evigan), and his passenger, a pet chimp named Bear. During the second season of the series, B. J. ran a trucking business in Los Angeles, where several beautiful women drove his trucks.

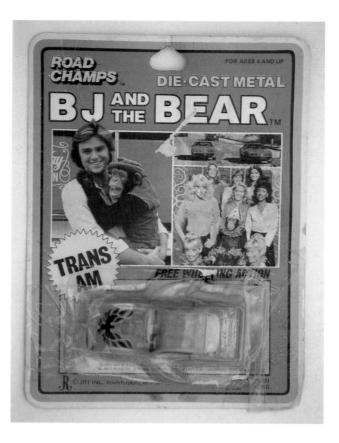

"B.J. and the Bear" die-cast metal Trans-AM car. © JRI Inc. and 1981 Universal City Studios, Inc. $8-10.

Baby Huey

(see "Matty's Funday Funnies.")

Baretta

"Baretta" was a popular crime drama which began its run on ABC on January 17, 1975. Former child star Robert Blake was cast as Tony Baretta, an undercover police detective. Other cast members included Tom Ewell and Dana Elcar. The show ended in 1978.

"Baretta Street Detective Game" was produced by Milton Bradley in 1976 to tie in with the show.

Barney Miller

"Barney Miller" was a successful situation comedy on the ABC network from 1975 to 1982. The action revolved around a Greenwich Village police station. Hal Linden played Captain Barney Miller; from 1975 to 1977 Abe Vigoda played Detective Phil Fish. Other characters included Det. Amenguale (Gregory Sierra), Det. Stanley Wojohowicz (Maxwell Gail), Det. Yemana (Jack Soo), Det. Dietrich (Steve Landesberg) and Det. Harris (Ron Glass).

A board game was produced in 1977 by Parker Brothers to take advantage of the show's popularity.

"Baretta the Street Detective Game." © Universal Television, a division of Universal City Studios, Inc., 1976. Produced by Milton Bradley Company. $15-20.

"How About a Game of Barney Miller with the 12th Precinct Gang?" © 1977 Parker Brothers, Division of General Mills Fun Group, Inc. © 1977 Four D Productions, Inc. $15-20.

Bat Masterson

"Bat Masterson" was another popular western from the 1950s. The program aired on NBC from 1957 to 1961. Gene Barry starred as William Bartley "Bat" Masterson, a law enforcement man of the West. Bat's trademarks-a gold tipped cane, a derby hat, and a special gun-were used by Barry in his characterization of the legendary law man.

Many children's products were produced to tie in with the Masterson program. Included were a cane (1958); a vinyl wallet featuring Gene Barry's picture; a playsuit costume by Ben Cooper (1960); a Hartland figure made by Hartland Plastics Inc. (circa 1960); a game produced by Lowell Toys (1958); and a coloring book published by Saalfield (1959). Most products carry a copyright from ZIV Television Programs, Inc.

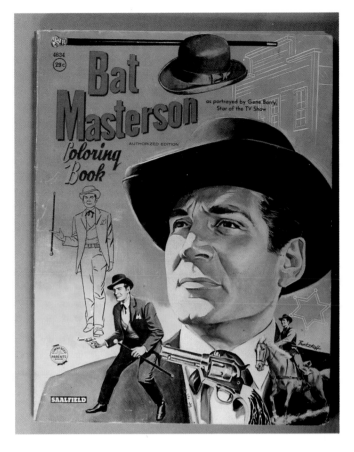

Bat Masterson Coloring Book (#4634). MCMLIX (1959) ZIV Television Programs, Inc. Published by The Saalfield Publishing Company. California National Productions, Inc. $25-35.

"Bat Masterson , 3-D Western Game" made by Lowell, 1958. © California National Productions, Inc. © ZIV Television Programs, Inc. $100-125.

Batman

"Batman" was a "camp" television show from 1966 to 1968 when it was on the ABC schedule. Many celebrities asked to do guest spots on the program in order to get in on the fun. The show was based on the comic book character created by Bob Kane. Adam West played Bruce Wayne/Batman, the hero who fought for good against various evil characters. Dick Greyson/Robin was played by Burt Ward. Silent film star Neil Hamilton played Police Commissioner Gordon and 1940s Twentieth Century-Fox star Cesar Romero was the Joker.

Numerous Batman toys have been produced through the years, but the only ones that can be considered tie-ins to the television show are the items made from 1966 to 1968. Some of these products include the following: Batman/Robin trash can by Chein Co.; figural Batman night lamp, 11" tall; Batman Figure Set by Ideal; many different coloring books published by Whitman; milk mug; Batman, Robin Model Kits by Aurora; Batmobile pin; Batman board game made by Milton Bradley (1966); Batman frame puzzles made by Whitman (1966); Batman "Star Dust" velvet art set made by Hasbro (1966); Batman Trace-A-Graph Drawing set by Emenee (1966); Batman Escape Gun by Lincoln International (1966); Batman Picture Pistol, Marx (1966); pencil case (1966); Batman slippers (1966); plastic Batmobile (1966); Soaky (1966); Batman Batmobile friction car (1966); and Batman and Robin lunch box and thermos made by Aladdin (1966). Because of the huge success of the program, the list of product tie-ins is larger than for any other television series except for the Roy Rogers and Hopalong Cassidy shows. Products should be marked with the copyright of National Periodical Publications, Inc.

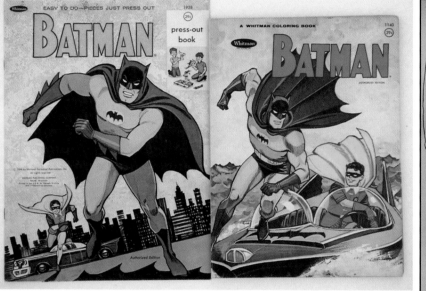

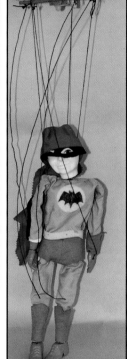

Batman marionette, marked "Batman Characters," © 1966 National Periodical Publications, Inc. $45-55.

Batman Press-Out Book (#1928), $20-25, and Batman Coloring Book (#1140), $15-20. Both published by Whitman, © 1966 by National Periodicals Publications, Inc.

Pow! Robin Strikes for Batman (#1833). © 1966 by National Periodical Publications, Inc. Published by Watkins-Strathmore Company. $15-20. ✦
Robin in the Batcave with Batman (#1833-2), 1968. © National Periodical Publications, Inc. Published by Watkins-Strathmore Company. $15-20.

"Batman Cartoon Kit," National Periodicals Pub., Inc. © 1966 Colorforms. $35-40.

Battlestar Galactica

"Battlestar Galactica" was a science fiction series which aired on ABC from September 17, 1978 to August 4, 1979. Lorne Greene starred as Commander Adama, who was in charge of the spaceship Galactica. The crew fought battles against the Cylons.

Many toy products were manufactured to promote this short-lived program. Most are copyrighted by Universal City Studios, Inc. Parker Brothers produced a board game in 1978. Aladdin Industries was responsible for a lunch box in the same year. Other products include several action figures by Mattel, Inc., a Medic Kit and a Periscope Scanner both by Larami Corp., and a Lasermatic Pistol by Mattel. All of these items were made in 1978.

"Battlestar Galactica: Parker Brothers Game." © 1978 Universal City Studios, Inc. $20-25.

"Battlestar Galactica" watch set. © 1978 Universal City Studios. Made by Larami Corp. $12-15.

"Battlestar Galactica" jigsaw puzzles. © 1978 Universal City Studios, Inc. Produced by Parker Brothers. $8-12.

The Beany and Cecil Show

"The Beany and Cecil Show" aired on ABC from January 6, 1962 to September 3, 1967. The cartoon series featured Beany, Cecil, Captain Horatio K. Huffenpuff, and Dishonest John. The characters were created by Bob Clampett for an earlier show called "Time For Beany," which was first run as a local show on KTLA in Los Angeles in 1949. In 1950 it became a syndicated series. Beany was a boy whose trademark was a cap with a propeller on top. Cecil was a sea serpent.

Many tie-in toys were produced for this children's show. One of the most popular is the Beany talking doll made by Mattel, Inc. in the early 1960s. The 17" doll has a vinyl head and molded cap with a propeller on top. Mattel also produced Cecil as a talking doll as part of this same series. Other products include a lunch box and thermos made by The American Thermos Prod. Co.; record player by Vanity Fair (1961); Beany and Cecil Beany-Copter made by Mattel, Inc. (1961); "Talk to Cecil" Mattel talking adventure game (1961); and "Beany-Cecil" animated clock. Most products carry the Clampett copyright.

"Beany and Cecil Match It Game" made by Mattel, 1961. Trademark and © 1961 Mattel, Inc. Cartoon characters © Bob Clampett. $20-25.

Bob Clampett: Beany's Coloring Book. © 1951. Whitman Publishing Company. $20-25. ✦ Bob Clampett's Beany: Cecil Captured for the Zoo. © 1954 by Bob Clampett. Whitman Publishing Company. $5-8.

Beat the Clock

"Beat the Clock," a popular game show of the 1950s, had its beginning on the CBS network on March 23, 1950. The program continued until February 16, 1958. The host was Bud Collyer. His assistant was Dolores Rosedale (Roxanne). The show then aired on the ABC network from October 13, 1958 until September 26, 1962. Later a new version of the show was run in syndication.

Lowell Toy Corp. produced a game based on the program and a doll was manufactured to represent Roxanne.

"Beat the Clock Game" by Lowell Toy Corp. © 1954 by Beat the Clock, Inc. A Goodson-Todman Production in association with CBS Television. $20-25. ✦ Hard plastic Roxanne doll, 21" tall, with a tag reading "Beat the Clock Roxanne's T.V. Walking Doll." Back of tag reads "See Roxanne walk this doll every week on 'Beat The Clock', Sylvania's outstanding T.V. show." A Mona Lisa Exclusive by Valentine Dolls, Inc. Head and body are marked "210." The doll has sleep eyes, a Saran wig and is circa 1953. Roxanne (born Dolores Rosedale) was the hostess on the show. $150-175.

Ben Casey

"Ben Casey" was one of the popular medical television programs of the early 1960s. The sixty-minute show aired on ABC from 1961 to 1966. The series made Vincent Edwards a star for his role as Dr. Ben Casey. His boss was portrayed by Sam Jaffe, and Betty Ackerman played Dr. Maggie Graham.

Several television collectibles come from this medical series. They include the "Ben Casey M.D." board game by Transogram (1961); charm bracelet by Gerald Sears Co., Inc. (1962); truck model kit by MPC (1968); and a Doctor Kit by Transogram containing a stethoscope, syringe, thermometer, microscope, smock, and otoscope (1962). Most products are copyrighted by Bing Crosby Productions.

"Ben Casey Junior Jigsaw Puzzle." © 1964 Bing Crosby Productions. Inc. Made by Milton Bradley Company. $15-18. ✦ "Ben Casey's Own Doctor Bag by Transogram." $25-35.

"Ben Casey M.D. Game" by Transogram Company, Inc. © 1961 Bing Crosby Productions. $30-40.

Ben Casey Coloring Book (#9532). Published by Saalfield Publishing Company, 1963. © Bing Crosby Productions, drawings by Ray Quigley. $15-20. ✦ Ben Casey Film Stories (#1), published by K.K. Publications, Inc. © 1962 by Bing Crosby Productions. $8-12.

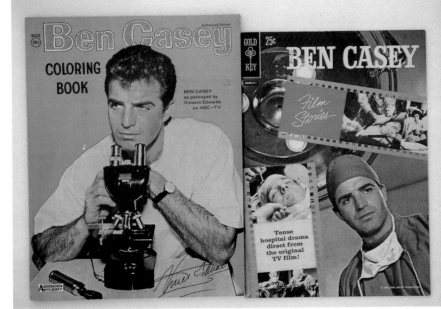

The Beverly Hillbillies

"The Beverly Hillbillies" was a highly rated television program during its most successful seasons. It was often listed among the top ten most watched TV shows in the nation. The show was about the Clampett family, hillbillies who had become millionaires when oil was discovered on their home property. Suddenly rich, the family packed up and moved to Beverly Hills, California where they purchased a mansion and tried to combine two lifestyles-hillbilly and wealthy-with unexpected results. Characters included Jed Clampett (played by Buddy Ebsen), Granny (Irene Ryan), Elly May (Donna Douglas), and Jethro (Max Baer). The show was ranked first in the Nielsen ratings for the seasons of 1962-1963 and 1963-1964 as the most watched series in the United States.

Many products were manufactured to tie in to this popular show. Most carry a copyright from Filmways TV Productions. Included are boxed puzzles by Jaymar (1963); hardcover books by Stein and Day (1964); lunch box and thermos by Aladdin Industries (1963); View-Master set (1963); truck model kit by MPC (1968); record (1960s); wind-up car made by Ideal (1963); and Colorforms set (1963). A doll was also produced in the likeness of Elly May Clampett by Unique. The 12" tall vinyl doll was marked "Unique" on the back of the head.

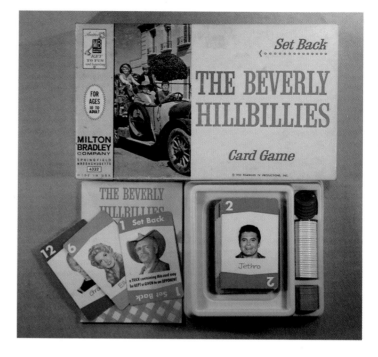

"The Beverly Hillbillies Card Game." Produced by Milton Bradley. © 1963 Filmways T.V. Productions, Inc. $20-25.

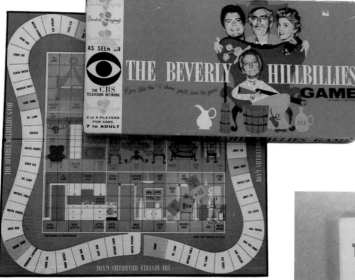

"The Beverly Hillbillies Game," © 1963. Filmways T.V. Productions, Inc. Standard Toykraft Inc. $45-55.

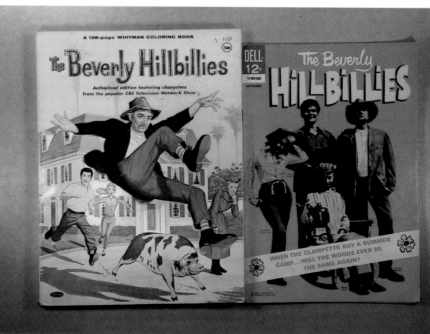

The Beverly Hillbillies coloring book (#1137). © 1963 Filmways TV Productions, Inc. Published by Whitman Publishing Company. $20-30. ◆
The Beverly Hillbillies comic book. September 1966. Published by Dell Publishing Company. © 1966 Filmways TV Productions Inc. $8-10.

Elly May paper dolls (#1819A). © 1963 Filmways TV Productions., Inc. Published by Watkins Strathmore Company. From the collection of Elaine Price. $35-45.

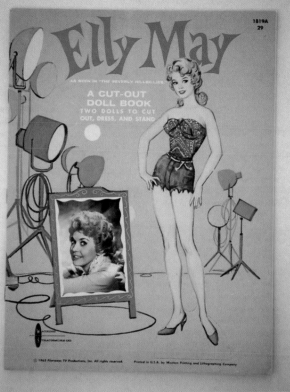

The Beverly Hillbillies Coloring Book (#1883). Published by Western Publishing Company, 1964. © Filmway TV Productions. Watkins-Strathmore Book. $20-30. ◆ Lunch box by Aladdin Industries circa 1964. © Filmway TV Productions. $50-60. ◆ *The Beverly Hillbillies Cut-Outs* #1955. Whitman Publishing Company, 1964. © Filmways TV Productions, Inc. $45-55.

TV Guide from March 12, 1966 featuring the Beverly Hillbillies on the cover. Published by Triangle Publications. $4-6. ◆ "Beverly Hillbillies Inlaid Puzzle." Made by Jaymar Speciality Company. © 1963 Filmways TV Productions., Inc. $15-20.

The Clampett Family Song Book. Alfred Music Company. © 1963 by Filmways TV Productions, Inc. $15-20. ◆ *The Beverly Hillbillies* comic book. © 1965 Filmways TV Productions, Inc. Dell Publishing Company, April-June 1965. $8-10. ◆ *The Beverly Hillbillies: the Saga of Wildcat Creek.* © 1963 Filmways TV Productions. Inc. Published by Whitman Publishing Company. $8-10. ◆ *Beverly Hillbillies Punch-Out.* © 1964 Filmways TV Productions., Inc. Whitman Publishing Company. $25-35.

Bewitched

The comedy series "Bewitched" joined other farfetched programs that spanned the airwaves in the early 1960s. The show featured a witch named Samantha (Elizabeth Montgomery), her normal husband Darren Stevens, and her mother Endora (Agnes Moorehead), also a witch. The plot revolved around the use of magic and the casting of spells by the women in the series. Advertising executive Stevens was played at different times by Dick York and Dick Sargent. The show ran on ABC from 1964 to 1972.

Two games were made to tie in to the "Bewitched" show. They are the "Bewitched Stymie Card Game," made in 1964 by Milton Bradley, and the "Samantha and Endora Game/Bewitched" made by T. Cohn in 1965. Books, coloring books, and comic books based on the series were published. Paper dolls which featured cast members were also produced. The boxed Samantha paper dolls were made in 1965 by Magic Wand and the Tabatha paper dolls were produced by the same company in 1966. The most expensive "Bewitched" item is the 12" tall vinyl doll dressed as Samantha the Witch, which was made by Ideal in 1965. Most of the Bewitched items carry the copyright of Screen Gems, Inc.

From the "Bewitched" TV show, *Tabatha Paper Doll*. © Screen Gems, Inc. 1966. Magic Wand Corp. $25-35 (cut).

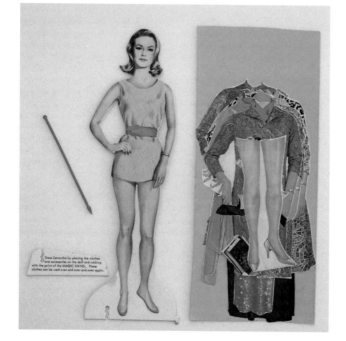

Bewitched Samatha Paper Dolls (#44) portraying Elizabeth Montgomery. Magic Wand, 1965. © Screen Gems, Inc. From the collection of Elaine Price. $25-35 (cut).

Bewitched Fun and Activity Book (#8908). Published by Treasure Books. © 1965 by Screen Gems, Inc. Illustrated by Tony Tallarico. $20-25. ◆ *Bewitched* comic book, July 1967. Dell Publishing Company. © 1967 by Screen Gems, Inc. $8-10.

The Big Valley

Famous movie star Barbara Stanwyck starred in the western television show "The Big Valley" from 1965 to 1969. The program ran on the ABC network and also starred Richard Long as Jarrod Barkley, Peter Breck as Nick Barkley, Lee Majors as Heath Barkley, Linda Evans as Audra Barkley, and Charles Briles as Eugene Barkley. Stanwyck played the part of Victoria Barkley, the head of the cattle ranching Barkley family. The plot was set in California, circa 1878, in an era when lawlessness prevailed.

The Big Valley book by Charles Heckelmann. Published by Whitman Publishing Company. © MCMLXVI (1966) by Four-Star Margate. $5-8.

The Bionic Woman

"The Bionic Woman" was a spin-off program from ABC's popular "Six Million Dollar Man." The main character, Jaime Sommers (played by Lindsay Wagner), was injured in a sky-diving accident, and though Dr. Rudy Wells (Martin E. Brooks) performed a bionic operation, she died anyway. Another doctor performed cryogenic surgery and brought her back to life-but with with bionic limbs. She then became an agent for the Office of Scientific Intelligence.

Other players included Richard Anderson as Oscar Goldman and Martha Scott as Helen Elgin. The show aired on ABC from 1976 to 1977 and on NBC from 1977 to 1978.

"The Bionic Woman" captured the imagination of toy makers, so many collectibles based on the show are available for today's collectors. Included are the A.M. Wrist Radio by Kenner (1976); sports car by Kenner (1977); and lunch box/thermos by Aladdin Industries. Most products carry a copyright from Universal City Studios.

"The Bionic Woman" game by Parker Brothers. © 1976 Universal City Studios, Inc. and Parker Brothers, Division of General Mills Fun Group, Inc. $20-25.

The Bionic Woman Coloring Fun Book. © 1976, Universal City Studios, Inc. Published by Treasure Books. $12-15. ✦ "The Bionic Woman" doll, 12" tall, made of vinyl. © 1974 Universal City Studios, Inc. © 1977 General Mills Fun Group. Made by Kenner. Came with Mission Purse. Fifteen different outfits for the doll were also available. The doll was made in the image of Lindsay Wagner, the star of the show. $40-50.

"The Bionic Woman" (Jaime Sommers) acrylic paint by number set by Craft Master, © 1976 Universal City Studios, Inc. Four different sets were made. $15-20.

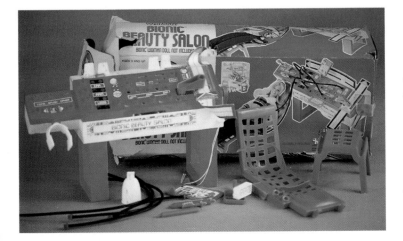

"Bionic Beauty Salon." The Bionic Woman, made by Kenner Products. © 1974 Universal City Studios, Inc. $20-25.

Blondie

Several different versions of a "Blondie" program have been broadcast on the television networks. The first show aired on NBC on January 4, 1954 and continued until December of the same year. The show was also shown on the same network from July 5, 1958 until October 4, 1958. The Bumstead characters were based on the comic created by Chic Young. CBS created a new "Blondie" program in 1968. The show lasted only a few weeks, airing from September 26, 1968 until January 9, 1969. Blondie was played by Patricia Harty, Dagwood by Will Hutchins, Alexander by Peter Robbins, Cookie by Pamelyn Ferdin, and Dagwood's boss by Jim Backus.

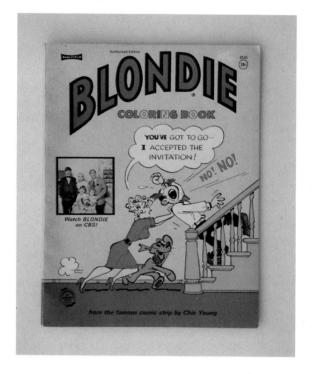

Blondie Coloring Book (#4541). © 1968 King Features Syndicate. Published by Saalfield Publishing Company. CBS television show cast is pictured on front of the book. From the famous comic strip by Chic Young. $10-15.

Blossom

"Blossom" was a situation comedy aimed mainly at teens. It starred Mayim Bialik as Blossom and Joey Lawrence as her brother Joey Russo. Blossom's pal, Six, was played by Jenna von Oy. The NBC comedy ended in 1995 after a run of five seasons. Joey Lawrence became a teen heart-throb as a result of his role in the show.

Dolls representing Blossom and Joey Russo from the NBC show "Blossom." A Six Le Muzere doll was also made. The dolls are all vinyl and come with extra clothing pieces. They are 9 1/2" tall. © Touchstone Pictures and Television. © Tyco Industries 1993. $40-50/pair.

The Bob Hope Show

"The Bob Hope Show" first appeared on television on October 12, 1952. The series used basically the same format as the star had used on his radio program. The variety show has continued on television, airing as specials on NBC, for over forty years. Guest stars have always played an important role on the program and Hope was always able to attract the best talent in the business.

Comic books and coloring books featuring Bob Hope were published during the 1950s.

Bob Hope Coloring Book published by Saalfield Publishing Company, 1954. $20-30. ✦ Autographed picture of Bob Hope, circa 1986. $20-30.

Bonanza

At the height of its popularity, "Bonanza" was seen in seventy-nine countries by 400 million people. It has become one of the most popular television programs of all time. According to the Nielsen ratings, it was the number one rated television show from 1964 to 1968. The ratings for the series dropped only after Dan Blocker's death in 1972.

The hour-long western began on NBC in September 1959 and ended after 440 episodes in January 1973. The story took place in Virginia City, Nevada in the nineteenth century. The main characters were widower Ben Cartwright, (played by Lorne Greene) and his sons Adam (Pernell Roberts), Hoss (Dan Blocker), and Little Joe (Michael Landon). The family lived on a thousand-square-mile ranch called the Ponderosa. Pernell Roberts left the show in 1965 but the program continued to be top rated even after his departure. It was the first major western to be filmed in color.

Since the "Bonanza" show was on for so many years, many tie-in products were produced to promote the program. Included were an Aladdin lunch box and thermos (1965); American Character 8" Hoss, Ben, and Little Joe dolls (1966); Little Joe, Ben, Hoss figure model kits by Revell (1966); "Michigan Rummy Game" by Parker Brothers (1964); Woodburning Kit by American Toy and Furniture Co. (1965); Bonanza gun and holster set by Halpern-Nicholas; Ponderosa Ranch set by Marx (late 1960s); movie viewer and film by Chemtoy Corp. (1961); and Bonanza record "Ponderosa Party Time" by RCA (1962).

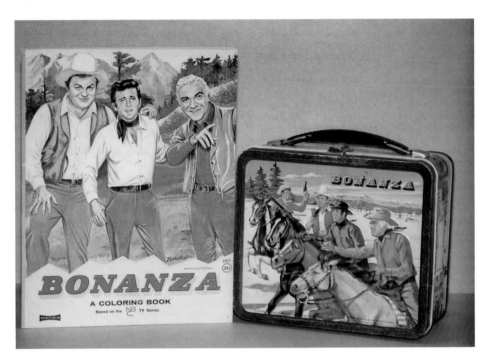

Bonanza: A Coloring Book (#1617). Published by Saalfield Publishing Company, 1960 and 1965. National Broadcasting Company, Inc. $20-30. ♦ Lunch box by Aladdin Industries, circa 1965. © National Broadcasting Company. $75-100.

Bonanza Coloring Book (#4635). Published by Saalfield Publishing Company, 1970. © National Broadcasting Company. $20-25. ♦ Comic book and scrapbook, both © National Broadcasting Company. The comic book was published by Western Publishing Company, Inc. and is dated May 1967. $8-10 each.

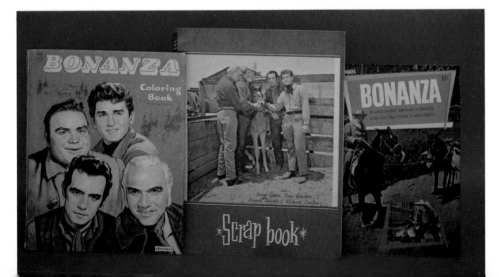

Bozo the Clown (Bozo's Big Top)

Bozo was a clown character that had been used by Capitol Records for its children's records. Larry Harmon purchased the rights to use the character on television in 1956. Bozo became a host for cartoon shows on local television stations. Each station used their own live "Bozo" clown. A Bozo lunch box and thermos were produced by Aladdin Industries in 1963.

Bozo Jr. Clown puppet. © Capitol Records, Inc. Made by Renall Dolls, Inc. $15-18. ◆ *Bozo the Clown,* A Little Golden Book. Golden Press © 1961 by Capitol Records, Inc. Western Publishing Company. $4-6. From the collection of Jeff Zillner.

The Brady Bunch Coloring Book published by Whitman Publishing Company, © Paramount Picture Corp., 1972. $20-25. ◆ *The Brady Bunch Coloring Book* (#1004), published by Whitman Publishing Company, © Paramount Pictures Corp., 1972. $20-25. ◆ *The Brady Bunch Activity Book* (#1252), published by Whitman Publishing Company, © Paramount Pictures Corp., 1974. $15-20.

The Brady Bunch

"The Brady Bunch" was a typical half-hour family sit-com that began on the ABC network in 1969 and continued until 1974. The premise of the show is the marriage of a widower with three sons to a widow with three daughters, who then set up a joint household. The diversified family was held together by the love of the parents for each other and their commitment to all six children. The term "Brady Bunch" came to represent clean-cut, privileged, well-behaved children. The term is still used in the vocabulary of many Americans, usually to explain that their own families had not followed the Brady example of child rearing. The Brady parents were played by Robert Reed and Florence Henderson. The children were Marcia (played by Maureen McCormick), Jan (Eve Plumb), Cindy (Susan Olsen), Greg (Barry Williams), Peter (Christopher Knight), Bobby (Michael Lookinland). The housekeeper Alice was played by Ann B. Davis.

This show is a favorite among television collectors and many products were manufactured which carry the show's name. These include a lunch box and thermos by King-Seeley (1970); puzzles by Whitman (1972); several sets of paper dolls and coloring books by Whitman; and "The Brady Bunch Fishin' Fun Set," copyright 1973 by Paramount Pictures, Inc.

The Brady Bunch Paper Dolls boxed set of two dolls. © 1973 by Paramount Picture Corp. Produced by Whitman Publishing Company. $10-15 (cut). ◆ *The Brady Bunch Paper Dolls* (#1976) in a larger set published by Whitman in book form, also in 1973. © Paramount Pictures Corp. $35-40 (uncut).

The Brady Bunch Coloring Book (#1657), published by Whitman Publishing Company. © 1974 Paramount Pictures Corp. $20-25. ✦ The Brady Bunch comic published by Dell Publishing Company, May 1970. © Paramount Pictures Corp., 1970. $7-10. ✦ The Brady Bunch in Adventure on the High Seas by Jack Matcha. Tiger Beat Publication. © 1973 by Paramount Pictures Corp. $5-8.

Branded

"Branded" was a short-lived western broadcast on NBC from January 24, 1965 to September 4, 1966. Chuck Connors starred as Jason McCord. The action took place in southwestern Wyoming during the 1870s and featured Indian uprisings of the time.

Milton Bradley produced a board game in 1966 based on the show.

Brave Eagle

"Brave Eagle" was another 1950s television show set in the West. The unusual plot was based on the viewpoint of the Indian during the early days of the white man's settlement of the West. Brave Eagle, a Cheyenne chief, was played by Keith Larsen. The show aired on CBS from September to June during the 1955-1956 season.

Despite the short run of the show, several items were made based on its characters. These include a lunch box and thermos from the American Thermos Bottle Co.; a Little Golden Book by Simon and Schuster (1957); a coloring book published by Whitman (1955); and View-Master reels (1956).

Brave Eagle comic book (#770). Published by Dell Publishing Company. © 1957 by Roy Rogers-Frontiers, Inc. $5-8.

Break the Bank

"Break the Bank" was a game show that aired on two networks during the early days of television. ABC carried the program from October 22, 1948 until September 23, 1949. Then the show was aired by NBC from October 5, 1949 until September 1, 1953. Both Bert Parks and Bud Collyer did stints as host for the show.

A game was produced by Bettye-B in 1955 to tie in with the program.

Broadside

"Broadside" aired on ABC from September 20, 1964 until September 5, 1965. As unlikely as it seems, the show was a comedy based in the South Pacific during World War II. The show was a spin-off from the more successful "McHale's Navy." The plot involved rivalry between the women assigned to the island Navy supply depot and the regular Navy men. Cast members include Kathleen Nolan as Lt. Anne Morgan, Lois Roberts as Private Molly McGuire, Joan Staley as Private Roberta Love, Sheila James as Private Selma Kowalski, Dick Sargent as Lt. Maxwell Trotter, and Edward Andrews as Commander Adrian.

An interesting board game was produced by Transogram in 1964 to tie in with the show.

Broken Arrow

"Broken Arrow" was another 1950s Western show, set in Tuscon, Arizona, in the 1870s. The main character, Tom Jeffords (played by John Lupton), was an Indian agent to the Apaches. The Indian chief Cochise was played by Michael Ansara. ABC carried the series from 1956 to 1960.

Built-Rite produced a frame tray puzzle honoring the show in 1958, and Hartland Plastics made figures of both Cochise and Tom Jeffords in the early 1960s.

The Buccaneers

"The Buccaneers" was an adventure series aired on CBS from September 22, 1956 to September 14, 1957. The hero of the program was Captain Dan Tempest, played by Robert Shaw. He was a buccaneer living in the Caribbean colony of New Providence in the early eighteenth century.

Several collectibles were made during the short time this series was on the air. They include a board game by Transogram in 1957, a Big Little Book by Whitman, comic books, and a lunch box also from 1957.

Buck Rogers in the 25th Century

"Buck Rogers in the 25th Century" is the title of two different television programs. The first one aired over ABC in 1950. The second series played on NBC from September 20, 1979 until April 16, 1981. The later science fiction show included Gil Gerard as Buck Rogers, Erin Gray as Wilma Deering, and Tim O'Connor as Dr. Elias Huer.

Several collectibles were produced to tie in with the program. They include a lunch box and thermos made by Aladdin Industries (1979); 12" hard plastic dolls by Mego Toys (1979); and "Buck Rogers Colorforms Adventure Set."

"Buck Rogers Colorforms Adventure Set." © 1979 Robert C. Dille. Made by Colorforms. $15-20. ♦ Lunch box © 1979 by Robert C. Dille. Made by Aladdin Industries Inc. $25-30.

Buffalo Bill, Jr.

"Buffalo Bill, Jr." was a syndicated television show produced by Gene Autry Flying A Productions in 1955. The series consisted of forty episodes geared to the young viewer. The program was a western based in Texas in the 1890s. The characters included Buffalo Bill, Jr. (played by Dick Jones); Calamity (Nancy Gilbert); and Judge Ben Wiley (Harry Cheshire).

Several items were produced to promote this series. They include: puzzles made by Built-Rite (1956); a 78 RPM record; View-Master pack; and "Buffalo Bill Jr's Cattle Round-Up Game" also by Built-Rite (1956).

A Buffalo Bill Jr. "Junior Picture Puzzle" from the "Famous TV Stars" series by Built-Rite. © 1956 Flying A Productions. $10-15.

Buffalo Bill Jr. Coloring Book (#1316). Published by Whitman Publishing Company, 1956. © Flying A Productions. $15-20.

C

The Californians

"The Californians" aired on the NBC network from September 1957 until September 1959. This western, based in San Francisco in 1851, starred Adam Kennedy as Dion Patrick, and later Richard Coogan as Marshal Matt Wayne. The story line involved law and order in San Francisco in its early years.

"The Californians" cards. © 1958 California Nat. Productions., Inc. © T.C.G. (Topps cards). $2-3 each.

Burke's Law

Although "Burke's Law" made a repeat appearance as a series on television in 1994, it was originally shown on the ABC network from September 20, 1963 to August 31, 1965. Both shows starred Gene Barry as Amos Burke the multimillionaire police investigator. The action in the series was based in Los Angeles, California.

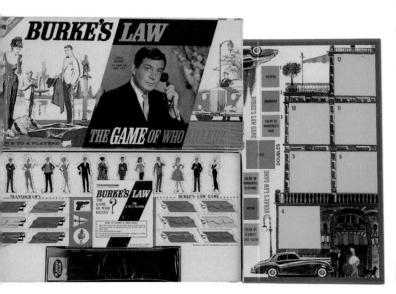

"Burke's Law: The Game of Who Killed?..." manufactured by Transogram Co., Inc. © 1963 Four-Star-Barbety. $35-40.

Candid Camera

"Candid Camera" was a unique program which included real people as its cast members. Unusual situations were arranged by the show's organizers and then ordinary people were lured into participating in the action. A hidden camera caught their reactions and the results were usually very funny. One of viewers' favorite scenes featured a talking mailbox which visited with people as they passed by. The show aired on ABC from 1948 until 1949; on CBS from 1949 to 1951; and again on ABC from 1951 to 1956. A later version appeared on CBS from 1960 to 1967. Alan Funt was the host on all of these programs.

A board game made by Lowell in 1963 was based on the "Candid Camera" program.

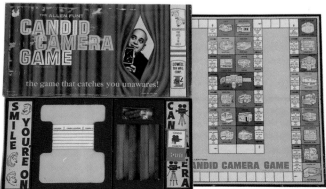

"The Allen Funt Candid Camera Game." © 1963 The Allen Funt Company. Made by Lowell Toy Manufacture Corp. $25-35.

The Captain and Tennille

Toni Tennille and her husband Daryl Dragon formed the duo "The Captain and Tennille." After winning a Grammy for the record "Love Will Keep Us Together" in 1975, they went on to have their own television show. The series, called "The Captain and Tennille," aired on ABC from September 1976 to March 1977. Tennille also had a syndicated variety show in 1980.

Captain Gallent, of the Foreign Legion

(see Foreign Legionnaire)

Captain Kangaroo

"Captain Kangaroo" was the longest running children's television program ever. It began on CBS in 1955, starring Bob Keeshan as the Captain and Lumpy Brannum as Mr. Green Jeans. The show continued until 1984. The series was a weekday show designed for preschool children. It featured puppets, animals, and animated features along with varied guests each day. Tom Terrific and Mighty Manfred became much-loved characters for children because of their exposure on the "Captain Kangaroo" television show. The cartoons featuring these characters were shown frequently as part of the regular broadcast. Tom Terrific was created by Terrytoons. Thirty of the four-minute films were made and they were syndicated in the early 1960s.

New products were produced nearly every year to tie in to the show. Some of the many collectibles include: Captain Kangaroo thermos and lunch box by King Seeley (1964); Captain Kangaroo board game by Milton Bradley (1956); View-Master Reel set (1957); and finger paint set by Hasbro (1956). Both Samuel Lowe Co. and Whitman Publishing Co. published coloring books featuring the Captain. Whitman also was responsible for several children's books based on Captain Kangaroo.

"Captain and Tennille Toni Tennille" doll. © 1977 Moonlight and Magnolias, Inc. Made by Mego Corp. Doll is 12 1/4" tall with rooted hair and painted features. $35-40. ✦ Autographed photograph dates from late 1980s. $20-25.

Captain Kangaroo Coloring Book (4967) Published by Samuel Lowe Company. © 1977 Robert Keeshan Associates. $10-15. ✦ *Captain Kangaroo Coloring Book* (1154) Published by Whitman Publishing Company. © 1957 by Keeshan-Miller Enterprises Corp. $10-15.

Tom Terrific with Mighty Manfred the Wonder Dog (#312). © 1957 CBS Television Film Sales, Inc. Published by Treasure Books. $15-20.

Captain Kangaroo's Picnic. Story by Mary Voell Jones. Illustrated by Mel Crawford. © 1959 Robert Keeshan Associates, Inc. A Whitman Tell-A-Tale Book. Western Publishing Company. C.B.S. Enterprises, Inc. $4-6. ✦ Tablet is not marked with the name of the maker. $5-10.

"Captain Kangaroo March" © MCMLVII (1957) by Lee Herschel and Leo Paris. $10-15. ✦ *Captain Kangaroo and the Panda* published by Golden Press. C.B.S. Television Enterprises. © 1957 Keeshan-Miller Enterprises Corp. $3-5.

Captain Kangaroo Trace and Color (#1413). Published by Whitman Publishing Company. © 1960 by Robert Keeshan Associates. $10-15. ✦ *Captain Kangaroo and Dancing Bear Presto Slate and Stylus.* Made by E. E. Fairchild Corp. © Robert Keeshan Associates. $10-15.

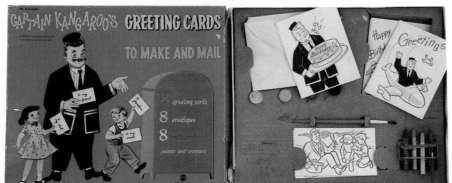

"Captain Kangaroo's Greeting Cards to Make and Mail." A Keeshan-Miller Enterprises Production. © 1956 Keeshan-Miller Enterprises Corp. CBS Television Enterprises. $20-30.

Captain Video and His Video Rangers

"Captain Video and His Video Rangers" was one of the first television shows for children. The program appeared on the DuMont network from 1949-1956. The show changed formats three times during this period. The science fiction program first starred Richard Googan as Captain Video, but Al Hodge took over the part in 1950.

Several products were made to tie in with the show. These included the "Rite-O-Lite Captain Video Gun," boxed figures by Lido, and "Captain Video Space Game" by Milton Bradley.

Car 54, Where Are You?

"Car 54, Where Are You?" was a unique police comedy whose two stars were reminiscent of the comic characters Mutt and Jeff. The action took place in the Bronx's 53rd precinct. The two policemen, Gunther Toody and Francis Muldoon, were played by Joe E. Ross and Fred Gwynne. Gunther's wife was played by Beatrice Pons, and Captain Martin Block was played by Paul Reed. The sixty episodes of the program aired on NBC from 1961 to 1963.

Although this program is a popular one for collectors, there were not many products made to tie in with the show. Whitman produced a coloring book in 1962, and Dell Publishing Co. published comic books in the same year. One of the hardest items to find is the board game manufactured by Allison Industries, Inc. in 1961. Another elusive toy is the metal friction car with a "54" on its side.

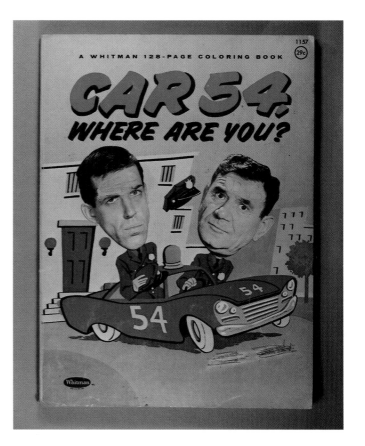

Car 54, Where Are You? (#1157). Coloring book drawings by Bob Jenney. © 1962, Eupolis Productions, Inc. Published by Whitman Publishing Company. $25-35.

"Car 54, Where Are You?" board game by Allison, 1961. © Eupolis Productions, Inc. $150-200.

Casper, The Friendly Ghost

"Casper, The Friendly Ghost" was the title of an animated cartoon series which first appeared in movie theaters under the Paramount banner. Casper was the star of the series; other characters were Wendy the Good Witch, and Spooky, another ghost. Two Casper cartoon series were aired on television. The first appeared on ABC from 1963 to 1967. The second was a spin-off series by Hanna-Barbera Studios which played on NBC during the 1979-1980 season.

Although there are many Casper products available to collectors, most are not associated with the television programs. Collectors do enjoy the Casper The Talking Ghost doll made by Mattel, Inc. (1961), as well as the Milton Bradley board game (1959).

"Casper the Friendly Ghost Game." © 1959 Harvey Famous Cartoons under Berne and Universal Copyright Conventions. Produced by Milton Bradley Company. $15-18.

Charlie's Angels

The success of "Charlie's Angels" was due primarily to the good looks of its stars. The hour-long crime program ran on ABC from September 22, 1976 to August 19, 1981, and starred Kate Jackson as Sabrina Duncan, Farrah Fawcett as Jill Munroe, and Jaclyn Smith as Kelly Garrett. The part made Fawcett so famous that she soon left the series, and a new character played by Cheryl Ladd (Kris Munroe) was added. When Jackson also left the show, Shelly Hack (playing the part of Tiffany Welles) was added to the cast. All of the young ladies worked for the Charles Townsend Private Detective Agency. The voice of Charlie Townsend was that of John Forsythe, who only communicated by telephone. Their contact man was John Bosley, played by David Doyle.

"Charlie's Angels" captured the attention of toy manufacturers, so there are many tie-in collectibes available. Included are the following: Farrah's Glamour Center with a model of Farrah's head along with accessories to style her hair, made by Mego Corp. (1977); Custom Van replica by Corgi (4 1/2" long); and Paint by Number set by Hasbro (1977).

"Charlie's Angels Dresser Set." © 1977 Spelling-Goldberg Productions © 1977 Fleetwood Toys, Inc. $15-18. ✦ Billfold © 1977 Spelling-Goldberg Productions, H. G. Toys, Inc. $15-18.

Charlie's Angels doll outfit on card made by Hasbro. © 1977 Spelling-Goldberg Productions. $20-25. ✦ A doll representing Jill (Farrah Fawcett-Majors), also produced by Hasbro and © 1977 Spelling-Goldberg Productions. $25-30.

8 1/2"-tall dolls representing "Charlie's Angels." Included are Kris (Cheryl Ladd), Kelly (Jaclyn Smith), and Sabrina (Kate Jackson). © 1977 Spelling-Goldberg Productions. Made by Hasbro. $25-30 each.

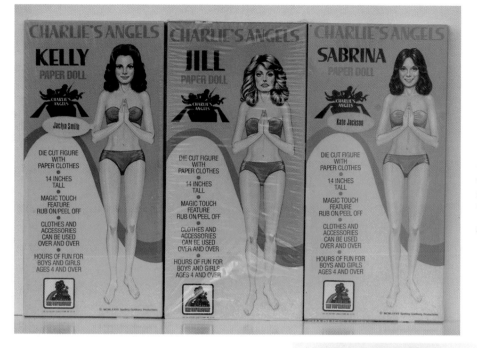

"Charlie's Angels" boxed paper dolls. The three boxes include Jill (Farrah Fawcett-Majors); Kelly (Jaclyn Smith); and Sabrina (Kate Jackson). The dolls are 14" tall. © 1977 by Spelling-Goldberg Productions. Made by The Toy Factory. $15-20 each.

"Charlie's Angels Game" by Milton Bradley. © 1977 Spelling-Goldberg Productions. $20-25.

"Charlie's Angels" lunch box and thermos made by Aladdin Industries, Inc. © 1978 Spelling-Goldberg Productions, Inc. $35-45. ✦ "Angels" cards, © 1977 by Spelling-Goldberg Productions. $2-3 each.

"The New Charlie's Angels" puzzle. © 1977 Spelling-Goldberg Productions. Made by H G Toys Inc. $12-15. ✦ "Revell Snap-Together Charlie's Angels Van." © 1977 by Spelling-Goldberg Productions, and © 1977 by Revell, Inc. $30-35.

Farrah doll, 12 1/4" tall. Vinyl with molded features and hair. © 1977 by Farrah. Made by Mego Corp. $35-40.

"Farrah Fawcett Casse-tête Jigsaw Puzzle." © 1977 Pro Arts, Inc. Distributor American Publishing Corp. Size 12" by 20". $8-12.

Cheyenne

"Cheyenne" was another of the westerns that were so important to the television schedules of the late 1950s. The sixty-minute show aired on ABC from September 20, 1956 to August 30, 1963. The action centered around the frontier scout Cheyenne Bodie (Clint Walker), and his adventures during the 1860s.

Several products were made to tie in to the Cheyenne image. They include a boxed set of three Milton Bradley puzzles (1957); board game made by Milton Bradley (1958); and Hartland Figure by Hartland Plastics (circa 1960).

Warner Bros.' Cheyenne. © Warner Bros. Pictures, Inc. 1958. A Little Golden Book published by Simon and Schuster. $5-8. ✦ Cheyenne comic book (Dec.-Jan. 1961) published by Dell Publishing Company. © 1960 Warner Bros. Pictures, Inc. $8-10.

"Cheyenne Game" by Milton Bradley. © by Warner Bros. Pictures, Inc., 1958. $35-45.

Chips

"Chips" was a not-so-typical crime show from the 1970s. It was unusual in that it lasted sixty minutes instead of a half hour, and it dealt with the adventures of the California Highway Patrol instead of city police officers. The series began on NBC in 1977. Leading characters were Jon Baker (played by Larry Wilcox) and Francis Poncherello (Erik Estrada). Robert Pine played the sergeant in charge of the officers. The series ended in 1983.

Associated products include a toy wristwatch by Imperial Toy Corp. (1980) and a board game by Ideal (1981). A set of dolls was made by Mego in 1981 in the likeness of characters from the series. The dolls were 8" tall and represented Erik Estrada, Larry Wilcox, and Robert Pine. The same characters were also made in figures 3 3/4" tall. Wheels Willy and Jimmy Squeeks were also included in the smaller size.

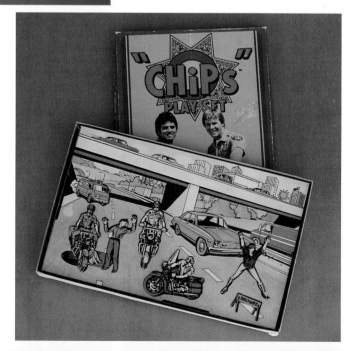

"Chips Playset," © 1981 Metro-Goldwyn-Mayer Film Company. Made by Colorforms. $15-20.

Chips Coloring and Activity Book (#402-2). Published by Playmore Publishing Inc. and Waldman Publishing Corp., © 1983 by M-G-M Inc. $10-15. ✦ "Ponch" Poncherello (Erik Estrada) doll, 8" tall. Dolls of Larry Wilcox and Robert Pine as Jon Baker and Sarge were also made. Made by Mego and © 1977 by M-G-M. Inc. $25-30.

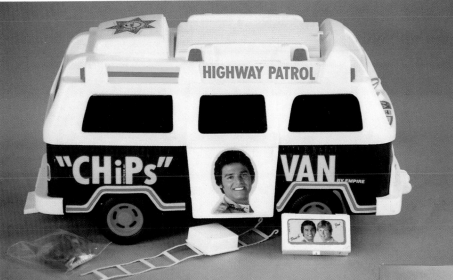

"Chips" Van, plastic, 19" by 11 1/2". © 1977 Metro-Goldwyn-Mayer, Inc. Made by Empire. $20-30.

Circus Boy

"Circus Boy" was a thirty-minute children's program broadcast on NBC from 1956 to 1957 and on ABC from 1957 to 1958. The story was about a boy named Corky whose parents had been killed in a circus accident. Corky became a water boy for Bimbo the elephant in a traveling circus. Cast members included Mickey Braddock as Corky, Robert Lowery as Big Tim Champion, Noah Berry, Jr. as Joey the Clown, and "Big Boy" Williams as Pete.

Since "Circus Boy" was a program for kids, several products were made which featured the characters. H.G. Toys manufactured a game in 1956 and Whitman Publishing Co. published several books and a coloring book based on the series.

Circus Boy Coloring Book (#1198). Published by Whitman Publishing Company, 1957. © Norbert Productions, Inc. Contains captioned pictures of the characters and animals from the television series. $15-20.

Cisco Kid

"Cisco Kid" was a thirty-minute syndicated television show from 1951 to 1956. There were 156 episodes in the series. The Cisco Kid was played by Duncan Renaldo and his companion, Pancho, was Leo Carillo. Their horses were Diablo and Loco. The action took place in New Mexico in the 1890s.

Related television products include coloring books produced by Saalfield Publishing Co., a white glass mug, a bowl, and other premium products issued for the local television programs.

Cisco Kid Coloring Book (#2428). Published by Saalfield Publishing Company, Doubleday and Company, and © 1954. ✦ Cisco Kid Coloring Book (#2078). Published and © by Saalfield Publishing Company, Doubleday and Company, 1950. $15-20 each.

Code Red

"Code Red" was on the ABC network from September 20, 1981 until September 12, 1982. The series starred Lorne Greene as firefighter Battalion Chief Joe Rorchek. Other Rorchek family members were also employed by the Los Angeles City Fire Department. They included Julie Adams as Ann, Andrew Stevens as Ted, and Sam J. Jones as Chris.

"Code Red" boat. © 1981 Columbia Pictures Industries, Inc. Matchbox, © 1981 Lesney Products Corp. Eight different vehicles were made including a helicopter, fire chief's car, snorkel, police car, police motorcycle, pumper, and ambulance. Die-cast metal. $8-10.

Columbo

Peter Falk created one of the great characters in television when he played the part of Lt. Columbo in this popular police drama. The "Columbo" series aired on NBC from 1972 to 1977 and has returned for specials through the years. Columbo worked for the Los Angeles Police Department. Driving an old car and wearing a rumpled trench coat, he acted as if he were so incompetent that the murderers he met need not fear detection. Still, the shrewd detective always solved the crime before the end of the show, after leading the viewing public through a string of unlikely clues.

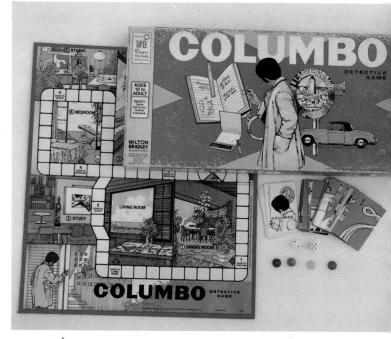

"Columbo Detective Game" produced by Milton Bradley Company. © Universal Television, 1973. $20-25.

"Columbo Mystery Puzzle Game" manufactured by American Publishing, A Division of LJN Toys LTD. © 1989 Universal City Studios Inc. Licensed by Merchandising Corp. of America, Inc. $8-10.

Combat

"Combat" appeared on the ABC network from 1962 to 1967. The sixty-minute show dealt with the story of the United States Infantry during World War II, and the action took place from the D-Day landing to the end of the war in 1945. Characters included Lt. Gil Hanley (Rick Jason), Sgt. Chip Saunders (Vic Morrow), "Wildman" Kirby (Jack Hogan), Caje (Pierre Jalbert), Littlejohn (Dick Peabody), Nelson (Tom Lowell), and Doc (Conlan Carter).

Several "Combat" products were manufactured during the life of the show. These included a book by Whitman (1964); board game by Ideal (1963); 66 gum cards (1963); coloring book by Saalfield Pub. (1963); card game by Milton Bradley (1964); puzzle by Jaymar (1966); and "Combat; Official Play Set" by T. Cohn (1963).

Concentration

"Concentration" was another of the early successful game shows. It aired on NBC from August 25, 1958 until March 23, 1973. Several different hosts were on the program, including Hugh Downs, Jack Barry, and Ed McMahon. A tie-in game was produced by Milton Bradley in 1958.

"The Fighting Infantry Game Combat" © 1963 Ideal Toy Corporation. ABC Television Network Show. © 1963 Selmur Productions., Inc. $25-30.

Combat! The Counterattack by Franklin M. Davis, Jr. Whitman Publishing Company. © 1964 by Selmur Productions. $5-6. ✦ "Combat Interlocking Picture Puzzle" made by Jaymar. $12-16.

Convoy

The World War II "Convoy" television program aired on NBC from September to December in 1965. There were only thirteen sixty-minute episodes of the series, which involved a convoy of 299 American ships on their way to England. Commander Dan Talbot was played by John Gavin and Captain Ben Foster was portrayed by John Larch.

The Cosby Show

"The Cosby Show" began on NBC in 1984 and ended in 1992. It was one of the most successful television shows of the 1980s. The series dealt with an upper-class black family, which included a father who was a doctor and a mother who had a career as a lawyer. Bill Cosby played the part of Dr. Cliff Huxtable, his wife Clair was played by Phylicia Rashad. The children were played by Lisa Bonet as Denise, Sabrina LeBeauf as Sandra, Malcolm-Jamal Warner as Theodore, Tempestt Bledsoe as Vanessa, and Keshia Knight Pulliam as Rudy. The show was one of very few that pictured a successful and happy black family through a situation comedy.

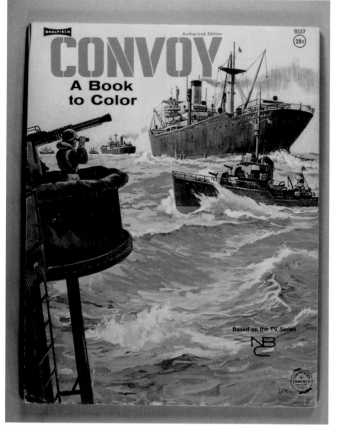

Convoy: A Book To Color (#9537). © 1965, Universal Television. Published by Saalfield Publishing Company. $15-18.

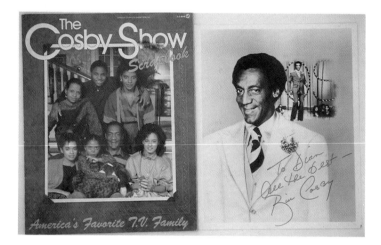

The Cosby Show Scrapbook. Sharon Starbooks. © 1986 by Sharon Publications, Inc. $3-5. ✦ An autographed picture of the show's star, Bill Cosby. $20-25.

The Courtship of Eddie's Father

"The Courtship of Eddie's Father" was a situation comedy that aired on ABC from September 17, 1969 until June 14, 1972. The story focused on the relationship between a widower, Tom Corbett (Bill Bixby), and his son Eddie (Brandon Cruz) as they strove to make a life for themselves.

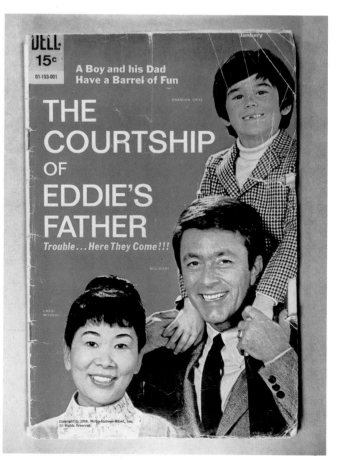

The Courtship of Eddie's Father comic book. © 1969 M-G-M Inc. Dell Publishing Company. January 1970. $5-8.

Curiosity Shop

"Curiosity Shop" was an interesting educational program which appeared on ABC from 1971 to 1973 in a sixty-minute format. The Saturday morning show contained sketches, cartoons, puppets, and Gittel the Witch (played by Barbara Minkus).

Saalfield Publishing Co. produced several books based on this show. They included "Follow the Dots Activity Book," "All Kinds of Things To Do," and coloring books (all in 1971). King Seeley manufactured a lunch box and thermos featuring the program in 1972.

D

Daktari

The action in "Daktari" took place in the Wameru Game Preserve and Research Center in Africa. Daktari means "doctor" in Swahili. The cast members included Marshall Thompson as Dr. Marsh Tracy, Cheryl Miller as his daughter, Headley Mattingley as the district Game Warden, and Yule Sommers and Hari Rhodes as zoologists. The show aired on CBS from 1966 to 1969.

Products using the show's name include "Daktari Play Set" made by Marx Toys (1967); pencil tablet (late 1960s); and Big Little Book by Western Publishing Co. (1968).

Dallas

"Dallas" was a prime time continuing drama which was first telecast on April 2, 1978 on the CBS network. The show was so successful it lasted over ten years. By the 1980-1981 season the program was the most watched series on television. The program was set in Texas and revolved around the wealthy Ewing family, headed by Jock Ewing (played by Jim Davis). His wife, Miss Ellie, was first played by Barbara Bel Geddes, but in 1984 Donna Reed took over the role. Their children were J. R. (Larry Hagman), Bobby (Patrick Duffy), and Gary (David Ackroyd; beginning in 1979, Ted Shackelford).

Larry Hagman, as J. R., became the star of the show. In the last episode of the 1980 season he was mysteriously shot and was taken to the hospital in critical condition. All summer the important question was asked: "Who shot J.R.?" When the new episode was shown, 41.5 million households watched as the character called Kristin (Colleen Camp) was shown to be guilty. The end of the series came in 1991.

"Curiosity Shop" lunch box, © 1972 American Broadcasting Company, Inc. Made by Thermos. $25-30. ✦ *Curiosity Shop Pictures To Color,* Artcraft (#5353). Adapted from the ABC TV Series. © 1971 American Broadcasting Company, Inc. $10-15.

"Daktari Jigsaw Puzzle" by Whitman Publishing Company. © 1967 Ivan Tors Films, Inc. $15-18. ✦ *Daktari* comic book, October 1968. Dell Publishing Company. © Ivan Tors Films, Inc. $5-8. ✦ *Daktari* by Jess Shelton. Ace Books, Inc. © 1966 by Ivan Tors Films, Inc. $5-8.

"Dallas Picture Puzzle Casse-tête" by Warren Paper Products. © 1980 Lorimar Productions. Inc. $10-12. ✦ "Dallas: The Television Role-Playing Game," © 1980 Lorimar Productions. Inc. SPI. $10-12.

TV Guide from June 16, 1979 featuring "Dallas" cast members on the cover. Published by Triangle Publications, Inc. $4-6. ✦ JR beer can, "J.R. Ewings' Private Stock." Pearl Brewing Company. J.R. Ewing name © 1980 by Lorimar Productions. Inc. $5-8.

Daniel Boone

"Daniel Boone" appeared on NBC as a sixty-minute program from 1964 until 1970. The show featured the adventures of pioneer Daniel Boone in Kentucky during the late 1700s. Fess Parker played the part of Daniel Boone, and Patricia Blair was his wife. Their children were played by Veronica Cartwright and Darby Hinton.

Program-associated products include the following: lunch box and thermos by King-Seeley (1965); "Fess Parker Trailblazers Game" by Milton Bradley (1964); "Fess Parker/Daniel Boone Color-Fun Book" by Saalfield Publishing Co. (1965); View-Master set; and frame tray puzzle (1960s). Remco made a 5" tall Daniel Boone doll in 1964.

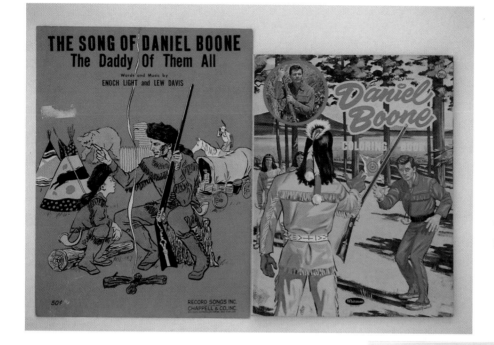

"The Song Of Daniel Boone: The Daddy Of Them All." Words and Music by Enoch Light and Lew Davis. © 1955 by Record Songs, Inc. $5-8. ♦ Daniel Boone Coloring Book, Walt Disney Edition (#1116). © 1961, Walt Disney Productions. Published by Whitman Publishing Company. $15-20.

The Danny Thomas Show

(see "Make Room For Daddy")

Dark Shadows

"Dark Shadows" was an unusual television serial that caught the attention of youngsters as well as adults. The thirty-minute afternoon show featured vampires, werewolves, and black magic in its story line. As in the case of most serials, there was a large cast of players. Included were Joan Bennett as Elizabeth Collins Stoddard, Alexandra Molke as Victoria Winters, Jonathan Frid as Barnabas Collins, and Nancy Barrett as Carolyn Stoddard. Both Roger Collins and Edward Collins were played by Louis Edmonds. The series aired on ABC from 1966 to 1971.

Program tie-ins include a soundtrack record album by Phillips (1969); comic books; "Barnabas Collins/Dark Shadows Game" by Milton Bradley (1969); "Dark Shadows Mysterious Maze Game" by Whitman (1968); puzzle by Whitman (1969); and "Barnabas Vampire Van" model kit made by MPC in 1969.

"Barnabas Collins Dark Shadows Game" produced by Milton Bradley Company. © 1969 Dan Curtis Productions., Inc. $40-50.

"Dark Shadows Game" by Whitman. © 1968 by Dan Curtis Productions., Inc. From the collection of Jeff Zillner. $40-50.

Dastardly and Mutley in Their Flying Machines

"Dastardly and Mutley in Their Flying Machines" was an animated cartoon set in the era of World War I. This Hanna-Barbera production was shown on CBS from 1969 until 1971. The characters included evil Dick Dastardly and his dog Mutley.

Davy Crockett

"Davy Crockett" was originally shown as part of the "Disneyland" series in 1955 on NBC. Fess Parker played the part of the famous frontiersman Davy Crockett. The show was a hit with kids and many products were produced as tie-ins, including the following: sheet music, pocket knife, hatchet, watch, and wallet. A lunch kit by Adco-Liberty, tool kit by Liberty, puzzle by Jaymar, coloring book by Whitman, and several items of clothing were also produced. All of the products were circa 1955.

"Dastardly and Muttley in Their Flying Machines," © 1969 Hanna-Barbera Productions. Inc. Made by Milton Bradley Company. $15-20.

"Davy Crockett" doll with plastic mask face and cloth body. Doll is approximately 33" tall. Circa 1955. Maker unknown. $15-20.

Walt Disney's Davy Crockett. Little Golden Book, Simon and Schuster. © 1955 by Walt Disney Productions. $8-10. ✦ Walt Disney's Davy Crockett comic books. Bottom left: © 1955 Walt Disney Productions. Western Publishing Company. Top right: Dell Publishing Company, 1955 (#631). © Walt Disney Productions. $8-10. ✦ Davy Crockett Christmas greeting card. © Walt Disney Productions. Made by Gibson, circa 1955. $10-15.

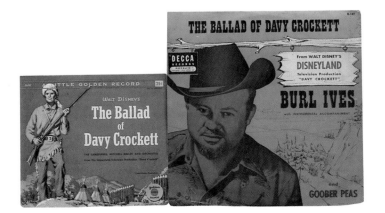

"The Ballad of Davy Crockett" 45 RPM record. © Walt Disney Productions. Featuring The Sandpipers and Mitchell Miller and his orchestra. Little Golden Records, Simon and Schuster. $8-10. ✦ "The Ballad of Davy Crockett" by Decca Records. From Walt Disney's Disneyland. Burl Ives vocalist. Decca Children's Series. $8-10.

Dennis the Menace

"Dennis the Menace" was one of the few television programs that appealed both to children and adults. The show was based on the comic strip by Hank Ketcham. The action revolved around Dennis Mitchell, a very mischievous little boy. The part was played by Jay North. His parents were portrayed by Herbert Anderson and Gloria Henry. George Wilson, a neighbor, was played by Joseph Kearns.

It is difficult to know what products were based on the television show and which were comic items. The show ran on CBS from 1959 until 1963. Some of the TV-related products include "Dennis the Menace Back-Yard Picnic" set-up kit by Whitman Publishing Co. (1960); TV soundtrack by Colpix (1960); board game by Standard Toy Kraft (1960); coloring book by Whitman Publishing Co. (1961); book by Random House (1960); and frame tray puzzle by Whitman, 1960. Several vinyl dolls of Dennis have also been produced.

"Dennis the Menace Frame Tray Puzzle" produced by Whitman. © 1960 by Hall Syndicate, Inc. $15-20. ✦ *Children's Playmate* magazine, September 1960. Published by Children's Playmate Magazine, Inc. Jay North is featured on cover. $8-10.

Dennis the Menace Back-Yard Picnic (#1991). © 1960 by Hall Syndicate Inc. Whitman Publishing Company. From the collection of Elaine Price. $50-60.

The Dick Van Dyke Show

Although the CBS situation comedy "The Dick Van Dyke Show" began in 1961 and ended in 1966, the format seemed much like the popular shows of the 1950s. The family involved in the action included a working father, Rob Petrie (played by Dick Van Dyke); a stay-at-home mother, Laura (Mary Tyler Moore); and a child Richie (Larry Matthews). The show was unusual in that it also focused on the father's comedy writing career. This aspect of the program featured characters Morey Amsterdam and Rose Marie as Van Dyke's fellow writers.

The "Dick Van Dyke Show" board game was made by Standard Toy Kraft in 1962. It is a very hard item to locate.

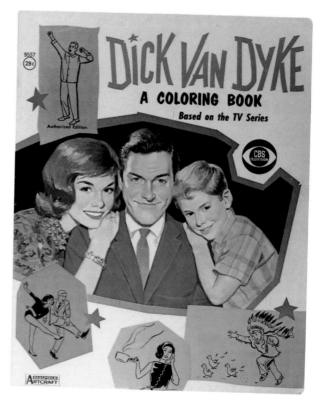

Dick Van Dyke A Coloring Book (#9557). Based on the CBS television series. © 1963 by Calvada Productions. Published by Saalfield Publishing Company. $75+.

"The Dick Van Dyke Show Board Game" made by Standard Toykraft, 1962. © 1962 by Calvada Productions. Courtesy of 52 Girls Collectibles. $175-200.

Diff'rent Strokes

"Diff'rent Strokes" was a situation comedy based in New York City. The show was a successful NBC series, beginning in 1978 and ending in 1986. The story line involved a white millionaire, Phillip Drummone (Conrad Bain), who adopted two black boys, Arnold and Willis Jackson. The star of the show was Gary Coleman, who played Arnold Jackson. Willis was played by Todd Bridges and Charlotte Roe was cast as the housekeeper.

The Dinah Shore Show

"The Dinah Shore Show" was a staple on NBC television from 1950 until 1962. The shows expanded from fifteen minutes to sixty minutes during this time. The popular variety programs included the finest in music and guests from the period. No retrospect of the best segments from television's past can be complete without some Dinah tape.

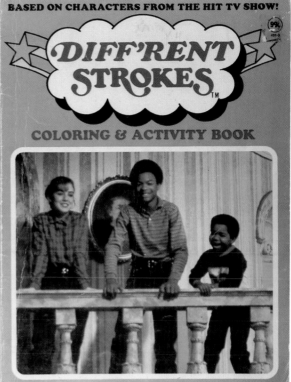

Diff'rent Strokes Color and Activity Book (#401-3). Published by Playmore Publishing, Inc. and Waldman Publishing Corp. © 1983 by Tandem Productions, Inc. $10-15.

Dinah Shore: 2 Cut Out Dolls and Clothes (#1963). Whitman Publishing Company, © 1958. $65-75. ♦ Dinah Shore and George Montgomery Cut-Outs (#1970). © 1959 by Whitman Publishing Company. Montgomery was Shore's husband at the time. $75-100.

Ding Dong School

A very popular kid's show from the early days of television was "Ding Dong School." It was shown on NBC from 1951 to 1956. The show was hosted by Miss Frances, who was really Dr. Frances Horwich. The preschool program featured simple games and instruction.

Several educational items were issued featuring the show's name. Included were books by Rand McNally and Co., Melody Bells by Knickerbocker, puzzles, RCA record player, and several Whitman books including sticker and activity types.

I Decided by Miss Frances. A Ding Dong School Book by Dr. Frances R. Horwich and Reinald Werrenrath, Jr., NBC and Rand McNally and Company. © 1953 by Frances Horwich and Reinald Werrenrath, Jr. $3-5. ♦ Ding Dong School "Let's Draw Pictures with Miss Frances." Created by Frances Horwich. © 1953 by Whitman Publishing Company. A National Broadcasting Co., Inc. Service and Trademark. $10-12.

Donny and Marie

Donny Osmond and his sister Marie starred in their own television variety show from 1976 to 1979 on the ABC network. Their brothers, billed as The Osmond Brothers, also appeared on the show as did the younger Osmond brother, Jimmy. Dolls were made in the images of Donny, Marie, and Jimmy. Puppets were also produced of both Donny and Marie.

Donny and Marie Osmond T.V. Show. Made by Mattel, Inc. © Osbro Productions., 1976. The case opens up to provide a stage. A piano, guitar, and lights were also to be used with the stage. $15-20.

Marie Osmond and Donny Osmond vinyl dolls. Each is approximately 12" tall. Made by Mattel, Inc., 1976. © Mattel, Inc. and © Osbro Productions. Inc., 1976. $25-30 each.

Donny and Marie: The Top Secret Project by Laura French. Published by Golden Press, Western Publishing Company, Inc. © Osbro Productions. Inc., 1977. $8-10. ◆ *Donny and Marie* coloring book (#1641), published by Whitman Publishing Company. © Osbro Productions. Inc., 1977. $15-20. ◆ *Donny and Marie* paper dolls, published by Whitman Publishing Company. © Osbro Productions. Inc., 1977. $15-20.

Dr. Kildare

The early 1960s brought many new medical shows to the television line-up. One of the best was "Dr. Kildare," based on the character made famous in a series of "B" films produced by M-G-M in the 1930s and 1940s. The program aired on NBC from 1961 to 1965 in a sixty-minute format, and then was shortened to half-hour segments during its last year, from 1965 to 1966. Dr. James Kildare (played by Richard Chamberlain) was an intern and later a resident physician at Blair General Hospital. His superior, Dr. Leonard Gillespie, was played by Raymond Massey.

Several tie-in products were manufactured with the Dr. Kildare name. Included are the following: board game by Ideal (1962); Dr. Kildare bobbing head figure (circa early 1960s); and a 12" tall doll made of vinyl. "Dr. Kildare" appears on the pocket of the doll's white uniform.

Dr. Kildare: Assigned to Trouble by Robert C. Ackworth. Whitman Publishing Company. © 1963 by Metro-Goldwyn-Mayer Inc. $5-8. ◆ *TV Radio Mirror*, May 1962. Published by Macfadden-Bartell Corp. $5-8. ◆ *Dr. Kildare: The Magic Key* by William Johnston. Whitman Publishing Company. © 1964 by Metro-Goldwyn-Mayer Inc. $5-8.

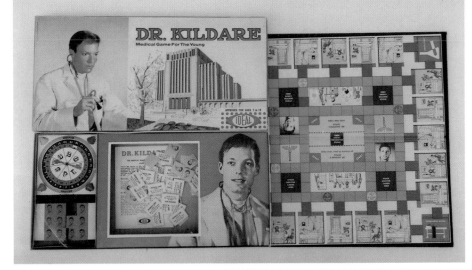

"Dr. Kildare Medical Game For the Young" by Ideal Toy Corp. Character © 1962 Metro-Goldwyn-Mayer Inc. $30-40.

Dr. Kildare and Nurse Susan paper dolls (#2740). Published by Samuel Lowe Company. © Metro-Goldwyn-Mayer Inc. $35-50. ◆ *Dr. Kildare* comic book. Dell Publications. © 1965 by Metro-Goldwyn-Mayer Inc. April-June 1965. $5-8. ◆ *Dr. Kildare Play Book* (#3092). © Metro-Goldwyn-Mayer. Published by Samuel Lowe Company. $15-18.

Dragnet

Although there have been many imitators, there has never been another crime show quite like "Dragnet." Perhaps its unusual style would not have made the program a hit in the 1990s, but it was just right for the 1950s. Most of its success was due to its star, Jack Webb. He played Det. Sgt. Joe Friday of the Los Angeles Police Department. Other officers included Frank Smith (played by Ben Alexander) and Bill Gannon (during the 1967-1970 run; played by Harry Morgan). The show aired on NBC from 1951 until 1959. It returned to NBC again from 1967 to 1970. The line "Just the facts" was a trademark of the show.

Many items were produced during the 1950s to take advantage of the show's popularity. Included were the following: "Official Dragnet Target" made by Knickerbocker (1955); "Dragnet Radar Action Game" made by Knickerbocker (1955); "Dragnet Crime Lab" by Transogram (1955); cap gun made by Knickerbocker; and "The Game of Dragnet" by Transogram (1955).

Dragnet told by Richard Deming. © Sherry T.V. Inc. 1957. Whitman Publishing Company. $10-12. ◆ "Dragnet Badge 714 Puzzle," produced by Transogram Co., Inc. © 1955 by Sherry T.V. Inc. $25-30.

"The Game of Dragnet." © 1955 by Sherry TV, Inc. Made by Transogram Co., Inc. $35-45.

The Dudley Do-Right Show

"The Dudley Do-Right Show" was an animated thirty-minute cartoon show on ABC from 1969 to 1970. Dudley was a naive boy who became a Canadian Mountie. The program depicted his attempts to catch bad guy Snively Whiplash.

Several television tie-ins were made during this time period. Included were frame tray puzzles made by Whitman and a coloring book made by Saalfield Publishing Co.

Dudley Do-Right Comes to the Rescue (#9571). Published by Saalfield Publishing Company in 1969. © P.A.T. Ward. $10-15.

The Dukes of Hazzard

"The Dukes of Hazzard" began on the CBS network in 1979. This is one series in which a car played a major role in the action. The Dodge Charger even had a name, "General Lee." The main characters were Bo Duke (played by John Schneider), Daisy Duke (Catherine Bach), and Luke Duke (Tom Wopat). The program lost some of its popularity when the two men quit the show in 1982 and were replaced by Byron Cherry and Christopher Mayer. The series ended in 1985.

This was another program that captured the fancy of toy manufacturers, and numerous products were produced to cash in on the program's popularity. Included were the following: action figures Cooter, Uncle Jesse, Daisy, Luke, Bo, Boss Hogg, Cletus, and Sheriff Rosco Coltrane (3 3/3" tall) by Mego; 8" tall Luke, Daisy, Bo, and Boss Hogg dolls by Mego; "General Lee Dodge Charger", Ideal (1981); General Lee car by Ertl (1981); lunch box and thermos by Aladdin Industries (1980); General Lee Model Kit by MPC (1981); and game by Ideal (1981).

"Dukes of Hazzard" cup, TM and © Warner Bros. Inc, 1981. $5-8. ✦ General Lee car made by ERTL Company. © Warner Bros. Inc., 1981. $15-20. ✦ Lunch box © Warner Bros. Inc., 1980. Made by Aladdin Industries, Inc. $15-20.

"The Dukes of Hazzard Electric Slot Racing Set." © Warner Bros., Inc. Made by Ideal Toy Company. $20-30.

The Dukes of Hazzard Scrapbook '83 by Roger Elwood. © Warner Bros., Inc. © 1982 Weekly Reader Books. $5-10. ✦ "Dukes of Hazzard Card Game," © Warner Bros. Inc. 1981. I.G.I. $8-12.

The Dukes of Hazzard Coloring and Activity Book. © Warner Bros. Inc. 1981. Published by Modern Promotions. $5-10 each.

E

Emergency

"Emergency" was a medical show with a difference. The action was handled by paramedics of Squad 51 of the Los Angeles County Fire Dept. The sixty-minute program was broadcast on NBC from 1972 until 1977. The doctors were played by Robert Fuller and Bobby Troup, and Julie London played nurse Dixie McCall.

Several products were produced during the show's run to take advantage of its name. In 1974 Milton Bradley made a board game; a lunch box was produced in 1973 by Aladdin Industries; and several "Emergency" trucks were issued by LJN and Dinky Toys.

Emergency (#1840) coloring book. Based on the television series created by Harold Jack Bloom and R.A. Cinader. Published by Saalfield, 1976. © Emergency Productions. $12-15.

"The Emergency! Game," © 1974 by Milton Bradley Company under Berne and Universal copyright conventions. $25-30.

F

F Troop

"F Troop" aired on ABC from September 1965 to September 1967. The setting for this unusual comedy was the end of the Civil War. After the war ends, Wilton Parmenter is sent to command F Troop at Fort Courage in Kansas. Ken Berry played the leading role. Forrest Tucker played Sgt. Morgan O'Rourke.

Products associated with the program include "F Troop Magnetic Action Fort Courage Playset" made by Multiple Toymakers (1966); "F Troop Card Game" made by Ideal (1965); coloring book by Saalfield (1966); and books and comic books.

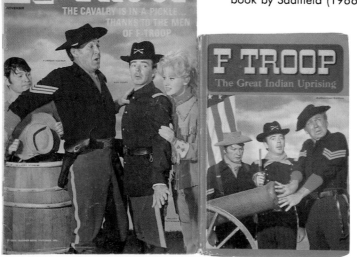

F Troop comic book, November 1966. Dell Publishing Company. © 1966 Warner Bros. Pictures, Inc. $5-10. ✦ *F Troop: The Great Indian Uprising* by William Johnston. Illustrated by Larry Pelini. Whitman Publishing Company. © 1967 by Warner Bros. Pictures, Inc. $5-10 each.

The Fall Guy

"The Fall Guy" made its debut as a television movie on October 28, 1981. It starred Lee Majors and Farrah Fawcett (who was then Mrs. Majors). The show was so successful it was made into a series. Lee Majors was co-producer and also sang the theme song, "The Unknown Stuntman." Majors also played the part of Colt Seavers, the stuntman. The show ended in 1986.

Associated products include a game made by Milton Bradley (1981); lunch box and thermos by Aladdin Industries (1981); and coloring books.

"The Fall Guy" game, © 1981 by Twentieth Century-Fox Film Corp. Produced by Milton Bradley Company. $12-15.

Fall Guy Coloring and Activity Book. © 1982, Twentieth Century-Fox Film Corp. Published by Modern Promotions. $8-10. ✦ Lunch box © 1981 Twentieth Century-Fox Film Corp. Made by Aladdin Industries. $15-20.

Fame

"Fame" centered on the students and teachers at New York City's High School for the Performing Arts. It was based on the movie *Fame* from 1980. Each story line gave young people a chance to showcase their talents in music and dance performance. The program began on NBC in 1982, with Debbie Allen doing both the choreography and playing the role of dance teacher Lydia Grant. The show won many Emmy awards, with Allen receiving two for her choreography. Although the show was a hit with critics, it did not seem to find an audience, and it was dropped by NBC after the 1982-1983 season. The program didn't die, however, as MGM/UA Television and Metromedia, Inc. continued to produce episodes to be used by independent stations until 1986.

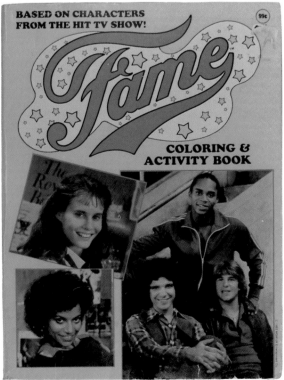

Fame Coloring and Activity Book. © 1983 MGM/UA Entertainment Company. Published by Playmore Publishing Inc., and Waldman Publishing Corp. $8-15.

Family

"Family" was a continuing drama that was first broadcast on ABC in 1976 and continued until the end of the season on June 25, 1980. The Lawrence family, who lived in Pasadena, California, was the focus of the series. Sada Thompson played the mother, Kate; James Broderick played the father, Doug; Elayne Heilveil was daughter Nancy (later replaced by Meredith Baxter-Birney); Gary Frank was son Willie; and Kristy McNichol played daughter Letitia (Buddy). While the show's story lines seemed much like ones used by the daytime soaps, the series did have a successful run and Kristy McNichol achieved good notices with her role as Buddy.

Family, © 1976 by Spelling-Goldberg Productions and Ballantine Books. $3-5. ◆ Vinyl doll portraying Kristy McNichol as Buddy from "Family," 9 1/4" tall. Made by Mattel, Inc., 1978. © 1978 Spelling-Goldberg Productions. $20-30.

Family Affair

CBS had a hit show with "Family Afair" for several years beginning in 1966. Brian Keith played an uncle who became guardian for his orphaned nieces and nephew, Cissy, Buffy, and Jody Davis. The twins, Jody and Buffy, were played by Johnie Whitaker and Anissa Jones. Kathy Garner was Cissy. Sebastian Cabot played the role of the family's manservant and Buffy's doll was Mrs. Beasley. The series ended in 1971.

Several products were produced to tie in to this successful show. Included are two sets of Buffy and Mrs. Beasley Dolls made by Mattel, Inc. (1965); Mrs. Beasley talking cloth doll with vinyl head and hands made by Mattel in 1967 (21" tall); lunch box by King-Seeley (1969); game by Whitman (1971); coloring books, and paper dolls.

Buffy Paper Doll (#1985). Published by Whitman. © 1969 Family Affair Company. $12-15. ◆ Buffy and Mrs. Beasley dolls. Made by Mattel, Inc. in 1967. Buffy is 6 1/4" tall. © 1965 by Mattel, Inc. © 1967 Family Affair Company. $50-75. Mattel also made a talking Buffy (10 1/2" tall) and Mrs. Beasley in 1969. ◆ *Buffy Paper Doll* (#1995). Whitman Publishing Company. © 1968 Family Affair Company. $12-15.

Hi! I'm Mrs. Beasley. © Family Affair Company. Color and Read book by Whitman. © 1972. $5-10. ◆ *Mrs. Beasley Coloring Book* (#1033) with doll and cut-out clothes. © 1972 Family Affair Company. Whitman Publishing Company. Mrs. Beasley dolls were also made in several styles and sizes by Mattel Inc. $10-15.

Family Feud

"Family Feud" was a popular game show from the 1970s and 1980s. The series aired on ABC from 1977 until 1985. The contestants included two five-person teams from different families. Richard Dawson was the host who asked the contestants quiz questions.

"Family Feud Question Game," © 1978 The Family Company. Made by Milton Bradley. $10-15.

"The Family Ties Game," © 1985-1986 Paramount Pictures Corp. Family Ties Registered Trademark of Paramount Pictures Corp. © 1987 Apple Street Inc. $10-15.

Family Ties

"Family Ties" is the situation comedy that made Michael J. Fox a star. The series first aired on NBC in 1982. The show centered around the Keaton family: Meredith Baxter-Birney as the mother, Elyse; Michael Gross as the father, Steve; Justine Bateman as daughter Mallory; Tina Yothers as daughter Jennifer, and Brian Bonsall (starting in 1986) as Andrew. The largest role on the show went to Fox as son Alex. The part was unusual, in that Fox played a conservative son dealing with liberal parents who had been flower children in the 1960s. The series ended in 1989.

The Famous Adventures of Mr. Magoo

Mr. Magoo animated cartoons were aired on the NBC network from September 19, 1964 to August 21, 1965. The stories dealt with past figures from history and literature. Jim Backus supplied the voice for Quincy Magoo.

Although there are many products carrying the Magoo image, most are not associated with this television series. Magoo had been a cartoon personality since 1949, and re-appeared on a later CBS television series called "What's New, Mr. Magoo" in 1977.

Mister Magoo Cut-out Coloring Book (#GF 186). © 1961 U.P.A. Pictures, Inc. Published by Golden Press. $20-25. ◆ "Mr. Magoo" doll. Vinyl head, hat, and cloth body, 14" tall. Marked "1962/UPA Pictures, Inc." $45-55.

Fantastic Voyage

"Fantastic Voyage" was an animated cartoon which aired on ABC from September 1968 until September 1970. The science fiction plot involved the Combined Miniature Defense Force (C.M.D.F.) run by the United States government. This force was able to make people very small and they were then able to travel in a tiny plane called the Voyager.

Fantasy Island

"Fantasy Island" was developed by ABC largely because of its success with "The Love Boat." Both programs aired on Saturday night. The "Island" stories were set on a resort island owned by Mr. Roarke (Ricardo Montalban), who was helped by his midget associate, Tattoo (Herve Villechaize). Guests on the island were mysteriously granted a chance to live out one of their fantasies, in which they generally learned a valuable lesson. During the later years, the plots became more bizarre and included magic spells, along with other occult twists. The program aired on ABC from January, 1978 until August, 1984.

A board game was produced by Ideal in 1978 using the "Fantasy Island" title.

"Fantastic Voyage Game" by Milton Bradley. © 1968 Twentieth Century-Fox Film Corp. $20-30.

"Fantasy Island Jigsaw Puzzle," © 1977 Columbia Pictures Television Div. of Columbia Pictures Indus., Inc. Made by H. G. Toys, Inc. $15-18.

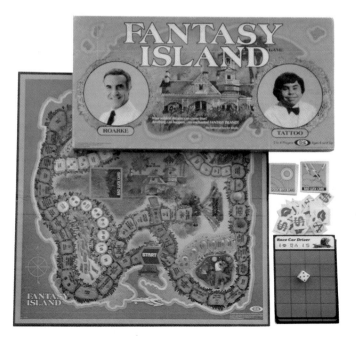

"Fantasy Island Game" by Ideal Toy Corp. © 1978 Columbia Pictures Television, a Division of Columbia Pictures Industries, Inc. $25-30.

Fat Albert and the Cosby Kids

"Fat Albert and the Cosby Kids" was a thirty-minute animated cartoon shown on CBS between 1972 and 1977. Bill Cosby was the executive producer for the show; he also was the host, and provided the voice for Fat Albert. Besides Albert, characters included Rudy, Weird Harold, Edward, Mush Mouth, Donald, Becky, and Russell. The program helped children to learn to solve problems and to enhance self-worth.

As with most children's television shows, this one also produced several tie-in products. Included are a game by Milton Bradley (1973); "Fat Albert and the Cosby Kids" record by Creativity (1980); View-Master Pack (1972); lunch box and thermos (1973).

"The Fat Albert and the Cosby Kids Game" produced by Milton Bradley Company. © William H. Cosby Jr. and Filmation Associates. $20-25.

Fat Albert and the Cosby Kids lunch box and thermos by Thermos. © 1973 William H. Cosby, Jr. and Filmation Associates. $25-30. ✦ Fat Albert and the Cosby Kids Getting it Together. © 1975 by William H. Cosby, Jr. and Filmation Associates. Whitman Publishing Company. $5-8.

Felix the Cat

"Felix the Cat" was an animated cartoon character which was first developed for movie theaters. These cartoons were syndicated in 1960 and were often shown on television. Felix was a black cat who owned a magic black bag that could grant wishes. Pat Sullivan was the inventor of the character.

Television tie-ins include a board game made by Milton Bradley (1960); soaky (1960s); frame tray puzzle by Built-Rite (1960s); wristwatch (1960s); and plastic cup.

Pat Sullivan's Felix on Television: A Flip-it Book. Told by Irwin Shapiro. Wonder Books. © Felix the Cat Productions, Inc. 1956. $8-10. ✦ Felix the Cat Coloring Book (#4655). © 1959 by King Features Syndicate. Produced by Felix the Cat Productions, Inc. Published by Saalfield Publishing Company. $20-25.

"Felix The Cat Game" by Milton Bradley. © 1960 by Felix the Cat Productions., Inc. $25-30.

The Flintstones

"The Flintstones" was a favorite animated cartoon series for many years and under several different formats. It began on ABC on September 30, 1960 and continued until September 1966. After syndication, the shows were rebroadcast on NBC from September 2, 1967 to September 5, 1970. Characters Pebbles and Bam-Bam starred in their own series on CBS from September 1971 until September 1972. "The Flintstones Comedy Hour" appeared on CBS from September 1972 until September 1973. CBS again featured "The Flintstones Show" in a shorter format from September 1973 until January 1974. All of the shows featured the Flintstone characters: Fred Flintstone, Wilma Flintstone, Barney Rubble, Betty Rubble, Dino (pet dinosaur), Pebbles (Flintstone daughter), and Bam-Bam (Rubble son). The characters lived in the Stone Age in the town of Bedrock, but their lifestyle more closely resembled that of the twentieth century.

There have been so many Flintstones products that a collector could never find them all. Some of these include a Fred Flintstone Marionette, 11" tall, made by Knickerbocker (1962); lunch box and thermos by Aladdin (early 1970s); Motorized Sports Car and Trailer Model Kit by Remco (1961); Fred Flintstone Radio (1973); drinking glasses, 14 issues, made as jelly jars for Welch's jelly (1962-1964); "Flintstones Circus Play Set" by Kohner (1965); puzzles by Whitman (1964); paper plates; Boxed Magic Paper Dolls by Whitman (1965); "Flintstone Stone Age Game" by Transogram (1961); "Flintstones TinyKins Set," Marx (1960s); View-Master Packs; "Dino the Dinosaur Game" by Transogram (1961); "Model Cast n' Color Set" by Standard Toy Kraft (1960); ceramic Fred Loves Wilma Bank (1960s); Punch Out and Sticker books by Whitman (1961); bowling set (1960s); "Flintstones Target Set" by Lido Corp. (1962); several different versions of Pebbles and Bam-Bam dolls made by Ideal; and "Fred Flintstone-Dino the Dinosaur," a Marx battery toy.

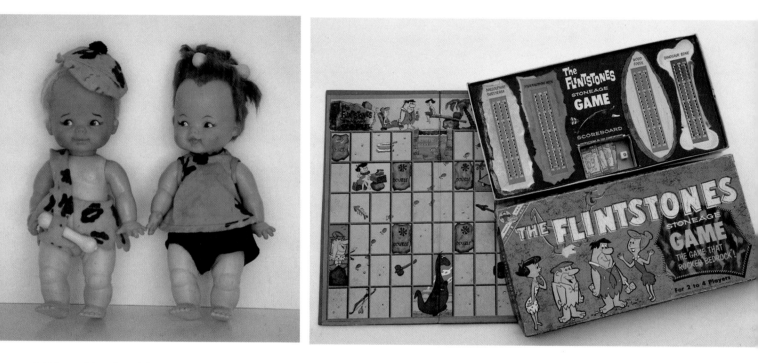

Pebbles and Bam-Bam dolls. Made by Ideal Toy Company, circa 1965. Hanna-Barbera Productions. The vinyl dolls are 9" tall and are wearing original clothing. $40-60/pair.

"The Flintstones Stoneage Game," manufactured by Transogram Co., Inc. Screen Gems Inc. © 1961 Hanna-Barbera Productions, Inc. $40-50.

"The Flintstones" puzzle. © 1978 Hanna Barbera Productions., Inc. Made by Warren Paper Products. $10-15. ♦ "The Flintstones Jr. Jigsaw Puzzle." © 1962 Hanna-Barbera Productions. Made by Whitman. $15-20. ♦ The Flintstones Coloring Book. © 1971 Charlton Publishing Inc., © 1971 Hanna-Barbera Productions., Inc. $8-10.

The Flip Wilson Show

"The Flip Wilson Show" made a star of host Flip Wilson. This variety show allowed Wilson to do sketches with many different guest stars. His "Geraldine" character was a favorite for viewers. The sixty-minute show ran on NBC from 1970 until 1974.

Flip Wilson doll, 15" tall, made by Shindana in the early 1970s. © Street Corner Productions, Inc. The talking doll is made of cloth, and when the ring is pulled he says famous "Flip" lines. The doll represents Flip Wilson on one side and his "Geraldine" character on the other. $20-25.

Flipper

"Flipper" provided young viewers with several seasons of a pet dolphin's sea antics. NBC showed the program from 1964 until 1967. The action took place in Coral Key Park, Florida, where ranger Porter Ricks and his sons Sandy and Bud spent their time keeping order and protecting the park. Flipper was the family's pet dolphin. Cast members included Brian Kelley as the ranger, Luke Halpin as Sandy, and Tommy Norden as Bud.

Related products include the following: "Flipper Spouting Dolphin" toy by Bandai Co. (1968); lunch box and thermos by King-Seeley (1966); View-Master Reels; books and coloring books by Whitman; "Flipper Flips" board game by Mattel (1965); and a jack-in-the-box type toy featuring Flipper made by Mattel (1966).

Flipper the Mystery of the Black Schooner by Richard Hardwick. Published by Whitman Publishing Company. © 1966 Ivan Tors Films, Inc. and Metro-Goldwyn-Mayer Inc. $5-8. ◆ *Flipper Paint With Water* (#1340). Published by Whitman Publishing Co, 1964. © Ivan Tors Films and Metro-Goldwyn-Mayer Inc. $12-15. ◆ "Flipper Frame-Tray Puzzle" by Whitman Publishing Company. © 1966 by Ivan Tors Films, Inc. and Metro-Goldwyn-Mayer, Inc. $12-15.

The Flying Nun

"The Flying Nun" was one of the most unusual situation comedies of the 1960s. Sister Bertrille (played by Sally Field) had discovered she could fly, and uses this strange ability in her efforts to do good deeds in her community in San Juan, Puerto Rico. This program was aired on ABC from 1967 to 1969.

"Flying Nun" products are especially attractive to today's collector. Items include a lunch box and thermos made by Aladdin Industries, and a record which includes the theme song (1967). The hardest item to locate is a 10 1/2" tall doll of Sally Field as "The Flying Nun," made by Hasbro in 1967. A 4 1/2" tall version was also produced by the same company.

Flying Nun Coloring Book (#4672). © 1968, Screen Gems, Inc. Published by Saalfield Publishing Company. $25-30.

The Flying Nun Paper Dolls (#4417). Artcraft. © 1968 Screen Gems, Inc. $30-40.

"The Flying Nun Game" produced by Milton Bradley Company. © Screen Gems, Inc., 1968. $30-35.

"The Flying Nun" paper dolls. Box contains five paper dolls. Included are Carlos Rameros, four children and clothes and stand-ups only of the nuns. © MCMLXIX (1969) Screen Gems, Inc. Published by Saalfield Publishing Company. $15-20 (cut).

Foreign Legionnaire

Early movie and Olympic star Buster Crabbe, who had achieved fame with a gold medal for swimming in the 1932 Olympics, played the lead role in this series. After his movie roles as Flash Gordon and Tarzan, the part of Captain Gallant fit Crabbe nicely. His real life son, Cullen, played Gallant's ward in this television program. The show, which aired on NBC from 1955 to 1963, took place in North Africa at the headquarters of the French Foreign Legion. It was shot on location in the Sahara, Spain, and Italy.

Related products include a board game made by Transogram (1955); "Captain Gallant Playset" by Marx; and a gun and holster set by Halco Toys.

Foreign Legionnaire From TV For You To Color (#1316). © Frantel, 1956. Published by Abbott Publishing Company. $20-25.

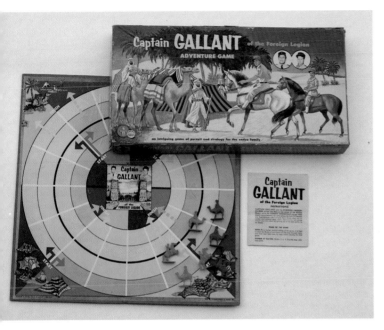

"Captain Gallant of the Foreign Legion Adventure Game." Made by the Transogram Company. © 1955 by Frantel, Inc. $30-35.

The Fugitive

"The Fugitive" was a drama that aired on ABC from 1963 until 1967. The plot involved Dr. Richard Kimble in the title role. His wife was murdered and Kimble was convicted of the crime. On the way to the penitentiary, there was a train wreck and Kimble escaped. He had caught a glimpse of the killer and knew the man had only one arm. The rest of the series deals with this hunt for the one-armed man. A movie based on this plot was released in 1994. David Janssen played the part of Kimble in the television series. "The Fugitive" board game was made by Ideal in 1964.

Full House

"Full House" appeared on ABC from 1987 until 1995. This situation comedy deals with a widower, Danny Tanner (played by Bob Saget), as he raises his three daughters. The daughters are D. J. (Candace Cameron), Stephanie (Jodie Sweetin), and Michelle (Mary Kate and Ashley Olsen). Needing extra help to deal with the girls, Danny asks his brother-in-law Jesse (John Stamos) and a friend Joey (David Coulier) to move in to help out. Jesse married Rebecca Donaldson (Lori Loughlin) in 1991 and the couple became parents to twins later the same year. The twins were named Nicholas and Alexander (Kevin and David Renteria).

Full House Paper Doll (#1696). © 1992 Lorimar Television. Golden Book–Western Publishing Company. $5-10. ✦ "Full House" dolls, © 1993 Lorimar Television. Made by Tiger Toys. Dolls include Jesse, Becky, Nicky and Alex. A Joey doll could be ordered by mail. $15-20.

Fury

"Fury" appeared on NBC from 1955 until 1966. The story involved an orphan boy named Joey (Bobby Diamond) and his friendship with a horse named Fury. Jim Newton (Peter Graves) adopted the young boy and the stories dealt with Joey and Fury and their life on Broken Wheel Ranch.

Several products were made based on characters from the show. These include comic books, Little Golden Book, coloring book (Whitman), and puzzles (Whitman).

"Fury Jr. Jigsaw Puzzle" made by Whitman. © Indep. Television Corp. $12-15. ✦ *Fury Coloring Book,* © 1958 Television Programs of America, Inc. Whitman Publishing Company. $15-20. ✦ *Fury,* © 1958 by Independent Television Corp. Whitman Publishing Company. $5-8.

G

The Gabby Hayes Show

"The Gabby Hayes Show" was first seen on NBC in 1950 and then on ABC in 1956. The children's program was hosted by Gabby Hayes, former cowboy movie star, who also acted as a storyteller for tales of the American West.

Gabby Hayes Coloring Book (#1313). © 1954, Gabby Hayes. Published by Abbott Publishing Company. $20-30. ✦ Gabby Hayes tablet, unmarked. $8-12.

Garrison's Gorillas

"Garrison's Gorillas" is an adventure series set in Europe during World War II. The characters are convicts sent to France to be commandos. If they are successful in their assignments, they will be pardoned for their crimes. The convicts are under the command of Lt. Graig Garrison, U. S. Army (played by Ron Harper). The show aired on ABC from September 5, 1967 until September 10, 1968.

A coloring book based on the series was made by Whitman in 1968, and a game was produced by Ideal in 1967.

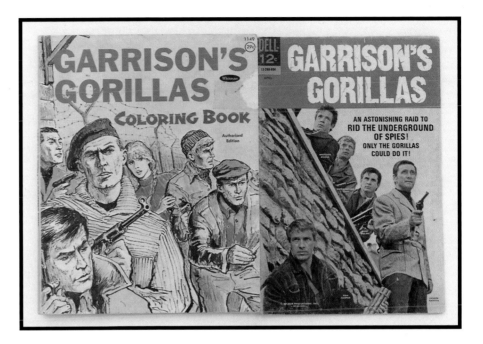

Garrison's Gorillas Coloring Book (#1149). © 1968 by Selmur Productions, Inc. Whitman Publishing Company. $15-20. ✦ Comic dated April 1968, © 1968 by Selmur Productions, Inc. Published by Dell Publishing. $5-8.

The Garry Moore Show

Although Garry Moore starred on several television programs, his most remembered is the sixty-minute variety show which aired on CBS from September 30, 1958 until June 16, 1964. The regulars on the program included Durwood Kirby, Ron Martin, Carol Burnett, Denise Lor, Dorothy Loudon, and Ken Carson. Carol Burnett received a big boost to her career from this series.

Garry Moore's Favorite Christmas Songs, marked "Compliments of the Hoover Company." © 1953 by Hoover Company. $3-5. ✦ Autographed picture of Gary Moore circa 1984. $15-20. ✦ TV Guide featuring Gary Moore, Jayne Meadows, and Faye Emerson on the cover, from April 7, 1956. Published by Triangle Publications. $3-5.

The Gene Autry Show

Cowboy star Gene Autry did a television series as well as movies and radio shows. "The Gene Autry Show" was shown on CBS from 1950 until 1956 and was a western set at Gene's Melody Ranch. There were 104 episodes in the series. Pat Buttram and Gail Davis were also in the show.

The television series made Gene Autry products popular once again. Included were comic books; View-Master Reels; cap guns by Leslie-Henry; spurs, billfold, clothing and boots; lunch box and thermos by Universal; wristwatch by New Haven; books and coloring books produced by Whitman.

Autographed picture of Gene Autry. $20-30.

Gene Autry Coloring Book (#1157). © 1949 by Gene Autry. Published by Whitman Publishing Company. $35-50. ◆ Gene Autry plastic doll made by Terri Lee Inc. in 1949. The doll is 17" tall and is wearing his original shirt and pants marked "Gene Autry." He originally sold for $10.95 through mail order. His hair and features are painted. $600+.

"Autry's Aces" fan club newsletter and membership card. Picture issue dates from Winter 1949-1950. Yellow issue from 1945. $40-60.

Jimmy and Jane Visit Gene Autry at Melody Ranch Cut-Out Dolls (#1184). Whitman Publishing Company. © 1951 by Gene Autry. $75-125. ◆ Gene Autry's Champion comic book, published by Dell Publishing, dated May-July 1955. © Gene Autry. $8-10.

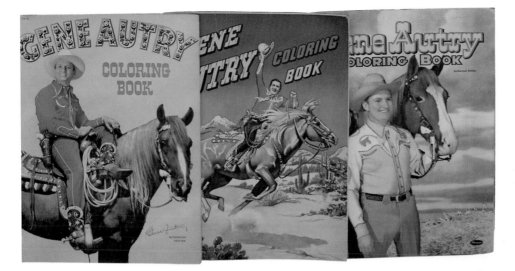

Gene Autry Coloring Book (#1124). ©
1950 by Gene Autry. ✦ Gene Autry
Coloring Book (#1157). © 1949 by Gene
Autry. ✦ Gene Autry Coloring Book
(#1860). © 1951 by Gene Autry. All three
books published by Whitman Publishing
Company. $35-50 each.

"Frosty the Snow Man" 78 RPM record with vocal by Gene Autry. Columbia
Record. ✦ "Rudolph, The Red-Nosed Reindeer" 78 RPM record also with
a Gene Autry vocal. Columbia Records, circa 1950. $10-12 each.

Gene Autry Comics. © 1952 Gene Autry.
Dell Publishing Company, dated January
1953. $15-18. ✦ Souvenir Program for
show which featured Gene Autry and his
horse Champion, © 1949 by David and
Kathleen Whalen. $25-35. ✦ Tablet with
Autry picture. No maker listed. $15-20.

General Hospital

"General Hospital" premiered on ABC in 1963 and became a very successful daytime soap. The story lines followed the lives of doctors and nurses who worked at the hospital. Dr. Steve Hardy (played by John Beradino) and nurse Jessie Brewer (played by Emily McLaughlin) were two of the many characters in the continuing series.

Cardinal Industries produced a "Role Playing Board Game" in 1982 based on "General Hospital."

Gentle Ben

"Gentle Ben" was first aired on CBS in 1967 and continuted on the network nearly two years until August 1969. This series dealt with the adventures of a game warden named Tom Wedloe (played by Dennis Weaver) stationed in the Florida Everglades, his son Mark (Clint Howard), and their pet bear, Gentle Ben. The Wedloe mother was played by Beth Brickell.

Products based on the series include a lunch box and thermos made by Aladdin Industries (1968), and comic books.

"Gentle Ben" lunch box made by Aladdin Industries, Inc. © 1968 Ivan Tors Films, Inc. $35-45. ✦ Ivan Tors' Gentle Ben comic. Published by Dell Pub., October 1969. © 1967 Ivan Tors Films, Inc. $5-8. ✦ Gentle Ben book by Walt Morey. Grosset and Dunlap, © 1965 by Walt Morey. $5-8.

The George Gobel Show

Comedian George Gobel starred in two variety shows in the 1950s. NBC aired the first show from October 1954 until June 1957. Jeff Donnell played Gobel's wife Alice in sketches in this earlier program. The second series was also on NBC and aired from September 1957 until March 1959, on an alternating basis with "The Eddie Fisher Show."

A board game called "I'm George Gobel" was made in 1955 by Edwards and Deutsch Lithographing Co.

TV Guide for May 5, 1956. Published by Triangle Publications. George Gobel and Mitzi Gaynor are featured on the cover. $4-6. ✦ Autographed picture of Gobel from the late 1980s. $15-20.

Get Smart

"Get Smart" was a successful NBC comedy from 1965 until 1969. In September 1969 the show was switched to CBS, where it played until September 1970. The action took place in Washington, D. C. and involved the agents for C.O.N.T.R.O.L. (an international spy organization). The agents were Maxwell Smart (played by Don Adams) and Agent 99 (Barbara Feldon). The comedy came from the bumbling efforts of Smart to carry out the assignments given to the pair by Thaddeus, "The Chief" (Edward Platt).

This show is popular among collectors of television-related products from the 1960s. Among the tie-in products are a lunch box and thermos by King-Seeley (1966); sheet music of the theme (1966); puzzle made by Jaymar (1966); "Get Smart Exploding Time Bomb Game," card game by Ideal (1966); "Get Smart, Secret Agent 99 Action Kit," and Plastic Car Model Kit by AMT (1967).

Get Smart comic, © 1966 Talent Assoc., Dell Publishing, dated October 1969. $10-15. ♦ Get Smart!: A Coloring Book (#9562). © 1965, 1966 Talent Assoc. Inc. Published by Saalfield Publishing. $35-40. ♦ Sorry Chief..., a paperback book by William Johnston. Tempo Books, Grosset and Dunlap. © 1966 Talent Associates. Paramount, Ltd. $5-8.

Gidget

The television series "Gidget" was based on the successful movie of the same name, which had starred Sandra Dee. The television version starred Sally Field as teenager Gidget and Don Porter as her father. The ABC series only lasted one season, from September 15, 1965 to September 1, 1966. Most of the action revolved around California surfing activities.

"Gidget Fortune Teller Game" by Milton Bradley. © 1965 Frederick Kohner, Screen Gems, Inc. $15-20.

Gilligan's Island

The "Gilligan's Island" show on CBS was one of the wacky situation comedies that seemed to dominate the television screen from 1964 to 1967. The plot followed a group of tourists who had been shipwrecked on an island in the South Pacific as they tried various plans to secure help. The fun came from the assortment of people marooned together, including the Skipper (played by Alan Hale, Jr.); Gilligan (Bob Denver); movie actress Ginger Grant (Tina Louise); Millionaire Thurston Howell III (Jim Backus); his wife, Lovey (Natelie Schafer); store clerk Mary Ann Summers (Dawn Wells); and Professor Hinkley (Russell Johnson).

Several products were manufactured using the show's name, including "Gilligan's Island Game" by Milton Bradley (1965), and a school tablet featuring the "Island" characters.

Gilligan's Island by William Johnston. Whitman Publishing Company. © 1966 by Gladasya-UATV. $8-10. ♦ Gilligan's Island coloring book (#1135). © 1965 by Gladasya-UATV. Published by Whitman Publishing Company. $40-45.

The Girl From U.N.C.L.E.

"The Girl From U.N.C.L.E." was a spin-off series from the successful "The Man From U.N.C.L.E." program. It first aired on NBC in September 1966 and continued until August 1967. Stephanie Powers starred as agent April Dancer, and Noel Harrison played agent Mark Slate. The two agents worked for an organization called the United Network Command for Law Enforcement.

Comic books, a paperback book, and the soundtrack of the show were offered as tie-in products in 1967.

The Gisele MacKenzie Show

"The Gisele MacKenzie Show" was an unsuccessful example of the variety shows that were so popular in the late 1950s and early 1960s. Singer Gisele MacKenzie was hostess. She had earlier been featured on "Your Hit Parade," the popular song program. Her variety series aired on NBC from September 28, 1957 until March 29, 1958.

The Girl from U.N.C.L.E. comic dated April 1967. © 1967 Metro-Goldwyn-Mayer Inc. K.K. Publications, Inc. $8-10. ♦ *The Girl From U.N.C.L.E.: The Birds of a Feather Affair* by Michael Avallone. Published by The New American Library. © 1966 by M-G-M Inc. $5-8.

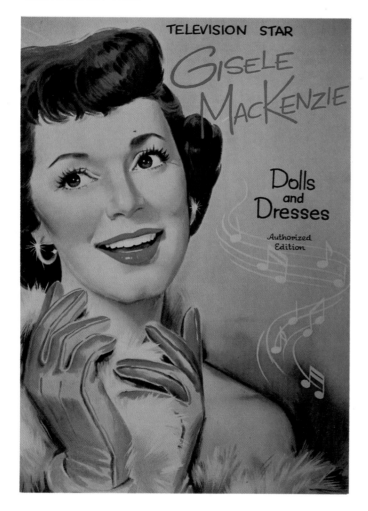

Television Star Gisele MacKenzie Dolls and Dresses (#4428). © 1958 MLM Enterprises, Inc. Saalfield Publishing Company. $65-85.

Gomer Pyle, U.S.M.C.

"Gomer Pyle, U.S.M.C." was a spin-off from "The Andy Griffith Show." Pyle was a gas station attendant in Mayberry, North Carolina before he joined the Marines. Jim Nabors played Gomer Pyle, a private at Camp Henderson in California. Frank Sutton played Sgt. Carter, who tried to straighten out the disasters caused by Gomer's antics. The show aired on CBS from 1964 to 1972.

Related products include a lunch box and thermos made by Aladdin Industries in 1966, and a board game made by Transogram also in 1966.

Gomer Pyle USMC comic. © 1967 by Ashland Productions. Inc. K.K. Publications, #3. $10-12.

"Gomer Pyle Game" by Transogram Company, Inc. © Ashland Productions, Inc. $40-45.

Good Times

"Good Times" was another spin-off from an earlier successful show. In this case, the new series was based on characters from "Maude," which itself was a spin-off from "All in the Family." "Good Times" followed the life of a lower-middle class black family who lived in a high-rise ghetto in Chicago. The series starred Esther Rolle as mother Florida Evans, John Amos as father James Evans, and Jimmie Walker as son James Evans Jr. (J.J.). Other children in the family were Thelma Evans (BernNadette Stanis) and Michael Evans (Ralph Carter). The series was on CBS from 1974 until 1979. The role model provided to young blacks by the J.J. character received criticism and caused Esther Rolle to leave the series for a while. J.J.'s phrase "Dyn-O-Mite" became popular during the early years of the program.

A cloth talking DYN-O-MITE J.J. doll was made by Shindana in 1975. The doll was 21" tall. A smaller J.J. doll was also made by Shindana the same year. It had a vinyl head with painted features and a cloth body. The dolls were copyrighted by Tandem Productions Inc.

Jimmie Walker talking cloth doll representing his J.J. character from the show "Good Times." The doll was made by Shindana Toys in 1975. © 1975 by Tandem Productions, Inc. The doll is 21" tall and said phrases like "Dyn-o-mite." A 15" doll which did not talk was also made by this company. $20-25.

The Governor and J.J.

"The Governor and J.J." was a situation comedy airing on CBS from September 1969 until December 1970. The show appeared again from June 1972 until August 1972, featuring re-runs. The series starred former movie actor Dan Dailey as Governor William Drinkwater, and Julie Sommars as his daughter J.J., who acted as her father's hostess during his time as governor and also worked at a zoo.

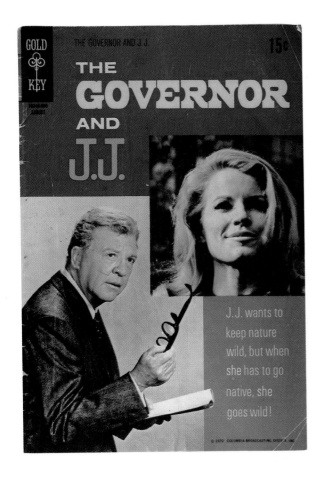

The Governor and J.J. comic dated August 1970. Published by Western Publishing Company. © 1970 Columbia Broadcasting Systems, Inc. $5-8.

Green Acres

The popular 1960s comedy series "Green Acres" featured a couple accustomed to a luxuriously rich New York life style. When they move to a farm, they begin to experience the trials of rural living—made all the worse by the broken-down condition of the farm they purchased (sight unseen) in Hooterville. Husband Oliver Douglas was played by Eddie Albert, and his glamorous wife Lisa was played by Eva Gabor. The show aired on CBS from 1965 to 1971.

Products with tie-ins to the series include a coloring book by Whitman (1967), paper dolls also by Whitman (1967), and a "Green Acres Tractor" made by Ertl.

Gunsmoke

"Gunsmoke" was the longest running television western ever. It began on CBS in 1955 and ran for twenty years until 1975. The story took place in Dodge City, Kansas during the 1880s. Like "Bonanza," the show featured an ensemble cast of excellent characters. These included Matt Dillon, a United States Marshall (played by James Arness); his deputies Chester Goode (Dennis Weaver) and Festus Haggen (Ken Curtis); Dr. Galen Adams (Milburn Stone); and Kitty Russell, owner of the Longbranch Saloon (Amanda Blake). "Gunsmoke" was first in the Nielsen ratings as the most watched show in America beginning in 1957 and lasting until 1960.

Since the series ran for so many years, many products were made which use the "Gunsmoke" name. These include a lunch box and thermos made by Aladdin Industries (1959); board game made by Lowell Toys (1958); Matt Dillon child's outfit (1958); Hartland Matt Dillon figure with horse; cowboy vest with badge; toy gun and holster; boxed puzzle made by Whitman; "Gunsmoke Target Game" by Park Plastic Co (1958); and Little Golden Book (1958).

"Green Acres Magic Stay-On Dolls." A boxed set of two paper dolls, produced by Whitman. © 1968 by Filmways TV Productions., Inc. $15-20 (cut).

"Gunsmoke Game." © 1958 by Columbia Broadcasting System, Inc. Made by Lowell Toy Mfg. Corp. $70-85.

"Gunsmoke" frame tray puzzle No. 1427. Whitman Publishing Company. © 1960 Columbia Broadcasting System, Inc. $15-25.

"Gunsmoke" trading cards. © 1958 by Columbia Broadcasting System. © TCG. Topps cards. $2-3 each.

"Gunsmoke Frame Tray Puzzle" made by Whitman. © Columbia Broadcasting System, Inc. circa 1958. $15-25. ◆ Comic book published by Dell Publishing and © 1959 Columbia Broadcasting System circa 1958. Dated Dec.-Jan. 1960. $8-10. ◆ Gunsmoke book published by Whitman circa 1958. © Columbia Broadcasting System. $8-12.

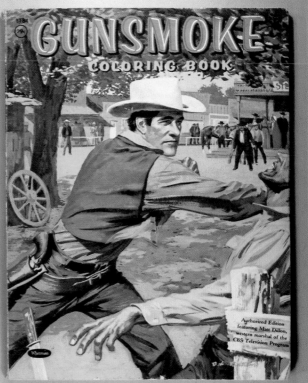

Gunsmoke Coloring Book (#1184). Published by Whitman Publishing Company, 1958. © Columbia Broadcasting System. $30-35.

H

H.R. Pufnstuf

"H.R. Pufnstuf" was a children's show broadcast by NBC from 1969 to 1971 and by ABC from 1972 to 1973. The program featured Jack Wild as Jimmy, and Billie Hayes as Miss Wichiepoo. The Sid and Marty Krofft puppets were also a part of the program. Jimmy had a talking flute which helped him when he was stranded on an island trying to find his way home.

Several products were made based on the show. They included comic books; coloring book; Cling or Clang Hand Puppet made by Remco Industries (1970); and a lunch box made by Aladdin Industries (1970).

Happy Days

The hit comedy series "Happy Days" premiered on ABC television in 1974. During its run it also provided a basis for several spin-off shows featuring several of its characters, including "Laverne and Shirley," "Mork and Mindy," and "Joanie Loves Chachi." The series was set in the 1950s and featured teenagers and their adventures at Jefferson High in Milwaukee, Wisconsin. The two main characters were Richie Cunningham, played by Ron Howard, and Arthur ("Fonzie") Fonzarelli, played by Henry Winkler. Winkler's portrayal of the drop-out mechanic who worked at Otto's Auto Orphanage became so popular, he soon dominated the show. Ron Howard left the program after the 1979 season and turned his attention to the directing of films. The series itself lasted a total of eleven seasons. The Fonz's leather jacket is now in the Smithsonian.

Many products were produced with tie-ins to this popular program. Included were: lunch boxes by King-Seeley; dolls by Mego (1976); game by Parker Brothers (1976); and other items as pictured.

H.R. Pufnstuf, published by Whitman Publishing Company. Sid and Marty Krofft Productions. Circa 1970. $5-10. ✦ H.R. Pufnstuf Coloring Book (1093). Published by Whitman Publishing Company, 1970. Sid and Marty Krofft Productions. $10-15.

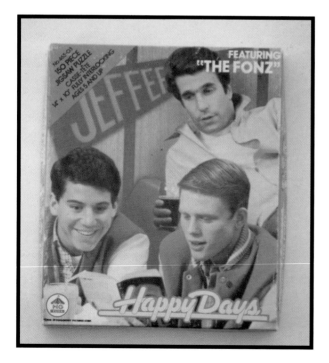

"Happy Days" puzzle made by H-G Toys Inc. Featuring the Fonz. © 1976 Paramount Pictures Corp. $10-12.

"Happy Days" game by Parker Brothers. © Paramount Pictures Corp., 1976. $15-20.

Two editions of the *Happy Days Coloring and Activity Book*, published by Playmore Publishing Inc. and Waldman Publishing Corp. © 1983 Paramount Pictures Corp. $8-10. ◆ *Happy Days: Fonzie Drops In*, by William Johnston. Tempo Books, Grosset and Dunlap. © 1974 by Paramount Pictures Corp. $3-5.

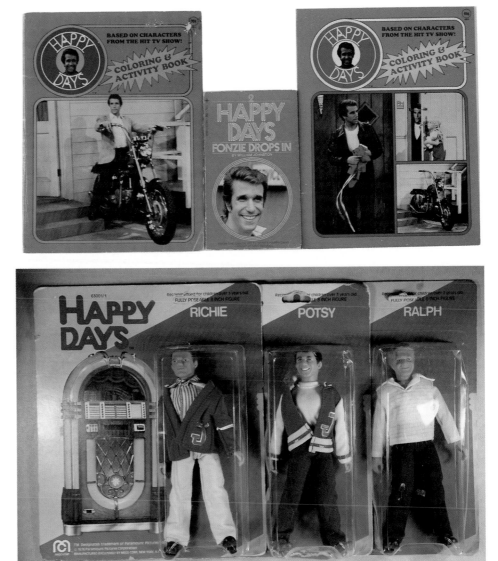

"Happy Days Fonzie Paper Doll." © 1976 by Paramount Pictures Corp. Made by The Toy Factory. $12-15. ◆ Lunch box made by King-Seely Thermos Company, with scene from "Happy Days" on one side and the "Fonz" on the other. © 1976 Paramount Pictures Corp. $30-35.

Dolls from "Happy Days." The dolls represent Richie, Potsy, and Ralph. They were made by Mego Corp. in 1976 and are 8" tall. © Paramount Pictures Corp. $20-25 each.

"The Fonz: Hanging Out At Arnold's." Platform Card Game by Milton Bradley. © 1976 Paramount Pictures Corp. $15-20.

Happy Days! Fonzie, Superstar, by William Johnson. Tempo Books, Grosset and Dunlap. © 1976 by Paramount Pictures Corp. $3-5. ◆ Fonzie doll made by Mego Corp. in 1976. The doll represents Henry Winkler and is 8" tall. © Paramount Pictures Corp. $20-30.

The Hardy Boys

Three different television shows have dealt with "The Hardy Boys." During the first run of "The Mickey Mouse Club" in the 1950s, the boys were the stars of a serial for that show. The boys were played by Tim Considine and Tommy Kirk. From September 6, 1969 to September 4, 1970 the boys were the lead characters on an animated cartoon for ABC. The third show aired on ABC from 1977 to 1979. In this series ("The Hardy Boys Mysteries") the two crime solvers were played by Parker Stevenson and Shaun Cassidy. The characters were based on mystery stories published by Grosset in 1927. Although the books were credited to Franklin W. Dixon, the Dixon name was a collective pseudonym for several authors who wrote the books.

Related products include dolls made in the likeness of Parker Stevenson and Shaun Cassidy in 1978. The dolls were 12" tall and were all vinyl with painted hair. The dolls were made by Kenner Prod. A lunch box and thermos were produced by King-Seeley in 1977, also as a product related to the 1970s show.

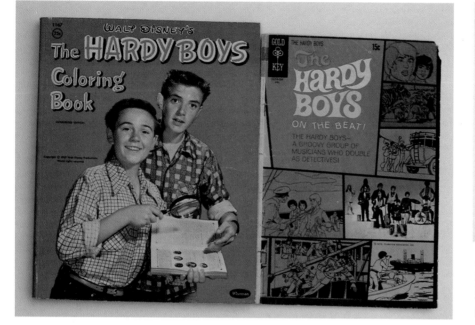

"The Secret of Thunder Mountain: The Hardy Boys Mystery Game." Made by Parker Brothers in 1978. Hardy Boys Trademark and Licensed by Universal City Studios, Inc. $15-20.

Walt Disney's The Hardy Boys Coloring Book (#1167). © 1957 Walt Disney Productions. Published by Whitman Publishing Company. $15-20. ◆ Comic book from the animated series "The Hardy Boys," which was shown on ABC beginning in 1969. © 1970 by Filmation Associates, Inc. A Gold Key Publication (Western Publishing Co., Inc.), April 1970. $3-5.

The Harlem Globetrotters

"The Harlem Globetrotters" was an animated cartoon based on the Harlem Globetrotters basketball team. A Hanna-Barbera production, the show made its debut on CBS in 1970 and continued until 1973.

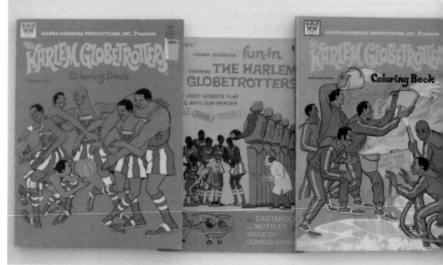

"The Harlem Globetrotters Game." © 1971 Columbia Broadcasting System, Inc. Produced by Milton Bradley Company. $15-20.

Two editions of The Harlem Globetrotters Coloring Book. © 1971 Columbia Broadcasting System, Harlem Globetrotters, Inc. Hanna-Barbera Productions, Inc. Published by Whitman. $10-12. ◆ Comic published by Whitman-Western Publishing Company. January 1972. © 1971 by Hanna-Barbera Productions, Inc. $3-5.

Have Gun-Will Travel

"Have Gun-Will Travel" was another popular western show from the late 1950s and early 1960s. The story line focused on Paladin, a professional gunman, based in San Francisco in the 1870s. Paladin is named after the white chess knight. His calling card reads: "Have Gun–Will Travel. Wire Paladin, San Francisco." Richard Boone was Paladin. The show first aired on CBS September 14, 1957 and remained on the air until September 21, 1963.

Like all of the 1950s western shows, this series attracted tie-in products. Included were the following: lunch box and thermos by Aladdin (1960); Hartland Paladin 4" tall figure with horse (1960); board game by Parker Brothers (1959); gun and holster set by Halco (1958); and plastic wallet (late 1950s).

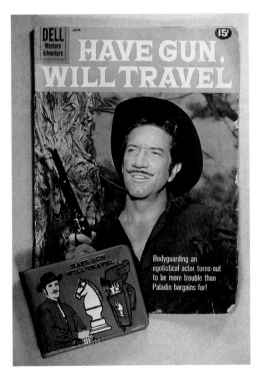

"Movieland Drive-In Theater" featuring six different films, including "Have Gun, Will Travel," "Heckle and Jeckle," and "Mighty Mouse." © 1959 CBS Inc., Terrytoons, Robert Keeshan Assoc. Inc. Made by Remco. $50-75.

"Have Gun, Will Travel" card. Series #32, card # 7 of a set of seven. © 1958 Columbia Broadcasting System. © TCG. $2-3. ♦ Have Gun, Will Travel. Whitman Publishing Company. © 1959 Columbia Broadcasting System. $10-12.

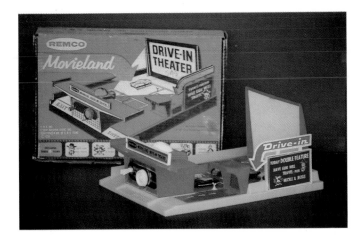

"Have Gun Will Travel: Wire Paladin San Francisco" game. Made by Parker Bros. © 1959 Columbia Broadcasting System. $70-85.

Have Gun, Will Travel comic book (April-June 1961) published by Dell Publishing. © 1961 Columbia Broadcasting System. $10-15. ♦Also pictured is a "Have Gun, Will Travel" billfold, © Columbia Broadcasting System. $20-30.

Hawaii Five-O

"Hawaii Five-O," set in Honolulu, Hawaii, featured Police Detective Steve McGarrett (played by Jack Lord). McGarrett worked with a special branch of the police department called "Hawaii Five-O." James MacArthur played Danny Williams, one of the detectives who worked with McGarrett. The series first aired September 26, 1968 and ended on April 26, 1980.

One of the most popular collectibles from this series is the game produced by Remco in 1968. A View-Master set and books were also marketed with the "Hawaii Five-O" name.

Hawaiian Eye

"Hawaiian Eye" was another television series set in Honolulu. The title of the series was also the name of the private detective agency featured in the program. The investigators were Tracy Steele (played by Anthony Eisley), Tom Lopaka (Robert Conrad), and Gregg MacKenzie (Grant Williams). Connie Stevens as singer Cricket Blake also contributed to the success of the show. The series first aired on ABC in the fall of 1959 and it ended in the fall of 1963.

Collectibles dealing with this series include the following: Connie Stevens/"Hawaiian Eye" paper dolls made by Whitman (1961); board game by Lowell (1963); and the soundtrack from the show by Warner Brothers (1960).

Hee Haw

"Hee Haw," the country variety show, began on CBS in 1969 and remained on that network until 1971. It is still seen on many stations through syndication. The many regulars have included Buck Owens, Roy Clark, Grampa Jones, Lulu Roman, and Minnie Pearl.

"Hee Haw" related products include a coloring book, paper doll book, King Seeley lunch box (1970), and record by Capitol (1970).

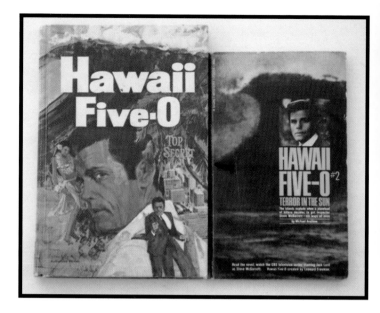

Hawaii Five-O: Top Secret by Robert Sidney Bowen. Whitman Publishing Company. © 1969 Columbia Broadcasting System, Inc. $5-8. ◆ *Hawaii Five-O #2: Terror in the Sun* by Michael Avallone. © 1969 by CBS Enterprises, Inc. Published by New American Library. $4-6.

Highway Patrol

"Highway Patrol" was a syndicated crime show from 1956 that used actual Highway Patrol experiences as the basis of its stories. Broderick Crawford played Don Matthews, the chief of the Highway Patrol.

Products related to this series include a tin lithographed friction car and a holster, revolver, and badge set which was made in England.

"Hee Haw" paper dolls. © 1971 Columbia Broadcasting System. Artcraft #5139. $35-40. ◆ *Hee Haw Coloring Book* (#4538). Published by Saalfield Publishing Company. © 1970, Columbia Broadcasting System. From the collection of Elaine Price. $10-15.

Hogan's Heroes

The comedy series "Hogan's Heroes" had a serious World War II setting: the German prison camp Stalag 13. The show aired on CBS from September 17, 1965 until July 4, 1971. Bob Crane played Air Force officer Col. Robert Hogan, a prisoner of war, who tried to run the German camp from the inside to help both the prisoners and the Allies.

Two of the Germans were Wilhelm Klink (played by Werner Klemperer) and Hans Schultz (played by John Banner).

Several interesting collectibles were made which were based on this series. Included are the following: "Hogan's Heroes' World War II Jeep" plastic model kit by MPC Models (1968); lunch box and thermos by Aladdin Industries (1966); and "Hogan's Heroes Bluff Out Game" made by Transogram (1966).

Hollywood Squares

"Hollywood Squares" was a game show based on tic-tac-toe. The program used nine celebrities as well as two people from the audience each day. The host was Peter Marshall. The show first aired on NBC in 1966.

A game was produced by Ideal in 1974 based on this series.

Hogan's Heroes comic book, dated October 1969. © 1966 Bing Crosby Productions., Inc. Dell Publishing. ✦ Another issue, from May 1967. $5-8 each.

"Hollywood Squares Game" made by Milton Bradley Company. © 1986 Century Towers Productions., Inc. $5-8.

Honey West

"Honey West" was a detective series which first aired on ABC in September 1965. It lasted only one season and was discontinued on September 2, 1966. Detective Honey West was played by Anne Francis. The setting for the series was Los Angeles.

One of the most sought after collectibles from this series is the "Honey West" doll produced by Gilbert in 1955. The 12" tall doll was dressed in black. Accessories for the doll were also available. Other series-related items include a game made by Ideal in 1965 and a soundtrack record from the same year.

Honey West #1 comic book. © 1966 Four Star Television. K.K. Publications, Inc. $10-20. ✦ Honey West: Dig a Dead Doll by G. G. Fickling. Pyramid Publications Inc. © 1960 by Gloria and Forrest E. Fickling. $5-10.

Hopalong Cassidy

William Boyd began appearing in Hopalong Cassidy films in 1935. The character was based on fiction stories by Clarence E. Mulford. The original character had a limp (which accounted for the name), but William Boyd changed the characterization and did away with the limp.

There were sixty-six films made in the series which were syndicated for television in 1948. A half-hour television show was begun in the same year. Ninety-nine episodes were used in the series.

The part of Hopalong Cassidy was played by William Boyd. His partner, Red Connors, was played by Edgar Buchanan. Topper was the name of Cassidy's horse.

The television show was so popular that numerous kid's products were made to tie in to the program. There were so many Hopalong products on the market during the early 1950s that a whole collection can be built on these items alone, including the following: white glazed ceramic cereal bowl, plate and mug; Aladdin lunch box and thermos (1950); Pop-Up Book (1950); milk bottle; party invitations; knife, fork, and spoon; records; bath towel and bathmat; Arvin radio; wristwatch (U.S. Time Corp.); Hoppy and Topper neckerchief; Marx tin target; wallpaper; bicycle horn; pencil case; roller skates (D.P. Harris Co.); wrist cuffs; chenille bedspread; Ideal Hoppy and Topper figures (plastic); cap guns and holsters; Hoppy Dominoes Set (Milton Bradley); Hoppy Dart Game (Toy Ent. of Amer. Inc.); pennant; Bar-20 Animated Lamp (Econolite Corp.); paper plates, napkins, cups, table cover; rocking chair; hand puppet; sweatshirt and other clothing; belt; and Lasso Game by Transogram (1950).

Hopalong Cassidy doll made in the likeness of William Boyd. The doll was made by Ideal in 1949, with a vinyl head and stuffed cloth body. He is missing his hat. The doll came in both 18" and 21" sizes. $350+. ◆ *Hopalong Cassidy Coloring Book Starring William Boyd* (#1200). © 1950 by Doubleday and Company. Published by Samuel Lowe Company. $40-50.

"Hopalong Cassidy Game" by Milton Bradley Company. © Wm. Boyd, 1950. $60-70.

Birthday card featuring Hopalong Cassidy. Buzza Cardozo/Hollywood issued a line of Hopalong Cassidy cards in the early 1950s. $30-50.

"Hopalong Cassidy Puzzles #4025" boxed, by Milton Bradley. © Wm. Boyd, circa 1950. The box contained three puzzles. $60-70.

"Hopalong Cassidy: 4 Television Puzzles." Manufactured by the Milton Bradley Company. © Wm. Boyd, 1950. The puzzles are 12" square. $50-60.

View-Master and View-Master reels of Hopalong Cassidy, circa 1950s. © Sawyer's. "Hopalong Cassidy in The Cattle Rustler" and "Hopalong Cassidy and Topper." $40-50.

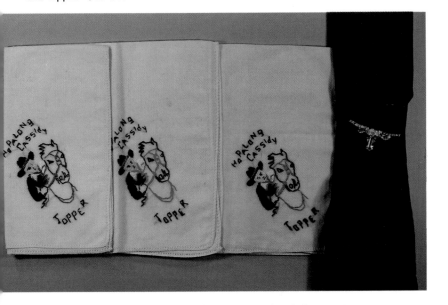

Three Hopalong Cassidy handkerchiefs with embroidered design, circa 1950. ✦ Necktie holder marked with the Hopalong name, circa 1950. $30-50.

Hopalong Cassidy Makes New Friends (#4059). A Bonnie Book published by Samuel Lowe, Inc. © Wm Boyd, circa 1950. $15-20.

House Party

"House Party" was a thirty-minute variety show hosted by Art Linkletter on CBS. The show aired from September 1, 1952 until September 5, 1969.

"Art Linkletter's House Party Game" was produced in 1968 by Whitman to tie in with the show.

How The West Was Won

Although *How the West Was Won* was a successful motion picture, the television series of the same name lasted only about a year. The show first aired on ABC on February 12, 1978 and ended on April 23, 1979. James Arness starred in the series as Zeb Macahan. The plot focused on a family's journey across America to the northwest during the 1860s.

In 1978, HG Toys issued puzzles based on the series and a doll was made by Mattel, Inc. in the image of James Arness as Zeb Macahan. The box reads "TV's How The West Was Won." Another doll, 9 3/4" tall, was made in the image of Ivan Naranjo, who played Lone Wolf. Earlier toys were probably made as tie-ins to the motion picture, rather than the TV show.

"Art Linkletter's House Party Game" by Whitman (Western Publishing Company). © 1968 Columbia Broadcasting System, Inc. $5-10.

Howdy Doody

"Howdy Doody," one of the first television programs made especially for children, soon became the most popular of them. It began on NBC in 1947 and remained a favorite for many years, leaving the air in 1960. At first it aired from Monday through Friday, but in 1956 it became a Saturday morning feature. The leading character of the program was a marionette named Howdy Doody. Helping out with the show were Buffalo Bob Smith (Bob Smith); Clarabell (Bob Keeshan, who later played Captain Kangaroo); Story Princess (Alene Dalton); and Tim Tremble (Don Knotts).

"Howdy Doody" inspired so many tie-in products that a collection can be built on them alone. Some of these collectibles include the following: wood and plastic puppet; Sand Forms by

Ideal (1950); keychain with Howdy take-apart puzzles by Lido Toy Co.; watch by Ingraham (1954); mask; night light; hand puppets of Howdy, Clarabell, and Princess; pencil case; ceramic bank showing Howdy riding a pig; wind-up acrobat toy; 20"-tall doll with a cloth body and composition head, made by Ideal; rocking chair; Christmas card; 7"-tall Flub-A-Dub String Puppet with compo lower body and vinyl head; Little Golden Books; white china plate by Taylor, Smith; Sip-a Mug by Gotham Ware; Television Game by Milton Bradley (1955); bandana; 4"-tall Howdy mechanical toy from "Tee-Vee Toy" series; ceiling light shade; bow tie; hankie; card game (Russell Mfg. Co.); and numerous coloring books, books, sticker books, and puzzles.

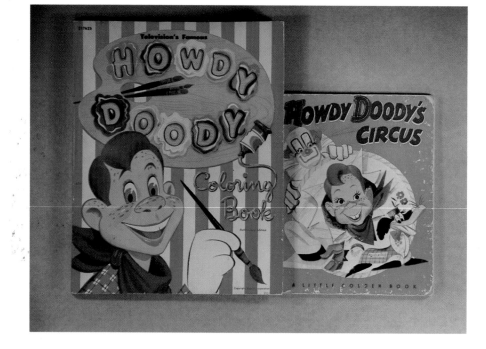

Howdy Doody Coloring Book (#217625). © Kagran Corp, 1952. Published by Whitman Publishing Company. $30-40. ✦ *Howdy Doody's Circus* by Edward Kean. Pictures by Liz Dauber and Dan Gormley. A Little Golden Book published by Simon and Schuster. © 1950 by Robert Smith. $8-10.

Push Out and Stick Howdy's Sticker Fun Circus. © 1955 Kagran Corp. Published by Whitman Publishing Company. $25-35. ✦ Hankie, © Kagran Corp. $30-40.

Autographed picture of "Buffalo" Bob Smith and Howdy Doody from the late 1980s. $20-25.

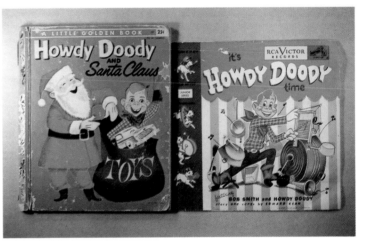

Howdy Doody and Santa Claus by Edward Kean. Pictures by Art Seiden. A Little Golden Book published by Simon and Schuster. © 1955 by Kagran Corp. $8-10. ✦ "It's Howdy Doody time" 45 RPM record featuring Bob Smith and Howdy Doody. © 1952 by Kagran Corp. RCA Victor. $10-15.

"Howdy Doody" lunch box, product of Adco-Liberty Mfg. Corp. © Kagran Corp. Circa early 1950s. $150+.

"Howdy Doody's Own Game," © Bob Smith. Made by Parker Brothers, Inc. Includes four wooden balls to be used to knock down the target cards of Clarabell, Flub-a-Dub, Howdy Doody, and Dilly Dally. Circa 1955. $55-75.

"Howdy Doody Picture Puzzle " frame tray inlay. Whitman Publishing Company. © Kagran Corp., 1952. $15-20. ✦ *Howdy Doody Coloring Book* (#217625). © Kagran Corp., 1952. Published by Whitman Publishing Company. $30-40.

Howdy Doody silverplate spoon made by Crown. © Kagran. Probably used as a premium during the 1950s. $20-25.

Howdy Doody marionette made by Peter Puppet Playthings, Inc. He is 15" tall and has a composition head. $100-125. The board from "Howdy Doody's TV Game" is in the background. Both items are from the early 1950s and are © Kagran Corp.

Howdy Doody doll, 32" tall, made by Eegee. National Broadcasting Company, Inc., 1972. Hard vinyl head and cloth body. $25-30. ✦ *Howdy Doody in Funland* by Edward Kean. Pictures by Art Seiden. A Little Golden Book published by Simon and Schuster. © 1953 by Kagran Corp. $8-10.

The Huckleberry Hound Show

"The Huckleberry Hound Show" was a Hanna-Barbera production dating from 1958. The syndicated series was an animated cartoon and featured Huckleberry Hound, a dog with a Southern accent.

Products that feature Huckleberry include a Colorforms Kit (1960); charm bracelet (1959); record titled "The Great Kellogg's TV Show" by Colpix (1960); plastic figural bank by Knickerbocker Toys (1960); two wind-up toys by Line Mar Toys; "Huckleberry Hound Western Game" by Milton Bradley (1959); and lunch box and thermos by Aladdin (1961).

I

I Dream of Jeannie

"I Dream of Jeannie" was another of the silly comedies that were so popular during the 1960s. The show featured a beautiful genie (Barbara Eden) who had been housed in a bottle for centuries. She is discovered when astronaut Captain Tony Nelson crashes on the desert island where Jeannie's bottle lies. She emerges from the bottle and secures help for Nelson. Jeannie returns to Florida with the astronaut and continues to protect him, even though her help is not always wanted. Nelson was played by Larry Hagman.

The most sought-after Jeannie item is a 19"-tall doll made by Libby Doll Corp. in 1966. The vinyl doll is dressed in a genie costume. A smaller 6 1/2"-tall doll was produced by Remco in 1977. Other collectibles include comic books and a board game.

Huckleberry Hound doll, 18" tall. Plush stuffed doll with vinyl head. Made by Knickerbocker Toy Company, circa late 1950s. Hanna-Barbera Productions. $25-35.

I Dream of Jeannie comic, © 1966 Sydney Sheldon Productions., Inc. Published by Dell Publishing Company. December 1966. $8-10. ✦ "I Dream of Jeannie" doll. Made by Remco Toys, © 1977. Doll is 6 1/2" tall and made of vinyl and hard plastic. Made during the time of the "Jeannie" animated show from Columbia Pictures Industries Inc. $35-45.

"I Dream of Jeannie Game" trademark of Screen Gems, Inc. © 1965 Milton Bradley Company. Characters © 1965 Sidney Sheldon Productions. Inc. $45-55.

I Love Lucy

The "I Love Lucy" television program is probably the most popular show that has ever been seen on any television network. Even though some of the episodes are over forty years old, they are still being shown all over the world on a daily basis.

The program began on the CBS network on October 15, 1951 and continued with a thirty-minute format until September 1956. Then "Lucy" was changed to an hour program, running from November 6, 1957 to September of 1958. The story centered on Lucy and Ricky Ricardo, who rented a New York City apartment from Fred and Ethel Mertz. Ricky Ricardo was a bandleader at the Tropicana Club. Although Lucy was a housewife in her daily life, she longed to join her husband in show business. Many of the episodes were based on this premise.

The show was so popular that forty-four million viewers watched the program the evening that Lucy's baby was born and the show was ranked first in the Nielsen ratings from 1952 to 1955 and again in 1957. It was rated second in 1956. Besides Lucille Ball and her real-life husband, Desi Arnaz, the cast included William Frawley and Vivian Vance as Fred and Ethel Mertz.

"I Love Lucy" products are some of the most collectible of the television tie-ins. Included are the following: 8"-tall Little Ricky Puppet doll attached to blanket by Zany Toys, Inc. (1953); Activity Book by Golden Press (1959); Tracing Book by Golden Press (1959); comic books; coloring books; paper doll books; 27" stuffed cloth doll with molded plastic face; several versions of Little Ricky dolls made by American Character as well as accessories for the dolls; and "Desi's Conga Drum" made of heavy cardboard.

See also "The Lucy Show."

Autographed picture of Desi Arnaz dating from the late 1980s. $50 & up.

Autographed picture of Lucille Ball from the late 1980s. $50 & up.

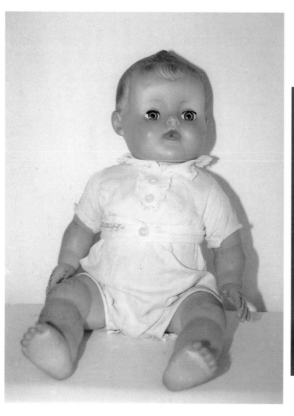

Little Ricky doll made by American Character in 1953. The all vinyl doll is 20" tall and has sleep eyes and molded hair. The mouth is open and the doll is fully jointed. He is wearing his original romper outfit with "Rickey Jr." embroidered on his belt. Marked "Amer. Char. Dol." on the back of his head. $125-150.

Look magazine featured Lucille Ball, Desi Arnaz, and television son Keith Thibodeaux (Richard Keith) on the cover for December 25, 1956. $10-15. ◆ Who's Who in TV and Radio (Vol. 1, No. 3) used a Lucille Ball cover for the 1953 annual issue. The magazine was a Dell Publishing Company publication. $15-20. ◆ TV Guide also used a Lucille Ball cover for its July 12, 1958 issue. The magazine was published by Triangle Publications. $8-10.

Lucille Ball–Desi Arnaz Coloring Book (#2079). © 1953 by Lucille Ball and Desi Arnaz. Published by Whitman Publishing Company. $50-75. ◆ *I Love Lucy: Lucille Ball, Desi Arnaz, Little Ricky Coloring Book.* © 1955 Lucille Ball and Desi Arnaz. Published by Dell Publishing Company. Printed by Western Printing and Lithographing Company. $40-50.

27" tall Lucy doll produced in 1953. The doll has a plastic face, orange yarn hair, and a cloth body. The apron is marked "I Love Lucy/Desi." From the collection of Dora Pitts. Photograph by Al Pitts. $140-160.

Lucille Ball Desi Arnaz Cut-Out Dolls with Little Ricky (#2116). Whitman Publishing Company, © 1953 by Lucille Ball and Desi Arnaz. $85-100. ◆ *I Love Lucy: Lucille Ball and Desi Arnaz* (#2101). "2 Statuette Dolls and Clothes." Whitman Publishing Company. © 1953 by Lucille Ball and Desi Arnaz. $85-100.

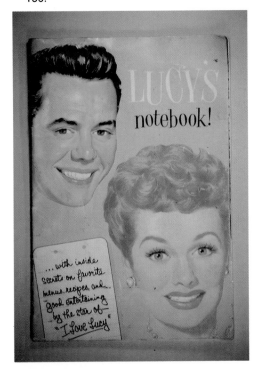

Lucy's Notebook, a premium offered by Phillip Morris Cigarettes (sponsor of television show). The book contained recipes and many pictures from the "I Love Lucy" show. From the collection of Elaine Price. $25-30.

I Love Lucy comic books based on the television show. The comics were published by Dell Publishing. Left: April-June 1960. Right: January-March 1957. $15-20 each.

I Spy

"I Spy" was one of the early television shows to co-star a black man (Bill Cosby) and a white man (Robert Culp). The two men played the parts of Alexander Scott and Kelly Robinson, undercover government agents. They used tennis as a cover for their investigations. Kelly portrayed a tennis champion while Scott assumed the role of his trainer. The series was shown on NBC from 1965 to 1968.

Ideal brought out a very collectible board game based on the show in 1965. The same company also produced an "I Spy" card game in 1966. Ray Line made an "I Spy Secret Agent Weapons Set" in 1966 and Warner Brothers released a program album in 1966.

Advertisements for the American Character Doll Company from the early 1950s picture two dolls associated with "I Love Lucy." The earliest doll, called the "I Love Lucy Baby," was produced during Lucy's pregnancy (circa 1952). It was similar to the Tiny Tears dolls made by the company. The doll was 16" tall, made of rubber with a hard plastic head. The doll could wet and blow bubbles. The hair was molded and the doll had sleep eyes. ◆ The second advertisement shows the doll that was made in 1953 after the birth of Little Ricky. Also shown is a doll carriage labeled "Ricky, Jr.," made by Play Time Products. A Trimble Doll Bath was also made for the 21" tall vinyl doll. Extra clothes for the doll could be purchased. Advertisements $8-10 each.

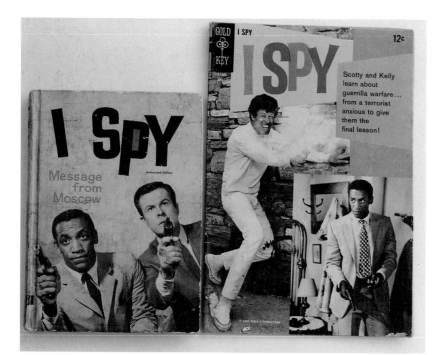

I Spy: Message From Moscow by Brandon Keith. © 1966 by Three F Productions. Whitman Publishing Company. $5-8. ◆ I Spy comic, © 1968 Three F Productions. June 1968. Western Publishing Company, Inc. $10-15.

The Incredible Hulk

"The Incredible Hulk" was based on a "Dr. Jekyll and Mr. Hyde" premise: because of a scientific mistake, main character Dr. Banner (Bill Bixby) changed into the Green Hulk when he was angry. He left his regular work to try to discover how he could keep from turning into the Hulk. The Hulk was played by Lou Ferrigno. The program was first aired on CBS in 1978 and ended in 1982. Because the character was originally a Marvel Comic product, many collectible items were based on that character and not on the television show.

Related series products include a plastic bank by AJ Renz Corp (1978) and an 8" action figure by Mego Corp. (1979).

Lunch box made by Aladdin Industries in 1978. © Marvel Comics Group, a Division of Cadence Industries Corp. $35-40. ◆ *The Incredible Hulk Coloring Book: At the Circus* (#1040). © 1977, Marvel Comics Group. Published by Whitman-Western Publishing Company. $10-15.

"The Incredible Hulk Tray," © 1979 Marvel Comics Group, a Division of Cadence Industries Corp. $15-20.

TV Guide featuring Jack Benny on the cover of the November 19, 1955 issue. Published by Triangle Publications. $4-6. ◆ Autographed picture of Benny from his later years. $50-75.

It's About Time

"It's About Time" was a science fiction series that aired on CBS from September 11, 1966 until September 3, 1967. The plot involved two astronauts, Mac and Hector, whose rocket crash-landed into the Prehistoric Era. When at last they were able to escape via their repaired rocket, the two men brought a cave family with them. Stories then dealt with the family's attempt to adjust to the ways of modern man. The two astronauts were played by Frank Aletter and Jack Mullaney. One member of the cave family was played by Imogene Coca.

A dome lunch box was made in 1967 based on this series.

I've Got a Secret

"I've Got a Secret" was a popular game show for many years. It was first shown on CBS in 1952 and continued until 1967. The host was Garry Moore, and later Steve Allen. Regular panelists included Bill Cullen, Henry Morgan, Jayne Meadows, Faye Emerson, Steve Allen, and Betsy Palmer. The later version with Steve Allen as host was syndicated in 1972.

A game based on this show was made by Lowell in 1956.

J

The Jack Benny Program

Popular radio comedian Jack Benny moved his show to television in 1950 and it continued airing on CBS until 1964. Then it was picked up by NBC, finally ending its run in 1965. The cast consisted of many of the same people who had been involved in the radio show, including Mary Livingston (his wife); Rochester (played by Eddie Anderson); vocalist Dennis Day; announcer Don Wilson; and Jack's violin teacher Professor LeBlanc (played by Mel Blanc).

The Jackie Gleason Show

Jackie Gleason was involved with several television shows through the years including "The Life of Riley," "Calvalcade of Stars," "The Honeymooners," and several versions of "The Jackie Gleason Show." His variety shows aired on CBS from 1952 to 1955 and 1956 to 1961. Gleason's most popular programs were the ones which featured segments of "The Honeymooners" with Art Carney, Audrey Meadows, and Joyce Randolph playing the parts of Ed Norton, Alice Kramden, and Trixie Norton. Jackie Gleason was Ralph Kramden.

The collectibles from any of the Jackie Gleason television programs are very much in demand. Included are the following products: "Jackie Gleason Story Stage Play Set" by Utopia (1955); "Jackie Gleason's Bus Driver's Outfit," by Empire Plastic Corp.; Gleason Marx figure, 3" tall (1955); "Jackie Gleason's TV Fun Game" by Transogram (1956); and a set of four paper dolls called "The Honeymooners," published by Lowe (1956).

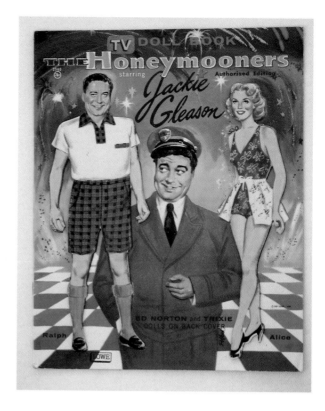

TV Doll Book: The Honeymooners starring Jackie Gleason (#2560). Published by Lowe. © VIP Corp., 1956. From the collection of Elaine Price. $150-175.

"Jackie Gleason's 'And Awa-a-a-a-y We Go' TV Fun Game." Made by Transogram, 1956. © VIP Corp., 1956. Courtesy of 52 Girls Collectibles. $125-150.

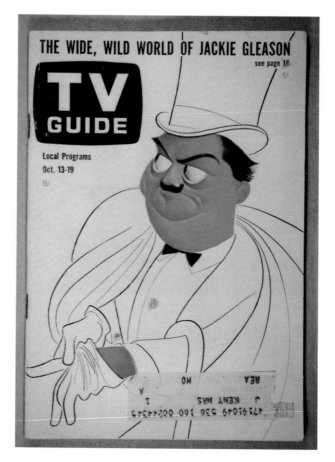

"Jackie Gleason, Story Stage Play Set" by Utopia, 1955. Includes standing figures of Gleason as Ralph and the Poor Soul. There are also figures of Norton, Alice, and other cast members plus tickets, stage set, and magnetic wand. Courtesy of 52 Girls Collectibles. $125-150.

TV Guide, published by Triangle Publications, October 13, 1962. Jackie Gleason is featured on the cover. $4-6.

"Songs I Sing on the Jackie Gleason Show" with Frank Fontaine and the orchestra conducted by Sammy Spear. 33 1/3 RPM record. ABC-442. ABC-Paramount Records, Inc. $10-15.

Jackie Gleason's Funny Book for Boys and Girls. © VIP Corp. 1956. Published by Samuel Lowe Company. $10-15. ◆ *Jackie Gleason's TV Show: An Entertaining Coloring Book* (#2614). Published by Abbott. © VIP Corp., 1956. $40-50.

An autographed picture of Jackie Gleason. $40-50.

An autographed picture of Art Carney. $15-20.

Jackpot

"Jackpot" was a game show that aired on NBC from January 7, 1974 until September 26, 1975. The host was Geoff Edwards. The game was based on riddles and the contestants competed to win up to $50,000 in prize money.

"TV Jackpot Game" by Milton Bradley Company. © 1974 under Berne and Universal copyright conventions. $5-10.

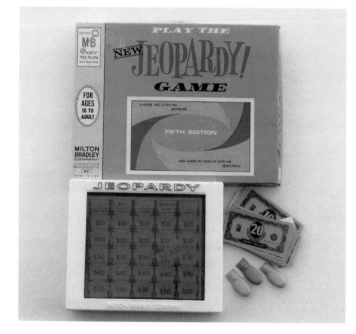

"New Jeopardy Game" by Milton Bradley. © 1964 January Enterprises, Inc. $5-10.

Jeopardy

The long-running game show "Jeopardy" began on NBC in 1964, hosted by Art Fleming. Contestants were read an 'answer' and had to reply with the correct 'question' to win. A game by Milton Bradley was produced the same year. An updated game was manufactured by the same firm in 1972.

The Jetsons

"The Jetsons" was a Hanna-Barbera animated cartoon with a science fiction story line. The Jetsons (father and mother George and Jane, and their children, Judy and Elroy) live on Earth during the twenty-first century. The series appeared on all three networks at different times from 1962 until 1975.

One of the most expensive products which features the Jetsons is the lunch box and thermos produced by Aladdin Industries in 1963. Several games based on the characters are also in demand. They include "The Jetsons Out of this World Game" by Transogram (1962); "The Jetsons Rosey the Robot Game With Astro," by Transogram (1962); and "The Jetsons Fun Pad Game" made by Milton Bradley (1963). Whitman also produced puzzles and a coloring book based on the Jetsons in the early 1960s.

The Jimmy Durante Show

Comedian Jimmy Durante was involved in several different television shows from 1952 until 1957. They included "The Buick Circus Hour" (NBC, 1952-1953); "The Texaco Star Theatre" (NBC, 1954-1955); and "The Jimmy Durante Show" (CBS, 1957). He also appeared on a short series for ABC called "Jimmy Durante Presents The Lennon Sisters Hour" from 1969 to 1970.

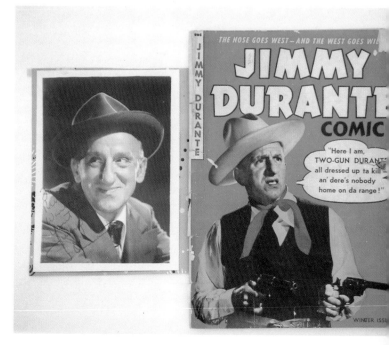

An autographed picture of comedian Jimmy Durante from the 1970s. $40-50.
◆ Jimmy Durante Comics, Magazine Enterprises, winter 1948. $5-8.

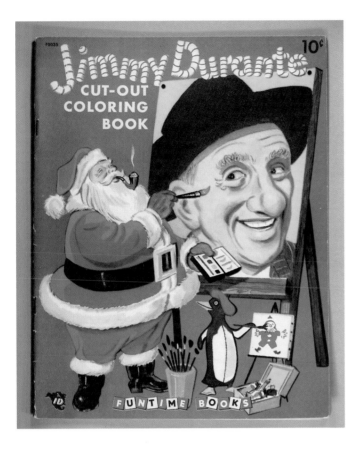

Jimmy Durante Cut-Out Coloring Book (F 5035). Published by Pocket Books, Inc., 1952. $30-40.

The Joe Namath Show

"The Joe Namath Show" was a syndicated interview show in 1969. The football star interviewed celebrities from both the sport and entertainment fields.

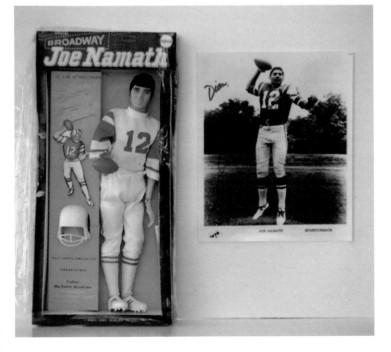

Journey to the Center of the Earth

"Journey to the Center of the Earth" was an animated cartoon appearing on ABC from 1967 to 1969. The story was based on the novel of the same name by Jules Verne. The show features Professor Lindenbrook, who leads a party to hunt for the center of the earth. While they are inside, an explosion seals the opening and they are trapped. The other episodes involve the party's various adventures as they try to find a way out.

Whitman Publishing Co. produced a coloring book and puzzles based on the program during the late 1960s.

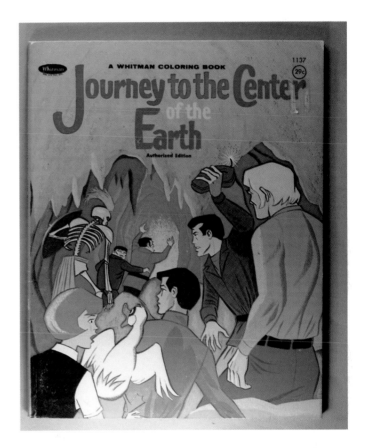

Journey to the Center of the Earth (1137). © 1968 by Twentieth Century-Fox Film Corp. Published by Whitman Publishing. $10-15.

Joe Namath doll, © Mego Corp. MCMLXX (1970). The doll is 12" tall and throws a toy football. Twelve different outfits were made that could be purchased for the doll. The head of the doll is soft vinyl while the rest is hard plastic. Back marked "Broadway Joe TM/ C Mego Corp. MCMLXX." $75-125. ✦ Also shown is an autographed photograph of the football star. $40-50.

Julia

"Julia" was the first television show to picture a black single mother (played by Diahann Carroll) working as an educated professional. Julia Baker was a nurse working at the Inner Aero-Space Center for Dr. Chegley (Lloyd Nolan). Her son, Corey, was played by Marc Copage. The show was on NBC television from 1968 to 1971.

The most sought after "Julia" collectible is the doll made by Mattel, Inc. in 1969. Other items include a Colorforms set (1969); lunch box and thermos made by King-Seeley Thermos (1969); two different styles of coloring books and a set of paper dolls made by Saalfield (1969 and 1970); and a View-Master set (1969).

Julia doll representing Diahann Carroll, made by Mattel, Inc. in 1969. The all vinyl doll is 12" tall and is marked on her hip "c 1966/Mattel Inc./U.S. Patented/ U.S. Pat. Pend./Made in/Japan." Wrist tag reads "© Savannah Productions, Inc." $65-85.

"Julia": A Coloring Book, published by Saalfield Publishing Company. © Twentieth Century-Fox Film Corp., 1968. $15-20. ✦ Corey Baker of Julia and His Show and Tell by Gladys Baker Bond. © 1970 by Twentieth Century-Fox Film Corp. A Whitman Tell-A-Tale Book. $5-8.

"Julia" Paper Dolls Based on the NBC TV Series (#4472). © 1968, 1969. Published by Saalfield Publishing Company. An Artcraft book. From the collection of Elaine Price. $30-40.

K

Knight Rider

"Knight Rider," created by Robert Foster, began its run on television during the 1982 season. David Hasselhoff starred as Michael Knight, a former policeman who becomes an investigator. A dying millionaire gives him a space-age car, Knight Industries Two Thousand (KITT), which he uses in his work. KITT can do all kinds of remarkable things. The series ended in 1986.

Products associated with the show include an AM radio made by Royal Condor in 1984, and a lunch box and thermos produced by Aladdin Industries the same year.

Knight Rider Color and Activity Book. © 1984 by Universal City Studios. Published by Modern Promotions. $5-10. ◆ "Knight Rider Sunglasses" by Larami Corp. © Universal City Studios. $10-15.

"Knight Rider" game by Parker Brothers. © 1982 Universal City Studios, Inc. $12-15.

Kojak

"Kojak" was a very popular crime series which starred Telly Savalas as Lt. Theo Kojak, a police detective working in New York for the Manhattan South Precinct. The show first aired on CBS in 1973 and continued until 1978.

"Kojak" products include a game; an action figure by Excel Toy Corp. (1976); a car made by Corgi Toys (1976); and an 8"-tall doll in the image of Kojak made by Excel Toy Corp. (1976).

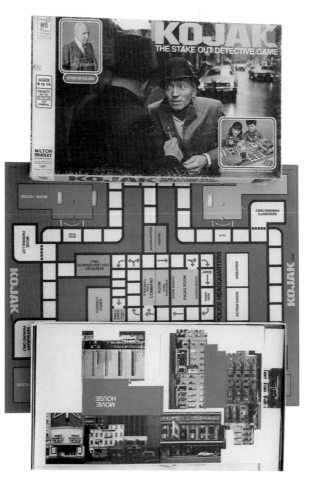

"Kojak: The Stake Out Detective Game" by Milton Bradley Company. © Universal Television a division of Universal City Studios, Inc. 1975. $20-25.

Kukla, Fran and Ollie

"Kukla, Fran and Ollie" first aired as a local children's television show in 1947 on the Chicago WBKB-TV station. It became a national show on NBC in 1949. Later it appeared on ABC until 1957. Kukla and Ollie were puppets, and Fran Allison was the hostess. Later versions of the show appeared on NBC during the 1961 season, on the NET network in 1969, and on PBS in 1970 and 1971.

Among the many products made to tie in to this show, the puppets of Kukla and Ollie produced by Parker Brothers in 1962 are very popular. Other items include a board game, also made in 1962 by Parker Brothers, and a toy wheelbarrow which dates from the early 1960s.

Kung Fu

"Kung Fu" was an unusual drama. David Carradine played Kwai Chang Caine, a Shaolin priest who traveled across America during the 1870s while looking for a lost brother. The priest has studied the art of Kung Fu. Flashbacks during the series trace the young man's earlier life when he lived in China. The series first aired on ABC in 1972 and continued until 1975.

"Kung Fu" products include a lunch box and thermos made by King-Seeley in 1974, and a doll as pictured.

"Kung Fu" doll made by Durham Industries, Inc. Doll is made of vinyl and is approximately 8 1/2" tall. $20-25 ✦ "Kung Fu" thermos. © 1974 Warner Bros. Inc. Made by King-Seeley Thermos Company. $10-15.

L

Lancer

"Lancer" was a sixty-minute western series that aired on CBS from September 1968 to September 1970. The program was syndicated, so the episodes were shown later on other stations. Andrew Duggan starred as Murdoch Lancer, the owner of a ranch in California in the 1870s. He had two sons, Scott (Wayne Maunder) and Johnny (James Stacy). The plot line centered on the two sons and their problems with each other and their father.

Remco produced a "Lancer" game in 1968.

Lancer: Blowup at Scorched Bend! comic. K.K. Publications Inc. September 1969. © Twentieth Century-Fox Television, Inc. $5-8.

Land of the Giants

"Land of the Giants" was a sixty-minute science fiction television show that debuted on ABC in 1968. In the program, the aircraft *Spindthrift* gets caught in a storm, leaves the Earth's atmosphere, and is forced to land in a forest. The three crew members and four passengers find that they have landed in a world of giants.

The episodes describe the group's adventures as they try to repair their craft to return to Earth while avoiding capture by the giants. The cast included Gary Conway as the captain; Don Marshall as the co-pilot; and Heather Young as the stewardess. The passengers were a thief, an heiress, a tycoon, and an orphan child. The program ended in 1970 after fifty-one episodes.

A number of products were produced to tie in to the show. Included were paperback books by Pyramid Books (1968); lunch box and thermos by Aladdin (1968); Movie Viewer made of hard plastic (1969); Wrist Flashlight by Bantam Lite (1968); Space Ship Spindrift by Remco (1968); game by Ideal (1968); puzzle by Whitman (1969); and Colorforms Kit (1968).

Land of the Lost

"Land of the Lost" was a science fiction television program involving a forest ranger and his children who were caught in a time vortex while on the Colorado River. They were transported back to the days of prehistoric creatures. The show revolved around their adventures as they tried to find their way back to civilization. The forest ranger and his children were played by Wesley Eure, Kathy Coleman, and Spencer Milligan. The show aired on NBC beginning in 1974.

Associated products include a lunch box by Aladdin Industries (1975); Safari Shooter by Larami (1975); prehistoric animals also by Larami (1975); puzzle by Whitman (1975); and board game by Milton Bradley (1975).

Land of the Lost (#1045). © 1975 by Sid and Marty Krofft Productions, Inc. Published by Western Publishing Company. (Whitman). $20-25.

Land of the Giants Coloring Book (#1138). © 1969. Kent Productions and Twentieth Century-Fox Film Corp. Whitman Publishing, a division of Western Publishing Company. $20-25. ♦ *Land of the Giants* by Murray Leinster. Pyramid Books. © 1968 Twentieth Century-Fox Television, Inc. and Kent Productions. $5-8.

"Land of the Giants Round Jigsaw Puzzle" © 1969 by Kent Productions and Twentieth Century-Fox Film Corp. Made by Whitman Publishing Company. $15-20.

"Land of the Lost Game" from Sid and Marty Krofft's Popular TV Show. © 1975 Sid and Marty Krofft Television Productions, Inc. Made by Milton Bradley. $30-40.

Laramie

"Laramie" was a western series dating from 1959, set in Laramie, Wyoming during the 1880s. The show featured John Smith as Slim Sherman and Robert Fuller as Jess Harper. The two characters were ranchers who also operated a stage depot. The program was carried by NBC until 1963.

A board game based on this show was produced by Lowell Toy in 1960.

Lassie

Just as the television program featuring the dog Rin Tin Tin had its beginning in the film world, so did the television series "Lassie." The original Lassie was the star of the M-G-M film *Lassie Come Home* in 1943. The television version of "Lassie" premiered on CBS in 1951. The show featured a boy named Jeff Miller (played by Tommy Rettig), his mother Ellen (Jan Clayton), his Gramps (George Cleveland), and his dog Lassie. The stories were mostly based on adventures shared by Jeff and Lassie.

This format lasted until 1957; then the story line changed to feature a new boy named Timmy (played by Jon Provost) and his adoptive parents (Cloris Leachman/June Lockhart and Jon Shepodd/Hugh Riley).

From 1964 until the end of this Lassie series in 1968, a third story line was followed. In this version, Lassie was given to a forest ranger named Corey Stuart (Robert Bray). Lassie was instrumental in helping to make rescues and in protecting the forest.

The fourth Lassie format was on CBS from 1968 to 1971. In this series Lassie was no longer owned by any one person; instead she was free to roam the California countryside helping both animals and humans when she was needed.

Because this children's show was aired for so many years, there are many products that tie in to its popularity. Included are a Lassie Knickerbocker doll (1964); frame puzzle by Whitman (1953); game by Lisbeth Whiting Creation (1955); View-Master Reels; pencil case (1950s); lunch box by King-Seeley; and numberous books and coloring books.

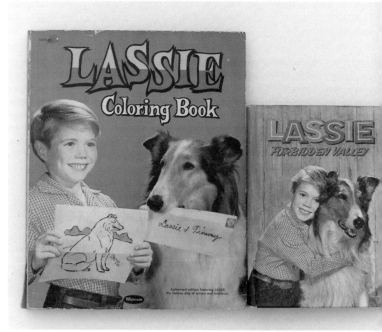

Lassie Coloring Book (#1039). Published by Whitman Publishing Company, 1958. Lassie Programs, Inc. $10-15. ✦ *Lassie: Forbidden Valley* by Doris Schroeder. Published by Whitman. © MCMLIX (1959) by Lassie Programs, Inc. $5-8.

Lassie stuffed doll, probably from early 1970s. Vinyl face with set-in eyes. Approximately 15" long. $15-20.

Lassie Coloring Book (#1114). Published by Whitman Publishing Company. © Lassie Programs, Inc. $10-15. ✦ *Lassie* comic published by Dell for January-March 1960. © 1959 by Lassie Programs, Inc. $5-8. ✦ *Hooray for Lassie* by Marion Borden. Published by Whitman. © 1964 Wrather Corp. $3-5.

Laugh-In

"Laugh-In" took the nation by storm when it appeared on television in 1968. Nothing like it had ever been seen on U.S. television. It was full of satire, political statements, and just plain silliness. Dan Rowan and Dick Martin served as co-hosts, but the show was peopled with wonderful cast members and unusual guests. Cast members included Ruth Buzzi, Judy Carne, Eileen Brennan, Goldie Hawn, Arte Johnson, and Henry Gibson. According to the Neilsen ratings, the series was rated as the most watched show by viewers in the years 1968-1969 and 1969-1970. The show ended in 1973. Despite several specials made after the show's demise, the original wit and entertainment has not been recaptured.

Several "Laugh-In" products were made during the run of the show. Included are the following: "Laugh-In Squeeze Your Bippy Game" by Hasbro (1968); lunch box and thermos by Aladdin Industries (1968); trash can (1968); record featuring gags and jokes from the show (1968); pencil case by Empire Pencil Co. (1968); "Laugh-In Sock It To Me Hat"; and "Laugh-In Electric Drawing Set" by Lakeside Toys (1969).

Rowan and Martin's Laugh-In, A Very Innnteresting Coloring Book (#4633). Published by Saalfield Publishing Company, 1968. George Schlatter-Ed Friendly Productions and Romart, Inc. $15-20. ◆ *Rowan and Martin's Laugh-In* paper dolls. Published by Saalfield, #1325. © MCMLXIX (1969) George Schlatter-Ed Friendly Productions and Romart, Inc. $25-35. ◆ *Rowan and Martin's Laugh-In #1.* New American Library. © 1969 by George Schlatter-Ed Friendly Productions and Romart, Inc. $3-5.

"Rowan and Martin's Official Laugh-In Squeeze Your Bippy Game" by Hasbro. National Broadcasting Company Trademark. © George Schlatter-Ed Friendly Productions and Romart, Inc. 1968. Coordinated by Schnur-Appel, Inc. $45-55.

Laurel and Hardy

The "Laurel and Hardy" television show was an animated cartoon based on the Stan Laurel and Oliver Hardy characters from the movies. Hanna-Barbera Productions and Larry Harmon Pictures produced the five-minute syndicated cartoons in 1966.

A game called "Laurel and Hardy Game of Monkey Business" was produced by Transogram in 1962.

Stan Laurel and Oliver Hardy dolls. The dolls are 10" and 8" tall. The heads are vinyl with cloth bodies over wire so they can bend. The dolls were made by Knickerbocker circa early 1970s. They are marked on the heads "c Larry Harmon Pictures Corp." $40-50/pair. ◆ *Laurel and Hardy Coloring Book* (#3883). © 1972, Larry Harmon Pictures Corp. Published by Saalfield Publishing Company. $15-20.

Laverne and Shirley

The Laverne and Shirley characters (played by Penny Marshall and Cindy Williams) had their beginning on the ABC "Happy Days" program. The women's series was developed from those characters and aired on ABC in 1976. In the show, Laverne and Shirley work at Shotz Brewery in Milwaukee, Wisconsin in the 1950s. Neighbors and sometimes friends Lenny and Squiggy were played by Michael McKean and David L. Lander. The show ran into trouble in 1983 after several successful seasons, when Cindy Williams quit the cast because of unresolved disagreements. The series ended the same year.

A set of dolls was produced by Mego in 1977. The dolls were 12" tall and represented Penny Marshall as Laverne, Cindy Williams as Shirley, Michael McKena as Lenny, and David L. Lander as Squiggy. The female dolls came in one set while the male dolls were packaged in another set.

"Laverne and Shirley" game made by Parker Brothers in 1977. Characters © 1977 by Paramount Pictures Corp. $15-20.

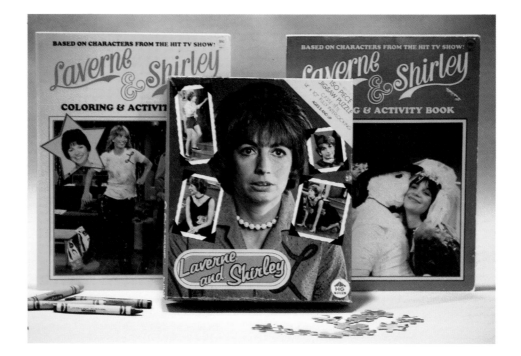

Laverne and Shirley Coloring and Activity Book (#405-2). Published by Playmore Pub., Inc. and Waldman Publishing Corp. © 1983 Paramount Pictures Corp. $8-15. ✦ The blue book is #405-4. $8-15. ✦ "Laverne and Shirley Jigsaw Puzzle" by H G Toys. Paramount Pictures Corp. circa 1983. $8-15.

Lawman

Like "Laramie," "Lawman" was a western series set in Laramie, Wyoming. The show was aired on ABC from October 1958 until October 1962. This program featured John Russell as Marshal Dan Troop and Peter Brown as Deputy Johnny McKay. The plot lines involved their efforts to bring law and order to the West.

A "Lawman" lunch box was produced by King-Seeley in the early 1960s.

The Lawrence Welk Show

"The Lawrence Welk Show" first aired on ABC in 1955. The show's re-runs are still being featured on most PBS television stations. The original shows ran until 1971 on ABC and then were syndicated. The musical variety show featured many performers during the years. Included were the "Champagne Ladies" (Alice Lon and Norma Zimmer), the Lennon Sisters (Diane, Peggy, Kathy, and Janet), Bobby Burgess, Larry Hooper, Myron Floren, and Jo Ann Castle.

Most of the collectibles associated with the Welk show center around their most popular performers, the Lennon Sisters. One exception is a doll called the "Champagne Lady," produced by the Effanbee Doll Co.

Lawrence Welk and the Lennon Sisters tray, measuring 9" by 13 1/2". Circa late 1950s. $20-25.

The Lennon Sisters: The Secret of Holiday Island by Doris Schroeder. Whitman Publishing Company. © 1960 Teleklew Productions., Inc. $3-5. ◆ "Lawrence Welk Presents The Lennon Sisters: Our Favorite Songs." Stereo Pickwick/33 record by arrangement with DOT Records. $5-8. ◆ *The Lennon Sisters Coloring Book* published by Whitman. © 1958 Teleklew Productions., Inc. $15-20.

The Lennon Sisters Cut-Outs (#1995). © 1963 by Teleklew Productions., Inc. Whitman Publishing Company. $25-35. ◆ *Janet Lennon Cut-Out Doll* (#1964). Whitman Publishing Company. © 1958 by Teleklew Productions., Inc. $20-30. ◆ *Lennon Sisters* (#1979). Four paper dolls. Whitman Publishing Company. © 1957 by Teleklew Productions. $30-40.

"Lawrence Welk's Champagne Lady" doll, 19" tall. The doll was made in 1957 by the Effanbee Doll Company. Her arms and head are vinyl, and her body and legs are rigid vinyl. The legs are jointed at the knees and ankles and she wears high heels. She is wearing her original clothing, including hat. Marked "Effanbee" on back of head. $150-200.

Leave It To Beaver

Although "Leave It To Beaver" was never a top-rated show while it was produced, it remains a much-loved nostalgic series in re-runs for present television viewers. The original program began on CBS in 1957 and then moved to ABC, where it remained until 1963. The half-hour situation comedy was a typical 1950s show that outlived its era. The Cleaver family had a housewife mother, a breadwinner father, and two average children. Perhaps it is a yearning for this comfortable family life that makes the re-runs so popular with current viewers. The program's continued success also comes from the excellent performances of the show's regulars, especially Jerry Mathers as "The Beaver" and Ken Osmond as Eddie Haskell (the obnoxious friend of Beaver's brother, Wally). Other characters were Beaver's father Ward (played by Hugh Beaumont), his mother June (Barbara Billingsley), and brother Wally (Tony Dow).

Besides several books and coloring books, three games based on the "Beaver" show were made, all by Hasbro: "Leave It To Beaver Money Maker" (1959), "Leave It To Beaver Ambush Game" (1959), and "Leave It To Beaver Rocket To the Moon" (1959).

Leave It To Beaver by Cole Fannin. Whitman Publishing Company. © 1962 by Gomalco, Inc. $15-20. ◆ *Leave It To Beaver: A Book to Color* (#5662). Published by Saalfield Publishing Company, 1958, 1963. Gomalco Productions, Inc. $50-60.

"Leave it to Beaver Money Maker Game" by Hassenfeld Bros., Inc. © 1959 by Gomalco Productions., Inc. $50-60.

Let's Make a Deal

This popular game show aired on ABC beginning in 1964 and ran until 1971. Monty Hall was the host and the studio audience provided the players. The show asked contestants to trade a known item for something unknown that might or might not be a better value.

"Let's Make A Deal" game . © 1974 Let's Make A Deal ABC. © 1974 Ideal Toy Corp. Stefan Hatos-Monty Hall Productions. $5-10.

Liberace

Wladziu Valentino Liberace first began his television career with a fifteen-minute local Los Angeles show in 1951. NBC began airing the program in 1952. By 1953 the show had expanded to thirty minutes for a syndicated production. ABC aired a later version of this Liberace show during the 1958-1959 season. Two more Liberace programs produced in England kept the famous piano player in front of the television audience during the 1960s.

Several products were produced in association with the "Liberace" show. Included are a charm bracelet featuring a piano; set of boxed Christmas cards; and a piano music box which plays "Somewhere My Love." All of these items were made in the 1950s.

The Life and Legend of Wyatt Earp

"The Life and Legend of Wyatt Earp" was one of many popular westerns during the 1950s. The show premiered on ABC in 1955 and continued on the same network until 1961. Wyatt Earp episodes were first based in Dodge City, Kansas and later took place in Tombstone, Arizona. Hugh O'Brien played the sheriff, Wyatt Earp. The 266 episodes were eventually syndicated.

Related products include the following: Crayon and Stencil set by Transogram (1958); Hartland Wyatt Earp and Horse figures (late 1950s); board game by Transogram (1958); and gun and holster set.

"Liberace plays Chopin Vol. II" extended play record. Columbia, B-449. ◆ Liberace Columbia 78 RPM record #39709. Columbia Recording. "September Song" and "I Want My Mama." $5-10. ◆ An autographed picture of the famous television star.

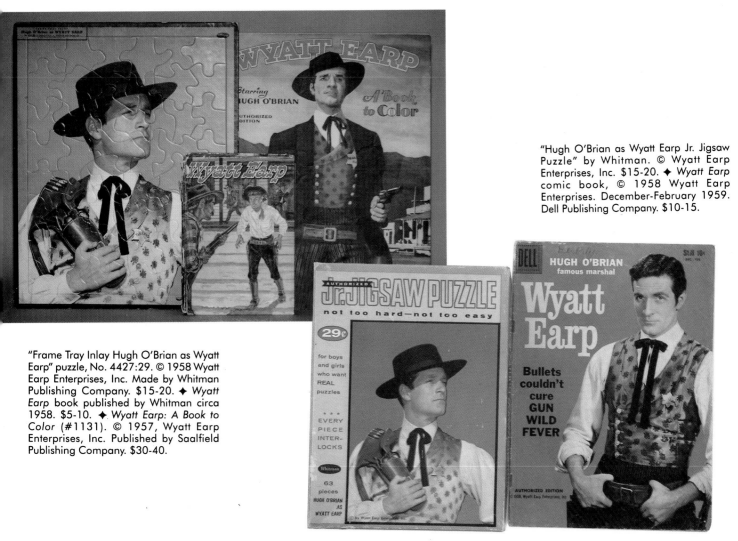

"Hugh O'Brian as Wyatt Earp Jr. Jigsaw Puzzle" by Whitman. © Wyatt Earp Enterprises, Inc. $15-20. ◆ Wyatt Earp comic book, © 1958 Wyatt Earp Enterprises. December-February 1959. Dell Publishing Company. $10-15.

"Frame Tray Inlay Hugh O'Brian as Wyatt Earp" puzzle, No. 4427:29. © 1958 Wyatt Earp Enterprises, Inc. Made by Whitman Publishing Company. $15-20. ◆ Wyatt Earp book published by Whitman circa 1958. $5-10. ◆ Wyatt Earp: A Book to Color (#1131). © 1957, Wyatt Earp Enterprises, Inc. Published by Saalfield Publishing Company. $30-40.

Little House on the Prairie

NBC's long-running hit series "Little House on the Prairie" began on September 11, 1974. The setting for the program was Walnut Grove in Plumb Creek, Minnesota during the 1870s. The plots were based on the "Little House" books by Laura Ingalls Wilder and dealt with the Ingalls family and their experiences as they homesteaded the land. Michael Landon played father Charles, Karen Grassle was mother Caroline, Melissa Gilbert was daughter Laura, Melissa Sue Anderson played the part of daughter Mary, and twins Lindsay and Sidney Green Bush were cast as daughter Carrie Ingalls. The series ended in 1982.

Some of the nicest "Little House" collectibles are the dolls based on the Ingalls daughters. The 12"-tall dolls had vinyl heads and cloth bodies, and were made by Knickerbocker in 1978. A game was produced by Parker Brothers the same year. Other products include a lunch box made by King-Seeley in 1978.

"Little House On The Prairie Colorforms Play Set." © 1978 Ed Friendly Productions., Inc. Licensing Representation by JLM Licensing Assoc. Inc. $15-20.

"Little House On The Prairie" game. Package and contents © 1978 Parker Bros., Division of General Mills Fun Group, Inc. Characters © Ed Friendly Productions, Inc. $10-15.

The Little Rascals

"The Little Rascals" series was made from old movie shorts. The kids gained new attention when the films were syndicated in 1955 and shown on television. Most of the series was originally shot in the 1930s and 1940s. The main characters included Spanky (George McFarland), Alfalfa (Carl Switzer), Darla (Darla Hood), Buckwheat (Billy Thomas), and Stymie (Stymie Beard).

Several new products were produced which featured "The Little Rascals" during the 1950s. Included were "Spanky and His Rascals Fun Game" by Lisbeth Whiteing (1956) and "Spanky and the Little Rascals Clubhouse Bingo" by Gabriel (1958).

Little Rascals: Spanky and Darla Paper Dolls (#2759). © 1957 by California National Productions, Inc. Published by Saalfield Publishing Company. $50-60.

The Lone Ranger

"The Lone Ranger" continued on television after being a success on radio and in the movies. The most famous TV Lone Ranger was Clayton Moore. Tonto was played by Jay Silverheels.

The first television presentation aired on ABC from 1949 to 1957 and then periodically until 1965. There were 221 episodes by the end of the series.

"Lone Ranger" products from the 1950s include books by Grosset and Dunlap; View-Master reels (1956); guitar by Jefferson; Jaymar puzzles; and various items of clothing.

Tonto horseshoe set with rubber horseshoes. © The Lone Ranger, Inc. $15-20.

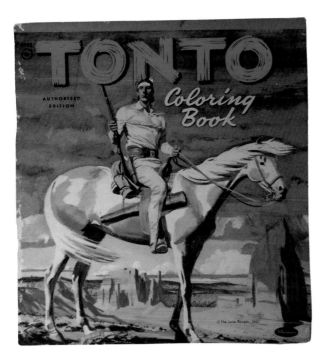

Tonto Coloring Book (#2953). © 1957 by The Lone Ranger, Inc. Published by Whitman. $15-20.

The Lone Ranger Coloring Book (#1117-15). © 1951 by The Lone Ranger, Inc. Published by Whitman Publishing Company. $20-25. ◆ "The Lone Ranger and Tonto" game. © Lone Ranger Television, Inc. Warren Paper Products, Inc., 1978. $15-20. ◆ The Lone Ranger Coloring Book (#208425). © 1953 by The Lone Ranger, Inc. Published by Whitman Publishing Company. $15-20.

The Loretta Young Theatre

"The Loretta Young Theatre" was hosted by former movie actress Loretta Young. She also was a frequent performer in the anthology series. The show aired on NBC from 1954 until 1961.

Loretta Young Coloring Book (#1108). Published by Saalfield Publishing Company, 1956. $30-40. ◆ An autographed picture of Loretta Young, signed circa 1986. $20-30.

Lost in Space

"Lost in Space" was a science fiction program that seems to have become more popular with today's collectors than it was with its original viewers. The show aired on the CBS network from 1965 until 1968. The plot line dealt with the adventures of the Robinson family as they explored space to find a new place for humans to dwell. The cast included Guy Williams as John Robinson, June Lockhart as Maureen Robinson, Mart Kristen as Judy Robinson, Angela Cartwright as Penny Robinson, and Billy Mumy as Will Robinson.

Related products include a boxed costume by Ben Cooper (1966); View-Master Reels; "Lost in Space Switch 'n Go" by Mattel (1966); "Lost In Space Robot" plastic battery toy by Remco; board game by Milton Bradley (1965); and model kit by Aurora (1966).

The Love Boat

In "The Love Boat" series, different stories of romance unfolded each week on a cruise ship called "Pacific Princess." The show featured different guest stars on each program. Most episodes were actually filmed on cruise ships and the passengers were sometimes asked to play "extras" in the television series. The show aired on ABC from 1977 until 1986. Regulars on the ship included Gavin MacLeod as Captain Stubing, Fred Grandy (who later went into politics) as Gopher, and Bernie Kopell as Doctor Adam Bricker.

Action figures of Capt. Stubing, Vicki, Isaac, Julie, Doc Bricker, and Gopher were made to tie-in to the show.

Space Family Robinson Lost in Space comic books from June 1968 and December 1968. Published by Western Publishing Company in 1968. $8-10 each.

"The Love Boat" Captain Stubing figure. © 1981 Aaron Spelling Productions, Inc. Made by Mego Corp. The figure is 3 3/4" tall. Figures were also made in the images of Vicki, Doc, Gopher, Julie, and Isaac. $8-15.

"The Love Boat World Cruise Game" made by the Ungame Company. © 1980 Aaron Spelling Productions. $15-20.

Love That Bob

Another movie star, Bob Cummings, gave his career a boost when he played the lead in the comedy series "Love That Bob." The show aired on NBC from 1954 to 1955; on CBS from 1955 to 1957; on NBC from 1957 to 1959; and on ABC from 1959 to 1961. The show dealt with Bob Collins (Cummings) and his romances as he went about his business as a professional photographer. Rosemary DeCamp played the part of his widowed sister, and Dwayne Hickman played her son.

The Bob Cummings Fashion Models: Statuette Dolls and Clothes (#2732). Bonnie Books © Samuel Lowe and Company, 1958. From "Love That Bob" television show. $75-85.

The Lucy Show

Lucille Ball–the "Queen of American Television Comedy"– began a new CBS television series in 1961, without her earlier partner, former husband Desi Arnaz. Although no other television comedy would ever be as popular as the original "I Love Lucy" series, the new Lucy program was very successful. Lucy chose Vivian Vance from the earlier series to work with her in the new show. The story line followed the day-to-day adventures shared by Lucy Carmichael (played by Lucille Ball) and Vivian Bagley (Vivian Vance) as they shared a home in Connecticut with their children.

In 1965, the series changed its format when Vivian left the show. In the new story, Lucy Carmichael worked as a secretary to Theodore J. Mooney (Gale Gordon) at the Westland Bank in San Francisco. This plot was the basis for the show until 1968.

Pictured are some of the related items produced during the run of "The Lucy Show."

Lucy and the Madcap Mystery by Cole Fannin. Published by Whitman Publishing Co, 1963. $10-15. ✦ The Lucy Show comic books published quarterly by K.K. Publications Inc. © Desilu Productions., Inc. Left: March 1964; Right: December 1963. $10-12 each.

The Lucy Show Cut-Out Coloring Book. Published by Golden Press, 1963. Desilu Productions. SF 227. $35-45. ✦ Lucy and her TV Family Paper Dolls (#1991). Published by the Whitman Publishing Company. © 1963 by Desilu Productions., Inc. Includes five dolls (Lucy, Vivian, and children from the TV series). $50-75.

M

The Magic Land of Allakazam

"The Magic Land of Allakazam" was a children's show which aired on CBS from 1960 to 1963 and then continued on ABC in 1964. Mark Wilson was the magician in the Magical Kingdom and the show involved many magical adventures.

Magic Land of Allakazam Paintless Paint Book (#1421). © 1962 by Mark Wilson Enterprises, Inc. Published by Whitman. $5-10.

Magnum P. I.

"Magnum P.I." was a popular detective series which began in 1980 on the CBS network. The show made a star of Tom Selleck, who played Thomas Sullivan Magnum. Other cast members included John Hillerman (as Jonathan Quayle Higgins III) and Roger E. Mosley (as T.C.). Thomas Magnum was a private investigator in Hawaii. He lived on the estate of Robin Masters (who did not appear in the series) in exchange for security he provided to the property. The last episode of the series was in May 1988.

A "Magnum" flashlight was produced in 1981 by Ja-Ru.

Make A Wish

"Make A Wish" was an acclaimed children's program that aired on the ABC network from 1971 to 1976. This Sunday educational series was hosted by Tom Chapin and the show was filled with educational animation, sketches, films, songs, and interviews. The program won a Peabody award in 1971 and an Emmy award in 1973.

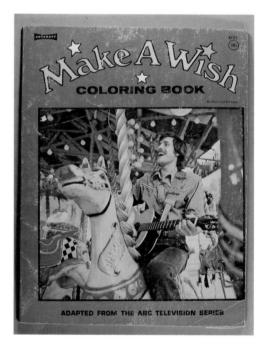

Make a Wish (#4655). © 1973 by the American Broadcasting Co., Inc. Published by Saalfield Publishing Company. $5-10.

Make Room For Daddy

"Make Room For Daddy" aired on ABC from 1953 to 1957. A second format was shown on CBS as "The Danny Thomas Show" from 1957 to 1964. The series featured Danny Thomas as Danny Williams, a New York nightclub entertainer. His wife was played by Jean Hagen, and the children were played by Sherry Jackson as Terry and Rusty Hamer as Rusty. When the series moved to CBS, Danny's wife had died and he married Kathy Williams (played by Marjorie Lord). She had a daughter named Linda (Angela Cartwright).

"An Evening with Danny Thomas" record, from Post Cereals. Includes TV family members Marjorie Lord, Rusty Hamer, and Angela Cartwright. Columbia LP recording. $8-10. ◆ A Linda Williams doll (Angela Cartwright). The first Linda Williams dolls were made as premiums for General Foods Corp. in 1959. Later, another doll was issued by the Natural Doll Company. Both dolls were approximately 15" tall, with dark rooted hair, sleep eyes and made of all vinyl. This doll's head is marked "Linda Williams." $50-60.

The Man From U.N.C.L.E.

"The Man From U.N.C.L.E." was a popular television show in the 1960s. The program began as a sixty-minute show on NBC in September 1964, and ended after 104 episodes in January 1968.

The letters in the title stand for United Network Command for Law Enforcement. The plot involved the U.N.C.L.E. agents' adventures as they clashed with the international organization THRUSH, in a quest to end the crime wave being waged by that organization.

Leading characters were Napoleon Solo (played by Robert Vaughn), Illya Kuryakin (David McCallum), and the head of U.N.C.L.E., Alexander Waverly (Leo G. Carroll). Many collectibles were produced in connection with this program, including a board game by Ideal (1965); card game by Milton Bradley (1965); books by Whitman (1966); "U.N.C.L.E. Secret Agent Watch" (1965); lunch box and thermos by King-Seeley (1966); "Man From U.N.C.L.E. Foto Fantastiks Set" by Faber (1965); "Secret Print Putty Gun" by Colorforms (1965); puzzle by Milton Bradley (1965); "U.N.C.L.E. Secret Code Wheel Pinball Game" by Marx (1966); Model Car Kit by AMT (1967); and a pistol by Ideal (1965).

"Napoleon Solo: The Man From U.N.C.L.E. Game." Characters © 1965 by Metro-Goldwyn-Mayer, Inc. © 1965 Ideal Toy Corp. $30-35.

"The Man From U.N.C.L.E. Card Game" by Milton Bradley. © 1965 Metro-Goldwyn-Mayer, Inc. $25-30.

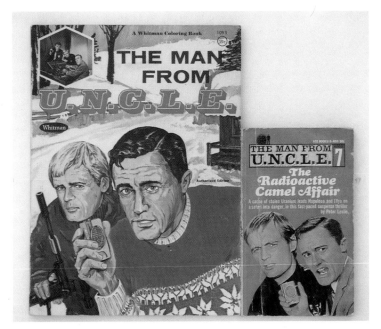

The Man From U.N.C.L.E. (#1095). © 1967 by M-G-M, Inc. Whitman Publishing Company. $20-25. ◆ The Man From U.N.C.L.E. #7 The Radioactive Camel Affair. Ace Books, Inc. © 1966 by M-G-M, Inc. $5-10.

Doll representing Illya Kuryakin (David McCallum) from "The Man From U.N.C.L.E." The figure is 12" tall and was made by A.C. Gilbert Company in 1965. © M-G-M, Inc. A matching plastic doll was made to represent Napoleon Solo. The figure could raise its arm and shoot a gun. $50-75. ✦ "Man from U.N.C.L.E. Illya Kuryakin Card Game." Made by Milton Bradley in 1966. © M-G-M Inc. $25-30.

The Many Loves of Dobie Gillis

The comedy series "The Many Loves of Dobie Gillis" appeared on CBS from 1959 until 1963. The show starred Dwayne Hickman as Dobie Gillis and Bob Denver as Maynard G. Krebs. The show followed the pair from their lives in Central City, through their experiences in the army, and into college after their military years were finished.

Related products include bobbing-head figures of Dobbie and Maynard that are 6 1/2" tall.

Mary Hartman, Mary Hartman

"Mary Hartman, Mary Hartman" was a prime time serial, and also a satire of popular soap operas. Louise Lasser played Mary Hartman, Greg Mullavey played her husband, and Claudia Lamb played her daughter, Heather. The show was syndicated in 1976 and received lots of publicity because of its unusual humor but it ended in the summer of 1977.

"Mary Hartman Mary Hartman: The Game of Life in Fernwood." Made by Reiss Games, Inc. © 1977 T.A.T. Communications Company. $30-40.

M*A*S*H

"M*A*S*H" was one of the most popular television series of the 1970s, first airing on CBS on September 17, 1972. Its cast members included Alan Alda as Hawkeye Pierce, Wayne Rogers as Trapper John McIntire, McLean Stevenson as Lt. Col. Henry Blake, Loretta Swit as Major Margaret Houlihan, Gary Burghoff as Corporal Radar O'Reilly, Larry Linville as Major Frank Burns, and Jamie Farr as Maxwell Klinger. The series was set in a Mobile Army Surgical Hospital in Korea in 1950, during the Korean War. The comedy is intertwined with serious situations as the medical team tries to save human lives. When the last episode was aired on March 2, 1983, it attracted 125 million viewers.

Like other popular shows, M*A*S*H spawned many tie-in products, such as sets including canteens and other gear made by Ja-Ru (1981); Canteen and Utility Belt by Tri-Star Inter. (1982); ambulance with Hawkeye figure by Tri-Star (1982); gum card set of 66 cards (1982); and "M*A*S*H Medic Set" by Ja-Ru (1980).

"M*A*S*H" 3 3/4" tall action figure representing Klinger. © 1970, 1982 Twentieth Century-Fox Film Corp. Tristar International, Ltd. Other figures were made to represent other members of the cast and the vehicles. $10-15.

"M*A*S*H" action figures portraying Loretta Swit and Alan Alda in their television roles. The dolls are 8 1/2" tall and were distributed by F.W. Woolworth Company, circa 1976. © Aspen Productions and Twentieth Century-Fox Film Corp. Hawkeye is missing his golf club and his hat. $25-50 each.

"M*A*S*H" jigsaw puzzles. Made by HG Toys Inc. © 1976 Twentieth Century-Fox Film Corp. $10-15.

"M*A*S*H" game made by Milton Bradley. © 1981 Twentieth Century-Fox Corp. $20-25.

The Match Game

"The Match Game" first appeared on the NBC network in 1962 and continued until 1969. The show was revived in 1973 by CBS. Gene Rayburn was the host for both editions. Each show also made use of celebrities in the completion of given sentences. A game was produced by Milton Bradley in 1963 which was based on the show.

Matty's Funday Funnies

"Matty's Funday Funnies" was shown on ABC from 1959 to 1962. The show used cartoons that had been made by Harvey Films for distribution by Paramount. Included were cartoons featuring "Little Audrey" and "Baby Huey." The show was hosted by characters Matty and Sisterbelle.

Baby Huey the Baby Giant Coloring Book (#4536). Saalfield Publishing Company, © 1959. Harvey Famous Cartoons. $15-20. ✦ *Baby Huey the Baby Giant* comic #96. Giant Harvey Comics. © Harvey Famous Cartoons. $5-8.

Little Audrey Coloring Book (#9535). © MCMLIX (1959) Harvey Famous Cartoons, published by Saalfield Publishing Company. $15-20. ✦ Little Audrey puzzle from the Tuco Work Shops Inc. $15-18. ✦ *Little Audrey TV Funtime* comic from October 1971. Harvey Picture Magazines, Inc. © Harvey Famous Cartoons. $5-8.

Maverick

"Maverick" was another popular western series from the late 1950s. The show first aired on ABC in September 1957 and finished its run in the summer of 1962. James Garner was cast as Bret Maverick, and Jack Kelly played his brother Bart. Although the show's background was the West of the 1880s, the series was as much comedy as it was adventure. The brothers were gamblers instead of lawmen, and satire played a part in many episodes of this atypical "western."

Related products include "Maverick Eras-O-Picture Book" by Hasbro (1958); cap guns; Hartland plastic figure (1958); Halloween costume (1959); string tie with stage coach clip (1959); "Maverick Saddle Rifle" by Marx; puzzle by Whitman (1959); and record (1958).

"Maverick Frame Tray Puzzle" made by Whitman, circa. © 1960 Warner Bros. Pictures, Inc. $15-20. ✦ *Warner Bros. Maverick* by Charles I. Coombs. Illustrated by Alexander Toth. Whitman Publishing Co. © 1959 by Warner Bros. Pictures, Inc. $8-10.

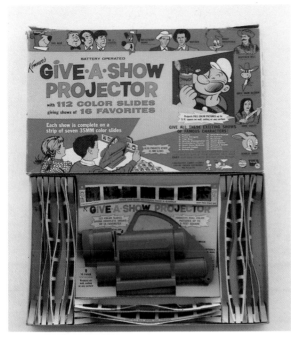

"Give-A-Show Projector" includes films on "Maverick", Popeye, Yogi Bear, Buffalo Bill, Wild Bill Hickok, and Wyatt Earp. Made by Kenner Products. © 1960. Includes sixteen different character filmstrips. Battery operated projector. $35-45.

McKeever and the Colonel

"McKeever and the Colonel" was aired on ABC for only one season, from September 1962 until September 1963. The action took place at the Westfield Military Academy for boys. Scott Lane played one of the cadets, while Allyn Joslyn played the school's head officer, Colonel Harvey Blackwell. Milton Bradley produced the "McKeever and the Colonel Bamboozle Hide and Seek Game" in 1962.

McHale's Navy

"McHale's Navy" was a television series based on the South Pacific island of Taratupa during World War II. It first aired in September 1962 and ended in September 1965. The war story starred Ernest Borgnine as Lt. Cdr. Quinton McHale. Joe Flynn and Tim Conway were also in the cast. Before the series ended, the action had moved to Southern Italy as the war neared its end.

A "McHale's Navy PT-73 Model Kit" was made by Revell in 1965.

McKeever and the Colonel comic. Dell Publication, Feburary-April 1963. © 1962 Four Star-Harlem. $5-8.

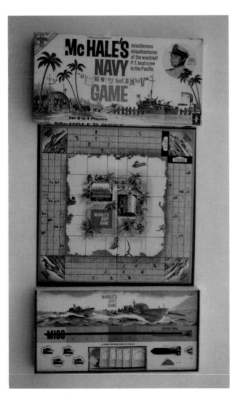

"McHale's Navy Game" © 1962 by Sto-Rev Company. Game made by Transogram Company, Inc. $30-35.

"Bamboozle: The Hide and Seek Game From NBC-TV McKeever and the Colonel." © 1962 Four Star-Harlem. Made by Milton Bradley Company. $30-35.

The Mickey Mouse Club

"The Mickey Mouse Club" began as an ABC television program on October 3, 1955. It ran until September 1959. Jimmie Dodd and Roy Williams were hosts. Some of the more famous Mouseketeers were Annette Funicello, Darlene Gillespie, "Cubby" O'Brien, Karen Pendleton, Bobby Burgess, and Cheryl Holdridge. The program had music, cartoons, children's news features, adventure serials, and guest celebrities. "The Mickey Mouse Club" was revived twice in syndication.

Besides the usual songs and games, the show also featured several different serials. Included were stories featuring "The Hardy Boys" (played by Tim Considine and Tommy Kirk); "Spin and Marty" (also featuring Tim Considine, with David Strollery); and "Annette" (with Annette Funicello).

Many products were made to tie in to this Disney show. They include coloring books and paper doll books made by Whitman, games, the "Walt Disney's Mickey Mouse Club Magazine," a "Mouseketeer Fan Club Typewriter," dolls, and a movie projector.

Walt Disney's Mickey Mouse Club: Old MacDonald Had a Farm (1863). © 1955 Walt Disney Productions. Published by Whitman Publishing Company. $15-20. ✦ Disney Mouseketeer girl, 12" tall. Vinyl with molded clothes. Marked "Walt Disney Productions./Sun Rubber Company." Circa 1950s. $45-55.

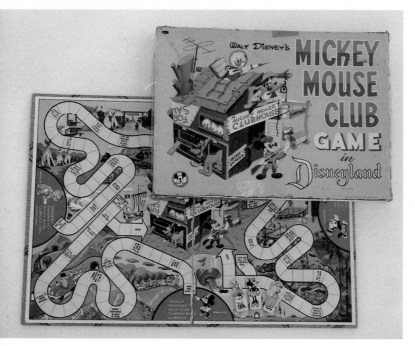

"Walt Disney's Mickey Mouse Club Game in Disneyland" © 1955 Walt Disney Productions. Made by Whitman. $40-50.

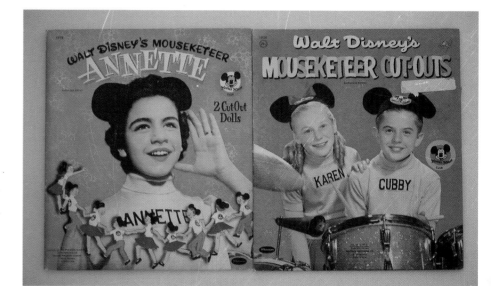

Walt Disney's Mouseketeer Annette (#1958). © 1956 Walt Disney Productions. Published by Whitman. $30-40. ✦ *Walt Disney's Mouseketeer Cut-Outs* (#1959). © 1957 by Walt Disney Productions. Published by Whitman. Both books from the collection of Elaine Price. $30-40.

Mickey Mouse Club Coloring Book (#1381, 1382, 1383). © 1977 Walt Disney Productions. Whitman Publishing Co. $10-15.

Walt Disney's Spin and Marty by Lawrence Edward Watkin. © Walt Disney Productions, 1956. Published by Whitman. $5-8.

"Mickey Mouse Club" projector, with four films (Model #488). © Walt Disney Productions. Made by Stephens Products Company. Circa 1950s. $40-50.

The Mighty Mouse Playhouse

"The Mighty Mouse Playhouse" aired on CBS from 1955 to 1967. The show featured animated cartoons starring Mighty Mouse, a Terrytoon character. The show ran for thirty minutes and included four six-minute cartoons.

Mighty Mouse handkerchief, © Terrytoons, Inc. $15-18. ✦ *Mighty Mouse*, a Wonder Book (#1502). Circa late 1950s. $4-6.

The Milton Berle Show

"The Texaco Star Theatre" was the first television series starring Milton Berle. The show was so popular that Berle received the title, "Mr. Television." The variety series aired on NBC from 1948 until 1953. Berle continued to star on various variety shows for NBC until 1959. A similar series for ABC which first aired on September 9, 1966 was not successful and ended on January 6, 1967.

The most important Berle collectible is the Milton Berle wind-up car, made by Marx during the 1950s.

Mission Impossible

"Mission Impossible" had a long run on the CBS network from 1966 until 1973. Cast members included Peter Graves as Jim Phelps, Steven Hill as Dan Briggs, Barbara Bain as Cinnamon Carter, Martin Landau as Rollin Hand, and Greg Morris as Barney Collier. All these characters worked for I.M.F. (Impossible Missions Force) which dealt with secret assignments for the U.S. government.

Ideal produced a game based on the series in 1966.

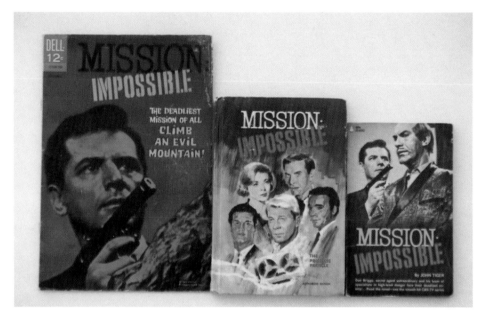

Mission Impossible: Climb an Evil Mountain comic by Dell Publishing. © Desilu Productions. Inc. September 1967. $8-10. ✦ *Mission Impossible: The Priceless Particle* by Talmage Powell. © 1969 by Paramount Pictures Corp. Whitman Publishing Company. ✦ *Mission Impossible* by John Tiger. Popular Library. © 1967 by Desilu Productions. Inc. $8-10 each.

Mister Ed the Talking Horse (#1135) coloring book. © 1963, Mister Ed Company. Published by Whitman Publishing Company. $30-40. ✦ *Mister Ed the Talking Horse*, a Little Golden Book by Barbara Shook Hazen. © 1962 by the Mister Ed Company. Published by Golden Press, Inc. $8-10. ✦ "Mister Ed the Talking Horse Puppet." © 1962 by the Mister Ed Company. © Knickerbocker Toy Company. $35-40.

Mister Ed

"Mister Ed" had one of the most far-fetched story lines of the silly sit-coms of the 1960s. In this thirty-minute show, Wilbur Post and his wife Carol discovered that a horse named Mister Ed came with their new house. This horse was not your usual horse; he could talk. However, he would only speak to Wilbur. The plots revolved around this premise.

The program was broadcast on CBS from 1961 to 1966 and consisted of 143 episodes. Wilbur and Carol Post were played by Alan Young and Connie Hines.

A talking Mister Ed hand puppet was made by Mattel, Inc. in 1962, and the show's theme song was produced as both sheet music and as a recording in 1962.

"Mister Ed The Talking Horse: A Game Based on the C.B.S. T.V. Show." Made by Parker Bros. © 1962 by the Mister Ed Company. $40-45.

Mister Peepers

"Mister Peepers" starred a timid character named Robinson J. Peepers, played by Wally Cox. Peepers was a biology teacher in Jefferson Junior High School in Jefferson City. Other faculty members were Harvey Weskitt (Joseph Foley/Tony Randall), Nancy Remington (Norma Crane/Patricia Benoit), and Mrs. Gurney (Marion Lorne). The series aired on NBC from 1952 until 1955. Peepers married Nancy Remington in 1954.

A "Mister Peepers School Bag and Game Kit" was produced by Pressman Toys in 1955 to tie in to this show.

"Mister Peepers Handy Andy Precision Microscope Set." Designed and developed by Skil-Craft Corp., Chicago. © 1954 by Skil-Craft Corp. $40-50.

The Mod Squad

"The Mod Squad" was a series focused on young people in Los Angeles. The cast included Michael Cole as Pete Cochran, Peggy Lipton as Julie Barnes, Clarence Williams III as Linc Hayes, and Tige Andrews as Adam Greer. The youngsters investigated local organizations in order to aid the police. The series aired on ABC from 1968 to 1973.

Related products include a View-Master set and a jigsaw puzzle produced by Milton Bradley in 1969.

The Mod Squad comic. January 1969, Dell Publications. © 1968 Thomas-Spelling Productions. ✦ The Mod Squad #3: The-Sock-It-To-Me-Murders by Richard Deming. Pyramid Publications, Inc. © 1968 by Thomas-Spelling Productions. $5-10 each.

The Monkees

"The Monkees," a comedy series about a rock-and-roll group, began on NBC in 1966 and aired until 1968. In 1966, the program won an Emmy as the year's best comedy series. When the show went off the air for NBC, the network received more letters of protest than had ever been received before by the network during a similar circumstance. CBS broadcast the show from 1969 to 1972. The series ended its life on ABC during the 1972-1973 season. The Monkees were played by Davy Jones, Mike Nesmith, Micky Dolenz and Peter Tork.

Because "The Monkees" were so popular among teens, many related products were produced bearing their likeness. Included were 5"-tall finger puppets with vinyl heads, made by Remco (1970); lunch box and thermos by King-Seeley (1967); model kits by Corgi toys (1967); board game by Transogram (1967); guitar by Mattel, Inc. (1966); and many records, magazines and other fan materials.

Monkees Who's Got the Button? by William Johnston. Whitman Publishing Company. © 1968 by Raybert Productions, Inc. Screen Gems, Inc. $12-15. ◆ Talking puppets of the Monkees. © 1966 Raybert Productions., Inc. © 1966 Mattel, Inc. $40-80 (depending on working condition.

The Monkees Big Beat Fun Book. Young World Productions LTD, London. © 1968, Raybert Productions, Inc. Screen Gems, Inc. $35-45.

"The Monkees Guitar." Produced by Mattel Inc., 1966. Made of plastic and 19" long. © Screen Gems, Inc. and Raybert Productions. $80-90.

"The Monkees" Colgems Record. RCA, Screen Gems, Columbia Pictures Corp. Includes theme of television show. © 1966. $15-20. ✦ Monkees puppet, 5" tall. Missing boots. © 1970, Columbia Pictures. Made by Remco Inc. ✦ "The Monkees Official Monkee Puzzle." Four different titles were made by the E.E. Fairchild Corp. © 1967 Raybert Productions. Inc. Screen Gems, Inc. $30-40

Monkees Go Mad, © 1967 by Raybert Productions, Inc. Popular Library.$12-15. ✦ The Monkees' "Last Train To Clarksville/ Take a Giant Step." RCA Colgems, Columbia Pictures Corp., Screen Gems, Inc. $10-15.

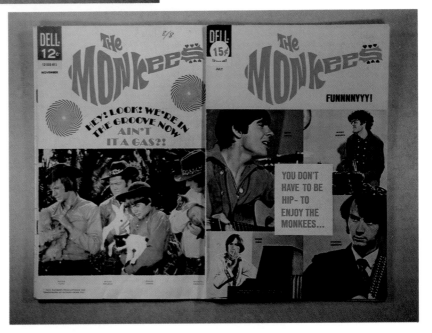

The Monkees comic books. © 1968 Raybert Productions., Inc. Trademark of Screen Gems, Inc. From November 1968 and July 1968. Dell Publishing Company. $12-15 each.

Mork and Mindy

"Mork and Mindy" was an instant hit when it aired on ABC in 1978. Mork (Robin Williams) came from the Planet of Ork. He landed in Boulder, Colorado where he became friends with Mindy McConnell (Pam Dawber). The episodes dealt with Mork's adventures as he learned about the alien culture of the United States.

The program's hit status was due largely to the talent of Robin Williams. The program ran until 1982.

This show was a hit with product manufacturers. Books, games, dolls, lunch boxes, and puzzles were just some of the many items made to tie in to this series.

"Mork & Mindy Card Game" by Milton Bradley Company. © 1978 Paramount Pictures Corp. $10-15.

"Mork & Mindy Rub n' Play" Magic Transfer Set by Colorforms. © Paramount Pictures Corp. 1979. $10-15.

"Mork & Mindy Game" by Parker Brothers. © 1979 Paramount Pictures Corp. $15-20.

"Pam Dawber as Mindy" doll. The vinyl doll is 9" tall and was made by Mattel, Inc. © 1979 Paramount Pictures Corp. $25-35. ✦ *Mork from Ork: An Outerspace Activity Book.* Published by Wonder Books. © 1979 Paramount Pictures Corp. $10-12. ✦ "Robin Williams as Mork" doll with talking spacepack. Made by Mattel, Inc. © 1979 Paramount Pictures Corp. The backpack says eight of Mork's phrases. The doll is 9" tall and made of vinyl. $25-35

"Mork & Mindy" puzzle. Made by Milton Bradley, © 1978 Paramount Pictures Corp. $10-12. ✦ "Mork & Mindy" lunch box and thermos. © 1979 Paramount Pictures Corp. Made by King-Seeley Thermos. $20-25.

Mr. Novak

"Mr. Novak" was another series dealing with high school teachers. Mr. Novak was an English teacher in Jefferson High School in Los Angeles. Dean Jagger played his principal, Albert Vane. The show ran on NBC from 1963 to 1965.

The Munsters

A popular 1960s show for collectors is "The Munsters," a comedy similar to "The Addams Family." The spooky characters in this series included Herman Munster (played by Fred Gwynne), Lily Munster (Yvonne DeCarlo), Grandpa (Al Lewis); Marilyn Munster (Beverly Owen, and later Pat Priest), and Edward Wolfgang Munster (Butch Patrick). The plots revolved around a family with members who seemed to come from old monster movies. Herman looked like Frankenstein, Lily was a vampire, Edward was a werewolf, and Grandpa was an elderly Dracula-type character. The only "normal" member of the family was the niece, Marilyn.

With such a wonderful source of material, many products were made to tie in with this series. Included were a Baby Lily doll made by Ideal (1965); comic books; "The Munsters Masquerade Party Game" by Hasbro; "The Munsters Colorforms Cartoon Kit" by Colorforms (1965); puzzles by Whitman (1965); Herman hand puppet by Mattel, Inc. (1964); 20"-tall Herman doll by Mattel, Inc. (1964); "The Munsters Drag Race Game" by Hasbro (1964); "The Munsters Picnic Game" by Hasbro (1964); lunch box and thermos by King-Seeley (1965); "The Munsters Drag Race Game" by Hasbro (1965); and various model kits made by AMT (1964).

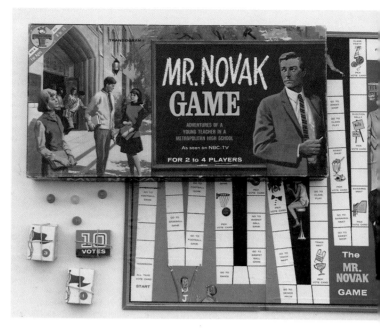

"Mr. Novak Game" made by Transogram Company. © 1963 by Metro-Goldwyn-Mayer, Inc. $22-25.

"The Munsters Card Game" by Milton Bradley. © 1964 Kayro-Vue Productions. $30-35.

The Munsters Sticker Fun published by Whitman. © 1965 Kayro-Vue Productions. $35-40. ✦ The Munsters Paper Dolls with five dolls (#1959). Published by Whitman. © 1966 by Kayro-Vue Productions. From the collection of Elaine Price. $75-100.

The Munsters comic, © K.K. Publications. December, 1966. © 1966 Kayro-Vue Productions. $10-15. ✦ The Munsters and the Great Camera Caper by William Johnston. Whitman Publishing Company. © 1965 by Kayro-Vue Productions. $10-15 each.

Murder, She Wrote

"Murder, She Wrote" first aired on CBS in September 1984. The successful murder mystery starred former movie star Angela Lansbury as murder-mystery writer Jessica Fletcher. The series ran for over ten years, with most of the action taking place in Jessica's home town, Cabot Cove, Maine. Other continuing characters included William Windom as Dr. Seth Hazlitt and Tom Bosley (later replaced by Ron Masak) as the sheriff. Beginning in 1991, Jessica spent part of her time in an apartment in New York where she taught criminology. Interestingly, each week the series revolves around guest roles, which are sometimes filled by former screen actors from the "golden years" of Hollywood.

My Favorite Martian

"My Favorite Martian" was a zany situation comedy from the 1960s. The show aired on CBS from 1963 until 1966. The story line involved a newspaper reporter named Tim O'Hara (Bill Bixby) who rescued a Martian professor after his UFO crashed on earth. The Martian (Ray Walston) pretended to be Tim's uncle while he repaired his space ship for a return to Mars.

Related products include the "My Favorite Martian Magic Tricks" set by Gilbert (1965); game by Transogram (1963); a coloring set by Standard Toy Kraft Inc. (1963); and coloring book by Golden Press (1964).

"Murder She Wrote" game by Warren Company. © 1985 by Universal City Studios, Inc. $10-15.

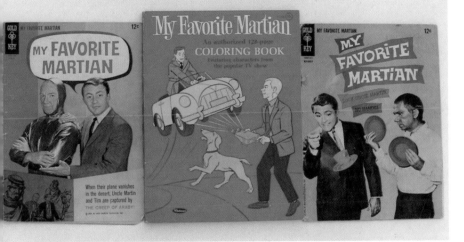

My Favorite Martian comics (at left and right). K.K. Publications Inc. From November 1965 and August 1965. © 1965 by Jack Chertok Television, Inc. $5-8. ◆ My Favorite Martian Coloring Book (#1148). © Jack Chertok Television, Inc. Published by Whitman Publishing Company. $20-25.

My Little Margie

"My Little Margie" was a successful early situation comedy which aired on CBS from 1952 to 1953 and on NBC from 1953 to 1955. Altogether there were 126 episodes. The show starred silent film star Charles Farrell as Vern Albright, and movie star Gale Storm as his daughter, Margie. The story depicted the problems of a father and daughter relationship.

My Little Margie Coloring Book. "Gale Storm and Charles Farrell Stars of the TV Show." © 1954, Rovan Films. Published by Saalfield Publishing Company. $20-25. ◆ My Little Margie Paper Dolls. Gale Storm dolls (#2737). Published by Saalfield in 1958. © Rovan Films. $60-75.

My Three Sons

"My Three Sons" was a favorite television situation comedy for over ten years. During its time on the air, new characters were added as the family was enlarged. The show aired on ABC from 1960 to 1965. Then it switched to CBS, where it remained until 1972. The original cast included Steve Douglas, a widower (played by Fred MacMurray), his sons Mike, Robbie, and Chip (played by Tim Considine, Don Grady and Stanley Livingston), and their grandfather (played by William Frawley). William Demarest replaced Frawley after several years, with a character called Uncle Charlie. The family also added another son when they adopted Ernie (Barry Livingston). The father, Steve, eventually re-married and became a stepfather to a daughter named Dodie (Dawn Lyn). The sons grew up on the series, eventually beginning college, careers, and families of their own.

One of the most sought-after items related to this series is the set of triplet dolls. The dolls represented the children of Robbie and his wife Kathleen. The boys who played the triplets were Joseph, Michael, and Daniel Todd. The dolls were made by Remco Ind. in 1969. They were 9 1/2" tall and were all vinyl.

"Myrtle Talking Handpuppet." Myrtle was Dodie's doll on "My Three Sons." Marked "© 1969 Mattel, Inc. Mexico" on back of neck. Tagged "Quality Originals by Mattel Murtle (Trademark) © 1969 Columbia Broadcasting System, Inc. © 1969 Mattel, Inc." From the collection of Cindy Sabulis. Photograph by Cindy Sabulis. $40-50.

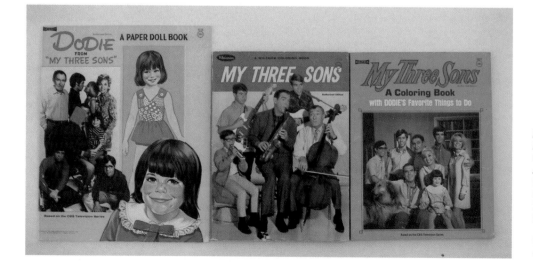

Dodie from "My Three Sons": A Paper Doll Book. Based on the CBS TV series. © 1971 Columbia Broadcasting System, Inc. Artcraft #5115. $20-25. ◆ My Three Sons (#1113). © 1967, Columbia Broadcasting System, Inc. Published by Whitman. $20-25. ◆ My Three Sons: A Coloring Book With Dodie's Favorite Things to Do (#3827). © 1971 by Columbia Broadcasting System, Inc. Published by Saalfield Publishing Company. $15-20.

N

Nanny and the Professor

"Nanny and the Professor" began on ABC on January 21, 1970. The thirty-minute program ended on December 27, 1971 after sixty-five episodes. The story focused on the household of widower Professor Harold Everett (Richard Long) and his children Hal, Butch, and Prudence (David Doremus, Trent Lehman, and Kim Richards). Their nanny was played by Juliet Mills, who seemed to have the ability to spread love and joy throughout the household.

Besides paper dolls and a coloring book, a paperback book and View-Master reels were also produced in 1970.

National Velvet

The "National Velvet" television series aired on NBC from 1960 to 1962. It was based on the M-G-M movie from 1944 which had starred a very young Elizabeth Taylor. The film had been made from the book written by Enid Bagnold.

The story was about Velvet Brown (Lori Martin) who was training her horse, King, to run in the Grand National Steeplechase. Velvet's father and mother were played by Ann Doran and Arthur Space in the television series.

Many products were produced to tie in to this children's show. Included are a game by Transogram (1961); King model kit by Revell (1962); King plush doll made by Smile Novelty Co. (1960); and a beautiful large doll representing Lori Martin as Velvet. The doll was 38" tall and was produced by Ideal Toy Co. in 1961. It has a vinyl head with dark brown hair. The rest of the doll is plastic.

Nanny and the Professor: A Paper Doll Book (#5114) by Artcraft. © 1970-1971 Twentieth Century-Fox Film Corporation. $20-25. ✦ *Nanny and the Professor: A Coloring Book* (#3835). © 1960, 1961 by Twentieth Century-Fox Film Corporation. Published by Saalfield Publishing Company. $15-20.

National Velvet Coloring Book (#2975-B). Based on NBC's television version of M-G-M's "National Velvet." © 1963 by Metro-Goldwyn-Mayer, Inc. Published by Whitman, Western Printing. $15-20. ✦ *National Velvet Cut-Out Doll* (#1958). Whitman Publishing. © 1961 by Metro-Goldwyn-Mayer Inc. $20-25. ✦ *National Velvet* by Dorothy Haas. Based on M-G-M's "National Velvet" as seen on NBC TV. © 1962 M-G-M Inc. Published by Whitman. $5-8.

Lori Martin doll representing Velvet Brown from the "National Velvet" television series. The Ideal doll is 38" tall and was made in 1961. She has rooted dark brown hair, a vinyl head, plastic body, and is jointed at the waist and ankles. The head is marked "Metro-Goldwyn-Mayer Inc./ MFG. By / Ideal Toy Corp." On her back is "© Ideal Toy Corp./ G-38." She is wearing her original clothing and boots. From the collection of Edith M. Wise. Photograph by James Wise. $600-800.

Northwest Passage

The television series "Northwest Passage" began on NBC in 1958 and continued until 1959. The story took place in 1754, during the French-Indian War. Major Robert Rogers (Keith Larsen) was searching for a Northwest passage in order to link the east with the west. Buddy Ebsen was also in the cast, playing the part of Sergeant Hunk Marriner.

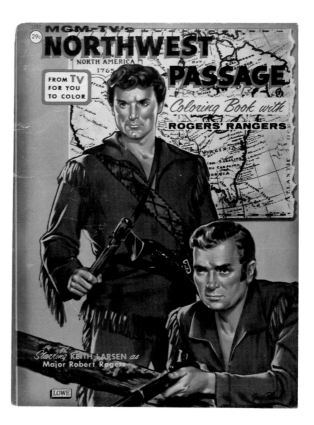

M-G-M-TV's Northwest Passage Coloring Book (#2852). Published by Samuel Lowe Company, 1959. $25-30.

The Nurses

The action in "The Nurses" centered around the Alden General Hospital in New York City. The main characters were Nurse Liz Thorpe (played by Shirl Conway), Nurse Gail Lucas (Zina Bethune), and Dr. Ted Steffen (Joseph Campanella). The show aired on CBS from September 1962 to January 1965. The show was then retitled as "The Doctors and the Nurses" and continued on CBS until September of 1965.

"The Nurses Game" based on the CBS drama. © 1963 Columbia Broadcasting System, Inc. © 1963 by Ideal Toy Corp. $30-35.

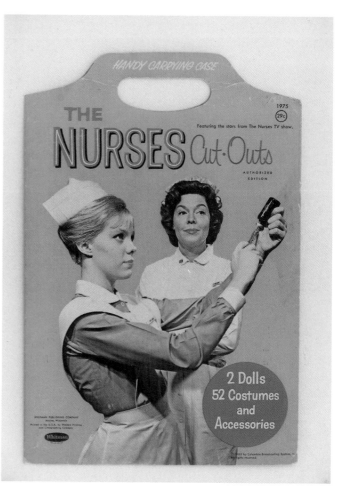

The Nurses Cut-Outs (#1975). Published by Whitman. © 1963 by Columbia Broadcasting System, Inc. $25-30.

O

Our Miss Brooks

"Our Miss Brooks" began airing on CBS in 1952 and continued until 1957 using two different formats. The most popular show starred Eve Arden as teacher Connie Brooks, Gale Gordon as Osgood Conklin, Robert Rockwell as Philip Boynton, and Richard Crenna as Walter Denton. Brooks was an English teacher in Madison High School and the plot involved her conflicts with principal Conklin and her efforts to impress biology teacher Boynton. The second format, which began in 1956, involved Brooks as a teacher in a private school in California. Gale Gordon continued to play the role of her principal.

Eve Arden Paper Dolls published by Saalfield Publishing Company, 1953. $55-75. ◆ *Radio-TV Mirror* featuring Eve Arden on the cover for October 1953. Published by Macfadden Publications, Inc. $8-10. ◆ *Eve Arden Coloring Book* (#2310). © 1953. Saalfield Publishing Company. $20-30.

Ozzie's Girls

"Ozzie's Girls" continued the story of Ozzie and Harriet Nelson's family. Since sons Dave and Ricky were grown, the Nelsons rented rooms to two college girls in this new series. The girls were played by Susan Sennett and Brenda Sykes.

The program was a syndicated show in 1973, but without the popular Nelson boys the show did not have much impact on viewers. Only twenty-four episodes were filmed.

Ozzie's Girls: A Coloring Book (#4687). Adapted from the television series. © 1973, Filmways Television Corp. Published by Saalfield Publishing Company. $15-20.

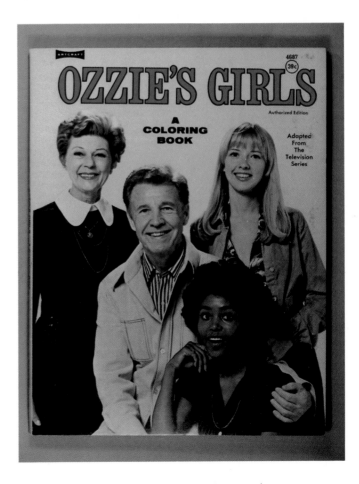

P

The Partridge Family

"The Partridge Family" was a hit show on ABC from 1970 to 1974. The mother, Shirley Partridge, was played by Shirley Jones. Much of the show's success was due to the fact that David Cassidy, who played the eldest son (Keith), became a teen idol. Besides Cassidy, the other children were played by Susan Dey (Laurie), Danny Bonaduce (Danny), Suzanne Crough (Tracy), and Jeremy Gelbwaks as Chris (later replaced by Brian Foster). The show focuses on the Partridges as they change from an ordinary family to a famous rock singing group.

This series was a hit with product manufacturers. Many different items were made to take advantage of the show's popularity, including a yellow hard-plastic bus; drum set, and guitar all made by Remco in 1973; lunch box by King-Seeley Thermos (1971); 16"-tall Patti Partridge doll made by Ideal (1971); and 19"-tall Laurie Partridge doll made by Remco (1973).

Laurie Partridge (Susan Dey) doll. Made by Remco, 1973. The doll is 19" tall and has a vinyl head, arms, and legs, rooted brown hair and painted eyes. Marked "© 1973/Remco Ind.Inc." Wearing her original clothes except shoes. $100+.

Susan Dey as Laurie paper dolls (#4218). © 1972 Columbia Pictures Industries, Inc. Published by Artcraft. From the collection of Elaine Price. $25-30.

"The Partridge Family Game" by Milton Bradley Company. © 1971 and trademark of Columbia Pictures Industries, Inc. $25-30.

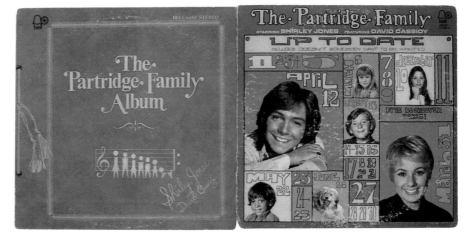

"The Partridge Family Album" from Bell Records, a Division of Columbia Pictures Industries, Inc. ✦ "The Partridge Family: Up To Date" by Bell Records, A Division of Columbia Pictures Industries, Inc. $8-10 each.

The Partridge Family (#5137). Paper dolls published by Artcraft. © 1971 Columbia Pictures Industries, Inc. $35-40. ✦ The Partridge Family: A Coloring Book. © 1970. Columbia Pictures Industries, Inc. ABC. Published by Saalfield Publishing Company. $20-25. ✦ Partridge Family comic for July 1971. © 1971 Chariton Press Inc. © 1971 Columbia Pictures Industries, Inc. $8-10.

Password

"Password" was another popular game show in the 1960s, airing on CBS from 1961 until 1967. It then moved to ABC, where it played from 1971 to 1974. Allen Ludden was the host for both shows. The program pitted two teams against each other, each team featuring a celebrity player as well as an audience contestant.

"Password as seen on CBS" game made by Milton Bradley Company. © 1962 Peak Productions, Inc. Goodson Todman Productions as seen on CBS. $5-10.

The Patty Duke Show

Patty Duke became a child star on Broadway when she played Helen Keller in the play *The Miracle Worker* in 1959. She was awarded an Oscar as best supporting actress in 1962 when she repeated her role in the United Artists film version of the play. She secured more fame, however, with her television program "The Patty Duke Show," which was shown on ABC television from 1963 to 1966. Patty played a double role as look-alike cousins Cathy and Patty. Patty was American while Cathy was from England.

One of the most popular Patty Duke items made during this series is the doll made by Horsman in 1965. The vinyl doll is 12 1/2" tall with rooted blonde hair and painted blue eyes. She came with her own phone.

"Patty Duke with Patty and Cathy Game" made by Milton Bradley Company. © United Artists Television, Inc. 1963. $25-35.

Patty Duke Paper Dolls (#1991), "Inspired by the Patty Duke Show." © 1964 by United Artists Television, Inc. Published by Whitman Publishing Company. $30-35. ✦ *Patty Duke Coloring Book* (#1122). Published by Whitman Publishing Company, 1964. © United Artists Television, Inc. $15-20.

Peanuts

Animated cartoons featuring the Peanuts' characters were aired on television as specials beginning during the 1965-1966 season. CBS carried the series, which included "It's the Great Pumpkin, Charlie Brown" and "A Charlie Brown Christmas" as well as several other titles. The characters were first created by Charles Schultz. Included are Charlie Brown, Linus, Lucy, Schroeder, Pig Pen, Frieda, Peppermint Patty, and Sally.

Although Peanuts products continue to be produced each year, it is the items from the 1960s that are most sought after by collectors.

Peanuts Pictures to Color (#5331). From the famous comic strip created by Charles M. Schultz. United Features Syndicate. Published by Saalfield Publishing Company, 1960. $15-20. ✦ Snoopy lunch box, © 1968 United Feature Syndicate, Inc. Made by American Thermos. $30-35. ✦ Billfold, © 1965 United Feature Syndicate, Inc. $10-12.

Pee-Wee's Playhouse

"Pee-Wee's Playhouse" was a very popular children's television show during the late 1980s and early 1990s. The show aired on CBS from 1986 to 1991. The star, Pee-Wee Herman, was a grown man (actually named Paul Rubens), but he acted like a child on the series. The show was cancelled in April 1991, just months before Herman's July arrest in a Florida adult movie theater. Although there were many products produced in Pee-Wee's image, the bad publicity generated by his arrest may make collectors shy away from this material, at least for now.

Pee-Wee Tee Shirt, © 1989 Herman Toys, Inc. $3-5. ✦ Lunch box, © Herman Toys, Inc. 1987. Made by Thermos. $10-12. ✦ Pee-Wee Herman doll, © Herman Toys, Inc. © 1987 Matchbox Toys (USA) Ltd. The talking doll has a vinyl head and hands and a cloth body. He is approximately 22" tall. $25-40.

Big Top Pee Wee: Life On The Farm. Scholastic, Inc. © 1988 Paramount Pictures Corp. $3-5. ✦ "Pee Wee Magic Catch Mitts" made by Synergistics Research Corp. © 1987 Herman Toys, Inc. $8-10. ✦ "Pee-Wee Yo Yo" by Spectra Star. © 1988 Herman Toys, Inc. $8-10.

People's Court

"People's Court" was a syndicated show from the 1980s that dealt with real cases that were headed for small-claims court. The show paid the settlement when the case was resolved. If no award was given, $500 was divided between the parties involved.

"The People's Court" game. © 1986 The People's Court, a Ralph Edwards Production. © 1986 Hoyle Products. $3-5.

Perry Mason

"Perry Mason" is probably the most popular "lawyer" series ever aired on television. Although the regular program ran on CBS from 1957 to 1966, the characters continued to surface in specials into the 1990s. The original show was sixty minutes in length. The characters were based on those created by Erle Stanley Gardner for his crime novels. Raymond Burr starred as Perry Mason, and Barbara Hale played his secretary, Della Street. Other memorable characters included William Hopper as Paul Drake and Ray Collins as Lieutenant Tragg. "The New Adventures of Perry Mason" (featuring Monte Markham instead of Burr as Mason) lasted only from September 16, 1973 until January 27, 1974.

"Perry Mason: Case of the Missing Suspect Game" by Transogram. © 1959 Paisano Productions. $50-55.

Peter Gunn

"Peter Gunn" was a crime drama based in Los Angeles. The action centered around private investigator Peter Gunn, played by Craig Stevens, and his girlfriend Edie Hart, played by Lola Albright. The show aired on NBC from 1958 to 1960. It then continued on ABC from 1960 until 1961.

A "Peter Gunn Detective Game" was made by Lowell in 1960, and a TV soundtrack representing the series was released.

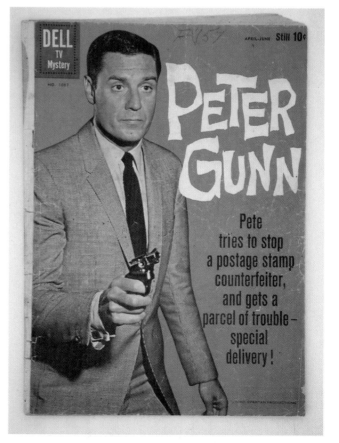

Peter Gunn comic by Dell Publishing. Dated April-June 1960. © 1960 Spartan Productions. $15-20.

Peter Potamus

"Peter Potamus" was a Hanna-Barbera syndicated animated cartoon from 1964. Characters included Peter the purple hippo and So So the monkey.

Products stemming from this series include a Yip pull toy made by Ideal; bubble bath figure of Yip; a puzzle; Spouty the Whale Soaky; bank by Ideal; and a book called *Peter Potamus Meets the Black Knight,* published by Whitman in 1965. Other character segments featured Yippie, Yappie, and Yahooey. three cartoon dogs.

Petticoat Junction

"Petticoat Junction" was a popular 1960s comedy for CBS from 1963 until 1970. The action took place in Hooterville, where Kate Bradley (played by Bea Benaderet) was owner of the Shady Rest Hotel. Other characters included her daughters Billie Jo (first played by Jeannine Riley, then Gunilla Hutton, and finally Meredith MacRae), Bobbie Jo (Pat Woodell and later Lori Saunders), and Betty Jo (Linda Kaye Henning). Their uncle, Joe Carson (Edgar Buchanan), was also an important part of the story line. Former Gene Autry sidekick Smiley Burnette played the part of Charley Pratt.

A game based on the series was produced by Standard Toy Kraft in the 1960s.

Peter Potamus coloring book (#1139). © 1964 by Hanna-Barbera Productions, Inc. Published by Whitman Publishing Company. $20-25.

The Pinky Lee Show

"The Pinky Lee Show" was a children's program that aired on NBC from 1950 until 1955. The program included music, circus acts, and comedy, with Pinky Lee as host.

Pinky Lee products include a television tray from 1954; View-Master reel; Party Packet; Paint Set; "Pinky Lee, Who Am I Game" by Ed-U; "Pinky Lee Game Time" by Pressman Toy Corp.; and a Pinky Lee doll made by Juro (Eegee). The doll is 25" tall with a vinyl head and a molded hat. The body is cloth (see picture under "That Girl" entry).

Petticoat Junction: 4 Cut-Out Dolls (#1954). © 1964 by Wayfilms. Published by Whitman Publishing Company. $35-45.

"Pinky Lee Xylophone" © 1955 NBC-TV. Emenee Musical Toys. $25-35.

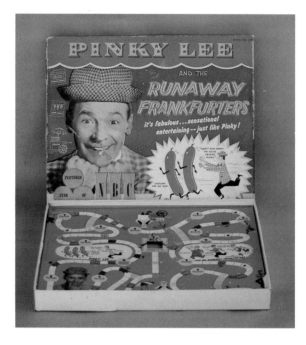

"Pinky Lee and the Runaway Frankfurters" game. © National Broadcasting Company, Inc. © 1954 Lisbeth Whiting Company, Inc. $40-50.

Planet of the Apes

The "Planet of the Apes" television series was adapted from the successful 1968 motion picture. It was first shown on television in September 1974 and ended in December of the same year after only thirteen episodes. In the science fiction story, a U.S. space capsule passed the time barrier and emerged in the year 3085. The capsule landed in a place ruled by apes. The surviving astronauts were befriended by one of the intelligent apes (Roddy McDowall) as they tried to return to their home. Ron Harper and James Jaughton were the astronauts.

A "Planet of the Apes" lunch box was made in 1974 by Aladdin, and dolls of the characters were made by Mego in the same year. The dolls are 8" tall and represent Roddy McDowall as Cornelius, Maurice Evans as Dr. Zaius, Kim Hunter as Zira, James Naughton as Peter Burke, and Ron Harper as Alan Virdon.

Planet of the Apes Cut and Color Book (#2434), © 1967, 1974 by Apjac Productions, Inc. and Twentieth Century-Fox Film Corp. It was published by Saalfield Publishing Company. ✦ Jigsaw puzzle produced by H-G Toys and copyrighted by Apjac Productions, Inc. and Twentieth Century-Fox Film Corp. These products may have been released earlier for the film, and then re-released for the TV series. $10-15 each.

Police Woman

Beginning in 1974 and ending in 1978, Angie Dickinson starred in "Police Woman" as Sgt. Suzanne "Pepper" Anderson. Anderson worked as an undercover police woman for the Los Angeles Police Department. The plot centered on her various cases and her personal life.

Angie Dickinson as Police Woman: #3–Death of a Call Girl by Leslie Trevor. Award Books. © 1975 by Columbia Pictures Industries, Inc. $5-8. ✦ Angie Dickinson as Police Woman doll, made by Horsman in 1976. The doll is 9" tall and is all vinyl. The head is marked "Horsman Dolls Inc./U/L/CPT/1976." © Columbia Pictures Television. $40-50.

Popeye

"Popeye" animated cartoons were a hit with movie-goers from 1933 until 1954. A total of 200 episodes were produced during these years. With the syndication of the cartoons in 1958, they also became popular with the youngsters of that era. Between 1961 and 1963, 220 Popeye cartoons were shown on television.

Popeye products made during the late 1950s and early 1960s are of special interest to television-related collectors. Included are the "Popeye the Weatherman" kit by Colorforms; Popeye "Jack-in-the-Box" by Mattel (1957); lunch box and thermos by King-Seeley Thermos (1964); and Popeye "Getar" by Mattel (late 1950s).

Popeye Coloring Book (#2834). © 1959, King Features Syndicate. Published by Samuel Lowe Company. $20-25. ◆ 13" tall Popeye vinyl doll. Marked "Cameo K.F.S." Circa late 1950s. Pipe has been replaced. $40-50. ◆ *Popeye Goes on a Picnic* by Crosby Newell. Pictures by Bud Sagendorf. Wonder Books. © 1958 by King Features Syndicate, Inc. From the collection of Suzanne Silverthorn. $5-8.

Punky Brewster

"Punky Brewster" aired on the NBC network from 1986 to 1988. The show starred Moon Frye as Punky Brewster and George Gaynes as Henry Warnimont. Punky had been abandoned as a child (along with her dog, Brandon) because her mother could no longer care for her. When Henry Warnimont found her living in an empty apartment in the building he managed, he took her in, and received temporary custody. The plot of the show revolved around their lives together, as well as Punky's continuing search for her mother.

Punky Brewster Paper Doll (#1532). © NBC Inc., 1986. Published by Western Publishing Company. $10-15. ◆ *Punky Brewster: A Coloring Book* (#1025). © NBC 1987, 1986. Published by Western Publishing Company. $8-10.

R

Ramar of the Jungle

"Ramar of the Jungle" was a syndicated television series set in Nairobi, Africa. The show centered on the experiences of Dr. Thomas Reynolds, a research scientist, and his assistant professor, Ogden. Dr. Reynolds (played by Jon Hall) was called Ramar–"White Witch Doctor". His assistant was played by Ray Montgomery. Fifty-two episodes of the program were syndicated in 1952.

Tie-in products include a game made in the 1950s by Dexter Wayne Co.; puzzles by Gabriel Toys made in 1955; and cards by Tru-Vue.

Ramar of the Jungle Coloring Book (#4529). © MCMLVI (1956), Saalfield Publishing Company. $15-20.

Rango

"Rango," a short-lived television series, was only on the air from January to June in 1967. Rango was played by comedy star Tim Conway. The show was a western comedy about a Texas Ranger named Rango who was comically inept compared to his fellow officers.

Rat Patrol

"Rat Patrol," a television series about World War II, ran on ABC from 1966 to 1968. The action took place in North Africa. Players included Christopher George, Gary Raymond, Justin Tarr, and Larry Casey.

Related products include a lunch box made by Aladdin Industries (1967); a motorized jeep made by Remco (1966); and "The Rat Patrol Desert Combat Game" made by Transogram (1966).

The Rat Patrol: A Story Book To Color (#9559). Based on the ABC TV series. Published by Saalfield Publishing Company. $15-20.

Rango: A Book To Color (#9575). © 1967, Thomas/Timkel Productions. Based on the ABC TV series. Published by Saalfield Publishing Company. $25-30.

The Real McCoys

"The Real McCoys" was another of the silly comedies that were so popular in the 1960s. It aired on ABC from 1957 until 1962, and then was picked up by CBS for a year from September 1962 until September 1963. The action took place in the San Fernando Valley in California. The McCoys were a family of poor farmers, headed by Grandpa Amos McCoy (Walter Brennan). Other family members included Luke (Richard Crenna), Kate (Kathleen Nolan), Hassie (Lydia Reed), and Little Luke (Michael Winkleman).

The Red Skelton Show

Red Skelton had a successful career in both radio and movies when he began his television show for CBS in 1953. He stayed with that network until 1970, when he moved to NBC until 1971. The program was a variety show that gave Skelton the chance to do his famous characters, including Freddie the Freeloader, Clem Kaddiddlehopper, and Junior, the Mean Widdle Kid.

The Real McCoys and Danger at the Ranch © 1961 by Brennan-Westgate Productions. Whitman Publishing Company. $8-10.

TV Guide from April 28, 1956 featuring Red Skelton on the cover. Published by Triangle Publications. $4-6. ✦ Autographed picture of Red Skelton dating from mid-1980s. $25-30.

The Restless Gun

During the heyday of the television western, film star John Payne joined the ranks of TV western heroes in a show called "The Restless Gun." His part was that of Vint Bonner, an ex-gunfighter who aided people in distress during the period shortly after the Civil War. The program was broadcast over NBC from 1957 to 1959.

Related items include a board game by Milton Bradley (1959), and a gun and holster set produced by Esquire Novelty Corp. (1958).

The Restless Gun: A Book To Color (#4828). © 1958 Window Glen Production Company. Published by Saalfield Publishing Company. $15-20. ✦ *The Restless Gun* "Starring John Payne." Whitman Publishing Company. © 1959 Window Glen Production Company. $8-10.

"The Restless Gun Game." Board game by Milton Bradley, 1959. © Window Glen Production Company. $25-30.

The Rifleman

"The Rifleman" aired on ABC from 1958 to 1963. The action centered on the activities of Lucas McCain (Chuck Connors) and his son Mark (Johnny Crawford) who were New Mexico ranchers in the late 1880s.

Tie-in products include a cap rifle made by Hubley, a "Rifleman" figure made by Hartland Plastics, and "The Rifleman Ranch" made by Marx Toys. This playset, like all television-related playsets, is a very much sought-after collectible.

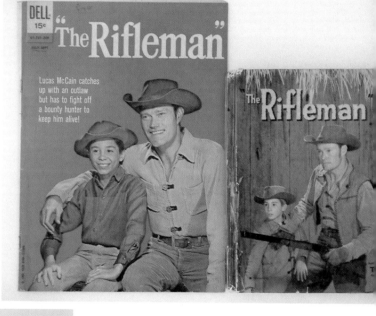

The Rifleman comic from Dell Publishing, dating from July-September 1962. © 1962 Four Star-Sussex. $8-10. ◆ The Rifleman by Cole Fannin. Whitman Publishing Company. © 1959 by Four Star-Sussex. $8-10.

"The Rifleman Game" by Milton Bradley. © 1959 Four Star Sussex. $50-60.

Ripcord

"Ripcord" was a program with an unusual plot line. The shows revolved around the experiences of sky-diving instructors. The sky-divers were Jim Buckley (played by Ken Curtis) and Ted McKeever (Larry Pennell). Ripcord was the name of their school. The show was syndicated in 1961.

Related products include a game made by Lowell in 1962 and a coloring book produced by Saalfield Publishing in 1963.

Romper Room

"Romper Room" was an educational program for very young children. The show was syndicated in 1953 but was filmed in such a way as to let local stations use their own teachers to help in the activities.

Related products include a "Kopeefun" kit made in 1964 by Embree Mfg. Co., and a "Do-Bee" wind-up toy from the early 1960s.

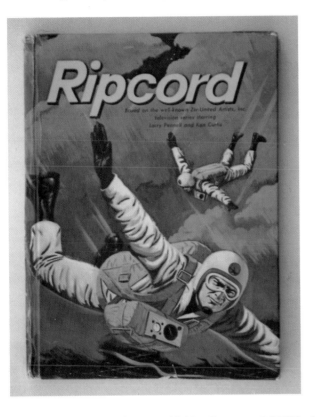

"Let's Play the New Romper Room Games" 33 1/3 record. © Romper Room Productions, 1950s. ✦ "Romper Room Singing Games" with Mitch Miller and the orchestra. © Romper Room Productions, 1950s. $3-5 each.

Ripcord by D. S. Halacy, Jr. Whitman Publishing Company. © 1962 by ZIV-United Artists, Inc. $5-8.

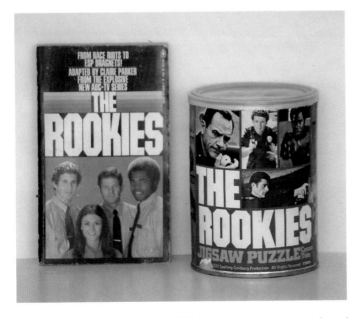

The Rookies

"The Rookies" was a crime drama that aired on ABC beginning in 1972. The sixty-minute program starred Gerald S. O'Loughlin as Lieutenant Edward Ryker; Michael Ontkean as Patrolman William Gillis; Georg Stanford Brown as Patrolman Terry Webster; Sam Melville as Patrolman Michael Danko; and Bruce Fairbairn as Patrolman Chris Owens. Kate Jackson played the part of Mike's wife. The patrolmen worked for Station Number Seven in Southern California. The show ended its run in 1976.

A 3"-long die-cast metal replica car was produced by L.J.N. Toys in 1973 to tie in to the show. A stamp set was made by Fleetwood Toys in 1975 as another tie-in. Dolls of the five male characters, 7 1/2" tall, were made by L.J.N. Toys Ltd. in 1976.

The Rookies by Claire Parker. © 1973 by Bantam Books, Inc. Adapted from ABC-TV series. $3-5. ✦ "The Rookies Jigsaw Puzzle Casse-tête" © 1975 Spelling-Goldberg Productions. $10-15.

Room 222

"Room 222" was broadcast on ABC from 1969 until 1974. The leading actor on the show was Lloyd Haynes, playing Pete Dixon, a black teacher at Walt Whitman High School in Los Angeles. The plots revolved around the conflicts in an integrated high school. Other cast members included Karen Valentine, Michael Constantine, and Denise Nicholas.

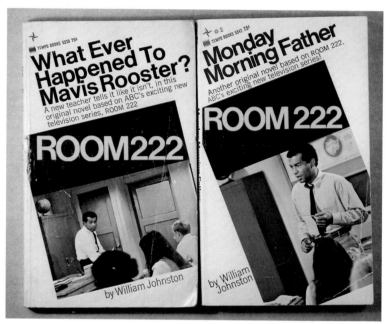

Room 222: What Ever Happened to Mavis Rooster? and *Room 222: Monday Morning Father,* both by William Johnston. Grosset and Dunlap, Inc. © 1970 by Twentieth Century-Fox Film Corp. $3-5 each.

Route 66

"Route 66" was a popular show that was broadcast on CBS from 1960 to 1964. The two original stars of the series, Martin Milner and George Maharis, played wanderers Tod Stiles and Buzz Mardock as they followed the highway to California. Later, Linc Case (played by Glen Corbett) replaced Mardock. The plot involved people they met along the way and the problems they helped to solve.

With the current interest in the old Route 66 highway that crossed the U.S. to California, collectors especially like items related to the "Route 66" television show. One of the most popular is the board game produced by Transogram in 1962.

"Route 66 Travel Game." Made by Transogram, 1962. © Lancer Productions. Inc. Courtesy of 52 Girls Collectibles. $90-100.

The Roy Rogers Show

The "King of the Cowboys," Roy Rogers began his own television show on CBS in 1951, continuing until 1964. The action took place on the Double R Bar Ranch in Mineral City. Other characters included his wife Dale Evans, Pat Brady as the diner cook, Harry Lauter as the mayor, and Harry Harvey, Sr. as the sheriff. The horses Trigger and Buttercup, the jeep Nellybelle, and Bullet the dog also had parts in the series.

There are so many Roy Rogers collectibles that a whole collection can be built around his career alone. For collectors of television memorabilia, the best products are those produced during the time of the television show. Some of those items are as follows: camera by Herbert George Co.; phonograph by RCA Victor; lamp by Plasto Mfg. Co.; trailer van, Rogers, Trigger, and Trigger Jr. made by Marx; boot bank by Almar Metal Arts; alarm clock by Ingraham; binoculars; bedspread; gloves; harmonica; Nellybelle jeep, Trigger, trailer set by Ideal; several different lunch boxes by King-Seeley; spurs; horseshoe set by Ohio Art Co.; white china dishes by Universal; and many other items of clothing.

Boy's western shirt with "Roy Rogers" embroidered on one side of the collar and "Trigger" on the other. Label reads "Roy Rogers Frontier Shirts, created by Rob Roy, Size 12." Circa 1950. $50-75. ✦ *Roy Rogers and Dale Evans Cut-Out Dolls* (#1950). Whitman Publishing Company. © 1954 by Frontiers, Inc. $85+. ✦ Roy Rogers and trigger billfold, never used. Pictures Roy and Trigger on front. Circa early 1950s. $40-50. ✦ Roy Rogers plastic souvenir cup. Could be purchased for thirty-five cents plus one trademark from Quaker Oats, circa early 1950s. $18-22.

8" tall Roy Rogers hard plastic doll made by Nancy Ann Story Book Dolls, Inc. Wearing original clothing and pictured with original box. Has sleep eyes and painted hair. Photograph and doll from the collection of Jackie Robertson. $150+.

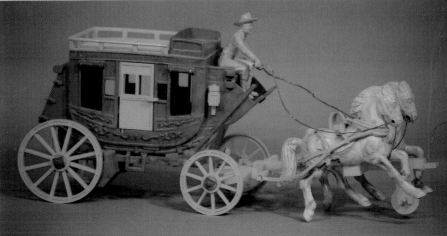

"Roy Rogers Fix-it Stage Coach" made by Ideal Toy Company, © 1955. Included stagecoach, horses, Roy Rogers figure, tool box with tools, rifle, and money chest. 5" x 6" x 15". $85+.

"Roy Rogers Ranch Set" made by Louis Marx and Company. Boxed set included a metal bunk house, cowboys, animals, fence, and furniture. No. 3979-3980. Produced in early to mid-1950s. $175+.

Matching 8" tall Dale Evans hard plastic doll made by Nancy Ann Story Book Dolls, Inc. Wearing original clothing and pictured with original box. Has sleep eyes and a wig. Photograph and doll from the collection of Jackie Robertson. $150+.

Roy Rogers cap guns and holsters, along with their original Classy Products Box. The guns are stamped "Geo Schmdt MFG/Made in USA L.A. 21 Calif." The name Roy Rogers is imprinted on the back of the holster belt. Circa mid-1950s. From the collection of James E. Werts. Photograph by James E. Werts. $250+.

Autographed picture of Roy Rogers and Dale Evans from the late 1980s. $35-45.

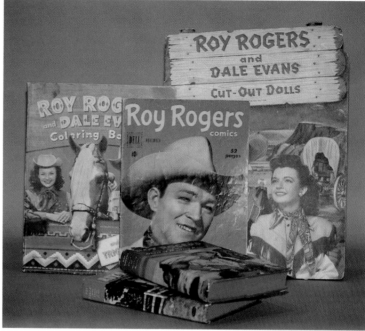

Roy Rogers and Dale Evans Coloring Book (#2171). © 1951 by Roy Rogers Enterprises, Inc. Published by Whitman Publishing Company. $35-50. ✦ Roy Rogers and Dale Evans Cut-Out Dolls (#1186). The set contains two dolls and Trigger, 1950. Published by Whitman Publishing Company. $85+. ✦ Roy Rogers Comics, November 1950. Volume 1, Number 35. Published by Dell Publishing Company. $15-18. ✦ Books: Roy Rogers and the Ghost of Mystery Rancho, © the Rohr Company, Whitman Publishing Company. $15-20. ✦ Roy Rogers on the Trail of the Zeros published by Whitman, © 1954 by Roy Rogers Enterprises. $15-25

"Roy Rogers Fan Club and Dale Evans Fan Club" membership cards from 1954 to 1956. $20-30.

"King of the Cowboys Roy Rogers Song Folio." © 1952 Famous Music Corp. $20-25. ✦ Fiberboard Roy Rogers guitar made during the 1950s. This Jefferson one is 29" long and pictures Roy, Trigger, and Dale Evans. $55-75. ✦ "Roy Rogers Picture Frame Tray Inlay Puzzle" No. 4426. Whitman Publishing Company. © 1958 by Frontiers, Inc. $25-35.

Roy Rogers and Dale Evans steel lunch box. Printing on box reads "Roy Rogers and Dale Evans Double-R-Bar Ranch." Made by the American Thermos Bottle Company, circa 1955-1958. $85+. ✦ Roy Rogers tablet, © Litho USA, circa early 1950s. $20-25. ✦ Roy Rogers pencil case. Includes labeled pencil plus pens. Has one drawer that opens. $50-60.

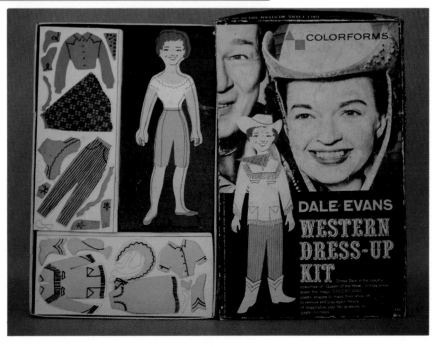

"Dale Evans Western Dress-Up Kit" made by Colorforms. © 1958 Roy Rogers Enterprises Inc. $20-25.

S

Sanford and Son

"Sanford and Son" was a situation comedy that aired on NBC beginning in 1972. The show brought stardom to Redd Foxx, who played lead character Fred Sanford. His son Lamont was played by Demond Wilson. The two characters were black junk dealers in Los Angeles. The plot revolved around their debate over keeping the business (as Sanford insisted) or quitting it (as Lamont demanded). The series ended in 1977.

Redd Foxx doll, 16" tall, made by Shindana in 1976. The doll had two sides and could talk with a string pull. It was cloth stuffed. $35-40.

Sea Hunt

Lloyd Bridges starred as Mike Nelson in "Sea Hunt," which was aired in syndication in 1958. He played a former Navy frogman who turned his experience into investigation work.

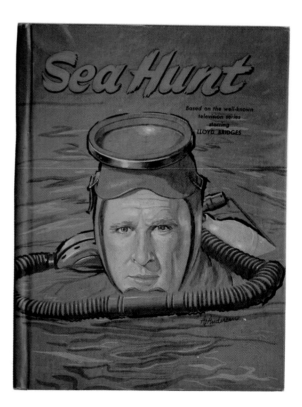

Sea Hunt, based on the television series starring Lloyd Bridges, by Cole Fannin. Whitman Publishing Company. © 1960 by ZIV-United Artists, Inc. $8-10.

Sergeant Preston of the Yukon

"Sergeant Preston of the Yukon" was a television series syndicated in 1955. Richard Simmons played the leading role of Sergeant William Preston. Preston became a Northwest Mounted Policeman when he went to the Yukon to find his father's killer. His dog, Yukon King, also played a prominent part in the action.

Milton Bradley made both a puzzle and a board game to tie in to this show during the 1950s.

Sergeant Preston Coloring Book (#1329). © Sergeant Preston of the Yukon, Inc. Published by Whitman Publishing Company, 1953. $20-25.

"Sergeant Preston Game" by Milton Bradley. © Sergeant Preston of the Yukon, Inc. $25-30.

Sergeant Preston of the Yukon comic books. Published by Dell Publishing. Dated Feburary-April 1954 and August-October 1958. © 1953 and 1958 by Sergeant Preston of the Yukon, Inc. $8-10.

Sesame Street

"Sesame Street," long-lasting educational television program for kids, premiered on the NET network on November 10, 1969. On November 9, 1970 it became affiliated with PBS, on which network it remains today.

The show, which is geared towards very young children, consists of cartoons, stories, songs, and puzzles used in an educational manner. Jim Henson's Muppets have played a big part in the success of "Sesame Street."

So many "Sesame Street" products are made each year, that no collector would ever be able to find them all, but some of the more desirable items include the older puppets and plush dolls, a lunch box by Aladdin Industries from 1983, and the various toys which featured "Sesame Street" characters.

"Sesame Street" lunch box and thermos made by Aladdin Industries, Inc. © 1979 Muppets, Inc. © Children's Television Workshop. $10-15. ✦ Bag also © Muppets, Inc. and Children's Television Workshop. $5-8.

"Miss Piggy; A Jim Henson Muppet Doll." Made by Fisher-Price Toys, a Division of the Quaker Oats Company. © Henson Associates Inc., 1977, 1979. The plush doll is 6" tall with a vinyl head and cloth body. $10-5. ✦ "Sesame Street Big Bird Jack-in-the Box." © 1982 Children's Television Workshop. © Muppets, © 1983 CBS Toys, a Division of CBS, Inc. Made by Child Guidance. $5-8. ✦ Bert cloth doll, 12" tall, also © Muppets-Jim Henson Associates Inc. $5-8.

"Miss Piggy Paper Doll." Made by Colorforms, 1980. © Henson Associates, Inc. $10-15. ✦ *Sesame Street Paper Doll Players,* © 1976 Children's Television Workshop. Muppet Characters © 1971, 1972, 1973, 1976. Whitman Publishing Company. $5-8. ✦ "Sesame Street Frame-Tray Puzzle" produced by Whitman. Cookie Monster © 1971, 1977 Muppets, Inc. $5-8.

77 Sunset Strip

"77 Sunset Strip" aired on ABC from 1958 to 1964. The sixty-minute show starred Efrem Zimablist, Jr. as Stuart Bailey and Roger Smith as Jeff Spencer, private investigators who had offices at 77 Sunset Strip. Edward Byrnes played parking-lot attendant Gerald Lloyd Kookson ("Kookie"), a role that became a hit.

"Music From 77 Sunset Strip" based on the TV show, featuring the hit "77 Sunset Strip." © Loew's Inc. Full Fidelity. Lion 33 1/3. Featuring the Aaron Bell Orchestra. $15-20.

"77 Sunset Strip: A 'Private Eye' Game of Mystery and Suspense" based on the Warner Bros. TV series. A Lowell Game. © 1960 Warner Bros. Pictures, Inc. Lowell Toy Manufacturing Corp. $45-50.

77 Sunset Strip, an original suspense novel by Roy Huggins. Published by Dell Publishing, © 1958, using characters from the TV show. $3-5. ◆ 77 Sunset Strip comic, December-February 1962. Published by Dell Publishing. © 1961 Warner Bros. Pictures Inc. $8-10. ◆ Edd "Kookie" Byrnes Cut-Outs (#2085). Whitman Publishing Company. © 1959 by Warner Brothers Pictures, Inc. $50-60.

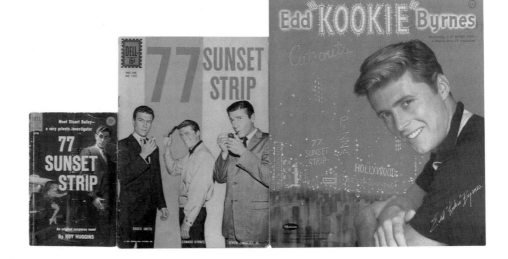

The Shari Lewis Show

"The Shari Lewis Show" was aired by NBC from 1960 to 1963. Shari Lewis was a famous ventriloquist who worked with her puppets Lamb Chop, Charlie Horse, and Hush Puppy. This show for children featured music, stories, and guests as part of its format.

One of the most desirable Shari Lewis collectibles is the doll made by Madame Alexander in 1959. The doll is all hard plastic with an auburn wig and high-heel feet. The doll came in both 14" and 21" sizes. Other collectibles include "Shari Lewis Magic Answer Cards," the "Shariland Game" by Transogram, a Lambchop costume from 1963, and many different puppets of Lamb Chop, Charlie Horse, and Hush Puppy.

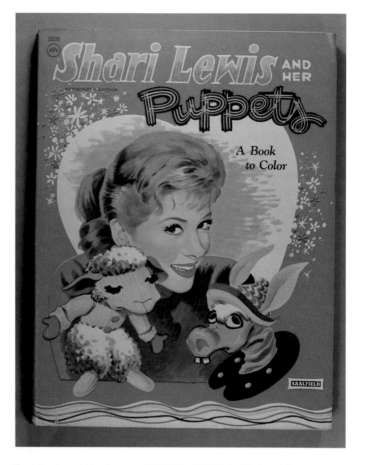

Shari Lewis and Her Puppets (#5335). © 1961 by National Broadcasting Company. Published by Saalfield Publishing Company. $15-20.

13.5"-tall Shari Lewis doll made by Madame Alexander in 1958. She is all hard plastic with high heel feet. Her dress is labeled "Shari." The back of her neck is marked "19 c 58/Alexander." Her shoes have been replaced. $250+

Inside page from "Shari Lewis & Her Puppet Friends."

"Shari Lewis and Her Friends" inlaid puzzle. © 1962 Tarcher Productions., Inc. Produced by Saalfield. $15-18. ✦ Lamb Chop and Hush Puppy puppets. © 1960 Tarcher Productions., Inc. Puppets from the collection of Jeff Zillner. $35-40/pair.

"Shari Lewis and Her Puppets," a boxed set of paper dolls. © 1962 Tarcher Productions, Inc. Produced by Saalfield/ Artcraft. $50-60. ✦ Shari Lewis (#4447). Paper dolls by Saalfield. © 1958 California National Productions., Inc. From the collection of Elaine Price. $50-60 each.

"Shari Lewis and Her Puppet Friends" A Colorforms Toy. © 1961 Tarcher Productions., Inc. © 1961 Colorforms. $20-25. ✦ Party in Shariland, A Little Golden Book. Golden Press. © 1959 by California National Productions, Inc. $5-8.

Shirley Temple's Storybook

Shirley Temple's show business career was rejuvenated when "Shirley Temple's Storybook" was broadcast on NBC as a sixty-minute show beginning in 1958. Although NBC's broadcast of the program ended the same year, it was continued on ABC from January to June in 1959, and then aired again on NBC from September 1960 until September 1961. The series was an anthology which used fairy tales as the basis for most of the programs. Shirley acted as hostess and also sometimes appeared as an actress in the shows.

With the return of Shirley Temple to the entertainment world, there was also a return of authorized Shirley Temple merchandise. The most important new collectible was the line of dolls which was again produced by the Ideal Toy Co. The dolls were made from the late 1950s into the early 1960s. The vinyl dolls featured Shirley's popular curls and came in sizes of 12", 15", 17", 19", and 35". Other important products included coloring books and paper dolls made by Saalfield Publishing Co. and various embroidery sets produced by Gabriel Sons and Co. Amsco Toys marketed a "Shirley Temple Magnetic TV Theater" in 1959, and Ideal produced a set of Shirley Temple plastic dishes during the same year.

36"-tall all vinyl Shirley Temple doll with jointed wrists, rooted curls, and amber-brown sleep eyes. She is wearing her original aqua and white nylon dress and black Mary Jane shoes. Made by Ideal circa 1958. From the collection of Mary Stuecher. Photograph by Werner Stuecher. $1200+.

The most popular doll in the new 1958 series of Shirley Temple dolls was the 12"-tall model pictured here. The doll is wearing a tagged Shirley Temple dress. Other tagged Shirley clothing is pictured in the trunk. The doll is marked on the back of the head "Ideal Doll/ST-12," and on the shoulder "ST-12N." The doll has rooted saran hair and sleep eyes. $225-250.

"Shirley Temple Movie Favorites Embroidry Set." Gabriel Sons and Company, Inc. Contains small "Heidi" and "Captain January" designs suitable for framing, along with embroidery hoop, thread and thimble. Circa 1960. $50-60. ◆ Two pot holders featuring Shirley as Wee Willie Winkie and Rebecca were also made by Gabriel Sons and Company, Inc. around 1960. The set also included dish towels to embroider. $30-40.

Shirley Temple Coloring Book (#4584). Published by Saalfield in 1958. $30-40. ◆ *Shirley Temple: An 18" Standing Doll.* The paper doll was made in two pieces and was published by Saalfield in 1959. The book is #1320. $75-85. ◆ *The Shirley Temple Play Kit* (#9859) produced by Saalfield in 1958. It included two paper dolls, lace-on dresses, as well as a coloring book and crayons. $50-75.

17"-tall all vinyl Shirley Temple doll wearing an original blue nylon dress with silver metal script pin and hang tag. Made by Ideal, circa 1958. Her saran hair is rooted and she has flirty sleep eyes. The black cardboard "make-up case" contains a card with curlers for keeping Shirley curly. From the collection of Mary Stuecher. Photograph by Werner Stuecher. $275+.

"Shirley Temple's Magnetic TV Theater" by Amsco Toys, 1959. Contains everything to stage The Three Bears, Red Riding Hood, and Sleeping Beauty. From the collection of Mary Stuecher. Photograph by Werner Stuecher. $100-125.

Book *The Shirley Temple Edition of The Littlest Rebel* by Edward Peple, published by Random House, 1959, features pictures of Shirley from the movie. $10-12. ◆ Book *The Shirley Temple Edition of Susannah of the Mounties* by Muriel Denison published by Random House in 1959, showing pictures from Shirley's film. $10-12.

Small advertising token (bottom center, near Dumbo's trunk) reads: "Shirley Temple's Storybook NBC-TV Show, 8-9 P.M. EST Wednesday, Nov. 12, 1958. $8-10. ◆ Records were produced to tie in to Shirley's television show. In 1960 RCA Records made this one called "Shirley Temple Tells the Story of Walt Disney's Dumbo." Shirley was the narrator. $15-20. ◆ Sheet music for "Dreams Are Made For Children," the theme song for Shirley's television show "Shirley Temple's Storybook." The lyric is by Mack David and the music is by Jerry Livingston. © 1958 by Fullarton Music Inc. $15-20.

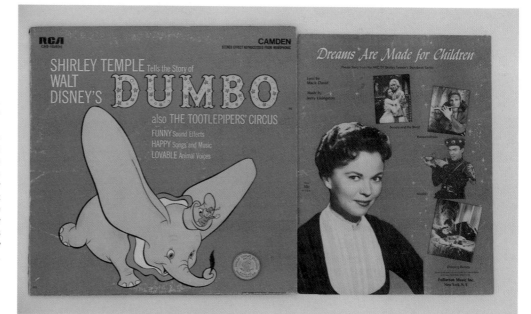

Pink plastic Shirley Temple tea set by Ideal, 1959. Not shown are the plates and saucers inscribed with the initials "S.T." From the collection of Mary Stuecher. Photograph by Werner Stuecher. $15-20 each piece.

Sigmund and the Sea Monsters

"Sigmund and the Sea Monsters" was a comedy program which aired on NBC from 1973 to 1975, It featured a sea monster named Sigmund (played by Billy Barty) who was rescued by brothers Johnny (Johnny Whitaker) and Scott (Scott Kolden). Sigmund's family had disowned him for not scaring people properly, so the boys took him home to their clubhouse and protected him from his sea monster family.

Sigmund and the Sea Monsters (#4634). Adapted from the TV series. © 1974, Sid and Marty Krofft Productions, Inc. Published by Saalfield Publishing Company. $15-20.

"Sigmund and the Sea Monsters Game" by Milton Bradley Co. © 1975 by Sid and Marty Krofft Productions, Inc. $25-30.

Simon and Simon

"Simon and Simon" was a detective show with a difference. The title characters, brothers A.J. and Rick Simon (Jameson Parker and Gerald McRaney), were partners in a detective agency, despite their differences. A.J. was conservative, neat, energetic, and ambitious, while Rick lived on a houseboat, drove a pickup truck, and tried to avoid work. The show aired on CBS beginning in November 1981.

Corgi made a replica of the '57 Chevy used on the show in 1982.

"Simon & Simon Walkie-Talkies With Telescoping Antenna." © 1983 Gordy International. © 1981 Universal City Studios, Inc. $15-18.

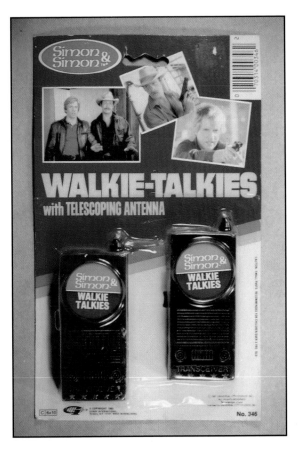

The Simpsons

"The Simpsons" is one of the few hit shows in television that was not broadcast on one of the "big three" networks. The show premiered on the Fox network on January 14, 1990 and quickly became not only a much-watched show but also a controversial one. The animated series is about an unusual family–Homer, the father; Marge, the mother; Bart, their ten-year-old eldest child; Lisa, the second-grade middle child; and a baby named Maggie. The behavior of Bart on the series has caused many parents to declare the program "off limits" to their children. The program is really aimed at adults but quite a number of toys have been developed to tie in to the show.

Bart Simpson Shirt. TM and © 1990 Twentieth Century Fox Film Corp. Matt Groening. $3-5. ✦ Five Simpson dolls, Matt Groening, © 1990 Twentieth Century Fox Film Corp. The dolls have vinyl heads and soft bodies. $15-20/set.

Six Million Dollar Man

The "Six Million Dollar Man" had its beginnings as a television movie in 1973. With that success, it was made into a series for ABC that aired from 1974 to 1978.

In the story, Steve Austin (played by Lee Majors) was injured in an airplane crash. The Office of Strategic Operations spent six million dollars to repair his injuries. Nuclear power was used on his replacement parts, and he turned out to be part human and part machine. His girlfriend, Jaime Somers (Lindsay Wagner), eventually had her own show called "The Bionic Woman."

Many tie-in products were produced for this popular show. Included are the Bionic Transport/Repair Station made by Kenner (1973); puzzle by APC (1975); vinyl bank by Animals Plus (1976); and lunch box and thermos made by Aladdin Industries, Inc. (1974). In 1977 Kenner made dolls in the likeness of Lee Majors as Colonel Steve Austin, Richard Anderson as Oscar Goldman, and Lindsay Wagner as the Bionic Woman.

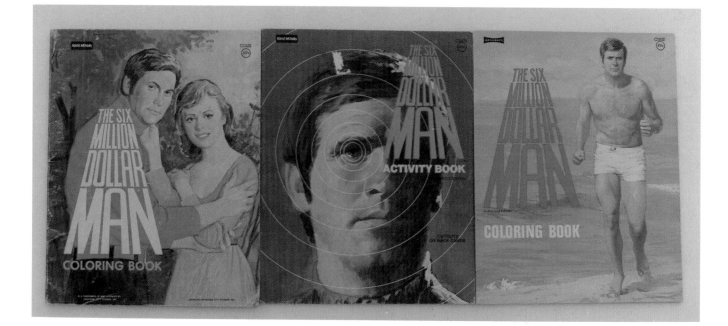

The Six Million Dollar Man Coloring Book (#C1520). Published by Rand McNally. © 1977 Universal City Studios. ✦ The Six Million Dollar Man Activity Book (#C2471). © 1977 Universal City Studios. Published by Rand McNally. ✦ The Six Million Dollar Man Coloring Book (#C1832). © 1974 Universal City Studios, Inc. Published by Saalfield Publishing Company. $15-20 each.

The Six Million Dollar Man comic for March 1978. Published by Charlton Publications, Inc. © 1978 Universal City Studios, Inc. $5-8. ✦ "Colonel Steve Austin, The Six Million Dollar Man: The Bionic Man" doll. Made by Kenner. © Universal City Studios, Inc. General Mills Fun Group, Inc., 1975. A "Bionic Transport and Repair Station" and a backpack radio were also made. $40-50.

"The Six Million Dollar Man: Bionic Crisis," a game made by Parker Brothers. Character © Universal Studios, Inc., 1975. $20-25.

"The Six Million Dollar Man: A Game by Parker Brothers." © Universal Studios, Inc., 1975. $20-25.

"The Six Million Dollar Man" lunch box and thermos. © 1974 by Universal City Studios, Inc. Made by Aladdin Industries, Inc. $40-50.

Skippy the Bush Kangaroo

"Skippy the Bush Kangaroo" was a syndicated thirty-minute show made in 1969. The action took place in Waratah National Park in Australia, where the Chief Ranger (Ed Devereaux) and his son lived. Skippy was a kangaroo that had been injured as a baby and the son (Garry Pankhurst) made a pet of him. The adventures centered around these characters.

The Smurfs

"The Smurfs" were first invented by a Belgian cartoonist named Peyo Culliford. The creatures were brought to television in the United States by Hanna-Barbera Prod. and the NBC network in 1981. The show won Emmy awards in both 1982 and 1983 for Outstanding Children's Entertainment. The Smurfs lived happily in the forest until their enemy, Gargamel, tried to capture them. The Smurfs were led by Papa Smurf. Other Smurfs included Brainy, Hefty, Handy, Greedy, Grouch, Smurfette, and Grouch.

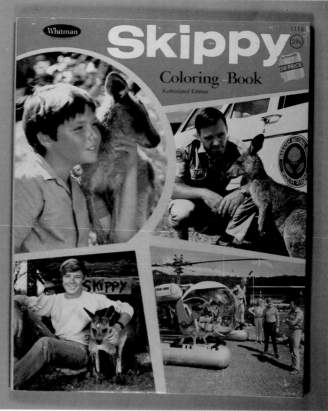

Skippy Coloring Book (#1116). © 1970 by Norfolk International Films Limited. A Whitman Book. Published by Western Publishing Company. $10-15.

"Smurf Colorforms Play Set" by Colorforms. © Colorforms and Peyo 1981. Licensed by Wallace Berrie and Company. $5-10. ✦ Smurfs lunch box by Thermos. © Peyo. $10-15.

Smurf plush doll, 12" tall. © Peyo, 1979. Wallace Berrie and Company, Inc. $5-10. ✦ "Smurfs Puzzle" licensed by Wallace Berrie and Company. © 1982 Playskool Inc. under Berne and Universal copyright conventions. $3-5. ✦ "The Smurfs Card Game" by Milton Bradley. © 1982 by Milton Bradley Company under Berne and Universal copyright conventions. $5-8.

The Sonny and Cher Show

"The Sonny and Cher Show" was aired over CBS from 1971 to 1974. The variety show featured Sonny (Salvatore) Bono and his wife Cher (Cheryl La Piere). The two stars sang, danced, and did comedy routines along with the help of regulars and guest stars.

Besides the dolls pictured, a dressing room for Cher was also produced.

12 1/4"-tall Cher and Sonny dolls made by Mego in 1976. The dolls are all vinyl and jointed. Cher is jointed at the waist and wrists in addition to the hips and shoulders. The dolls both have painted features. Cher has long rooted black hair. Sonny has painted hair. On the neck of the dolls is "C Mego Corp. 1976." $35-45 each.

One of the many outfits made for the Sonny and Cher dolls. This Cher number was designed by Bob Mackie. © 1976 by Mego Corp. $20-25.

Soupy Sales

"Soupy Sales" had several television shows for children over the years. He did local shows in Detroit beginning in 1953, in Los Angeles in 1959, and in New York in the mid-1960s. His network shows were "The Soupy Sales Show" on ABC from July 4, 1955 to August 26, 1955 and from October 3, 1959 to June 25, 1960. His New York show from WNEW-TV was syndicated from 1966 to 1968.

Milton Bradley produced a board game called "Soupy Sales Sez Go-Go-Go" during the early 1960s. A "Soupy Sales" doll was made by Knickerbocker in 1966. The doll had a vinyl head with molded hair and features. The body was cloth and the doll was 13" tall.

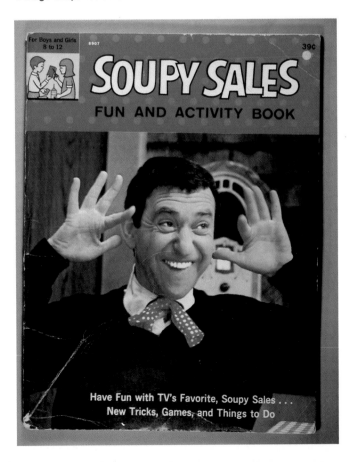

Soupy Sales Fun and Activity Book (#8907). © 1965 by Soupy Sales-WMC. Published by Treasure Books. $15-20.

Space: 1999

"Space: 1999" was a syndicated English-produced science fiction show that lasted from 1974 to 1976. Martin Landau played the commander and Barbara Bain played Dr. Helena Russell. The crew was thrown into outer space by a nuclear explosion on the moon and had to cope with the situation.

Related products include a Colorforms Set from 1976, and a lunch box and thermos by King-Seeley Thermos from the same year. Dolls were made by Mattel in 1975 to represent the main characters of the series. The dolls were 9" tall and included Martin Landau as Commander Loenig, Barbara Bain as Doctor Russel, and Barry Morse as Professor Bergman.

"Space: 1999, A Game Adapted From the Television Series." Milton Bradley Co. © 1976 ATV Licensing Limited. $20-25.

"Space: 1999 Eagle 1 Transporter." An MPC Product of the Fundimensions division of General Mills Fun Group, Inc. © 1975 ATV Licensing Limited. The model kit was made to be assembled. $30-40.

Space: 1999 Cut and Color Book (#C2484). Published by Saalfield. © 1975 ATV Licensing Limited. $15-20. ✦ Space: 1999 Coloring Book (#C1881). Published by Saalfield Publishing Company. ATV Corp. $15-20. ✦ Space: 1999, Rogue Planet, "#9 in the Spectacular New Science-Fiction Epic." Author E.C. Tubb. Pocket Book. © 1975 by ITC-Inc. Television Company Limited. Novelization © 1976 by E.C. Tubb. $3-5.

Space Patrol

"Space Patrol" was an early science fiction adventure series broadcast on ABC from 1950 to 1956. The action took place in the twenty-first century. Ed Kemmer played Commander Buzz Corey, the commander-in-chief of the Space Patrol. His co-pilot was Cadet Happy, played by Lyn Osborn.

Since this was an early show, tie-in products are hard to find. They include a "Rocket Lite" made by Ray-O-Vac Co. and several premiums that were issued by Ralston cereals during the run of the program.

Star Trek

"Star Trek" is one of the few television programs that has spanned the decades and remains popular even today. The show first aired on NBC in 1966 and was discontinued in 1969. The cast included William Shatner as Captain James T. Kirk, commander of the *Enterprise;* Leonard Nimoy as Officer Spock (half Earthling and half Vulcan); DeForest Kelley as Dr. Leonard McCoy; and Nichelle Nichols as Lieutenant Uhura. This science fiction show was set in the twenty-second century as the starship U.S.S. *Enterprise* explored the universe. The show spawned lots of tie-in products as well as movies and devoted fans from its short run on television.

Although there are many "Star Trek" products, not very many were actually made during the 1966-1969 run of the show. These products include a lunch box (dome) and thermos made by Aladdin Industries (1968); View-Master Reels (1968), and "Star Trek Numbered Pencil and Paint Set" by Hasbro (1967).

Star Trek

The animated version of the popular "Star Trek" television series aired on NBC from 1973-1975. This science fiction adventure took place in the twenty-second century aboard the starship U.S.S. *Enterprise.* Captain Kirk, Officer Spock, Lieutenant Uhura and Dr. Leonard McCoy were leading characters.

"Star Trek Game," © 1974 Hasbro Industries, Inc. $25-30.

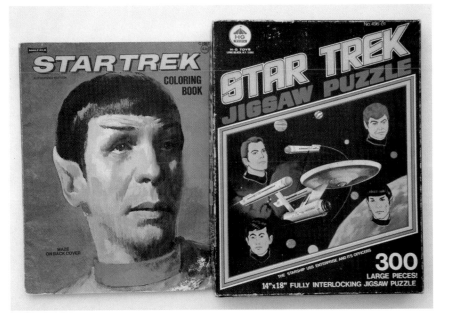

Star Trek Coloring Book (c1862). © 1975, Paramount Pictures. Published by Saalfield Publishing Company. $15-20. ✦ "Star Trek Jigsaw Puzzle" made by H-G Toys. © 1974 by Paramount Pictures Corp. $15-20.

"Star Trek" dolls (at left and right) made by Mego. The 8" dolls are © 1974 by Paramount Pictures Corp. Pictured are Captain Kirk and Mr. Spock. Also made were Dr. McCoy, Lt. Uhura, Mr. Scott, and Klingon. $25-30 each. ✦ *Star Trek Coloring Book* (c1856). © 1975 Paramount Pictures Corp. Published by Saalfield Publishing Company. $10-15.

Starsky and Hutch

"Starsky and Hutch" was a crime drama that aired on ABC beginning in 1975. The show starred Paul Glaser as Dave Starsky and David Soul as Ken "Hutch" Hutchinson. The two were plainclothes police detectives and the plot derived from their cases. The show lasted until 1979.

Related products include a "Starsky and Hutch Detective Game" made by Milton Bradley (1977); Corgi set that included a Ford Torino, plus figures of Starsky and Hutch and a criminal; and a water pistol made by Fleetwood Toys (1976). Mego produced dolls of the four main characters (1976). These included Starsky, Hutch, Captain Dobey (Bernie Hamilton), and Huggy Bear (Antonio Fargas). A "Chopper" doll was also made.

"Starsky and Hutch Detective Game" by Milton Bradley. © 1977 Spelling-Goldberg Productions. $20-25.

Starsky and Hutch: A Golden All Star Book. Golden Press-Western Publishing Company, Inc. © 1977 Spelling-Goldberg Productions. $5-8. ✦ *TV Guide* for November 15, 1975 featuring a Starsky and Hutch cover. Published by Triangle Publications Inc. $3-5.

"Starsky and Hutch Jigsaw Puzzles" made by H-G Toys Inc. © 1976 Spelling Goldberg Productions. $10-15.

Hutch, Chopper, and Starsky dolls made by Mego Corp in 1976. The company also made Huggy Bear and Dobey in doll form. The dolls are 7 1/2" tall, © Spelling-Goldberg Productions. $20-25 each.

Stingray

"Stingray" was a syndicated English-produced puppet show from 1965 that was filmed in "supermarionation." The World Aquanaut Security Patrol was an organization based on the océan floor. It played a big part in the action of the show, along with the futuristic submarine "Stingray."

Related products include a game by Transogram from 1966 and a puzzle by Whitman from 1965.

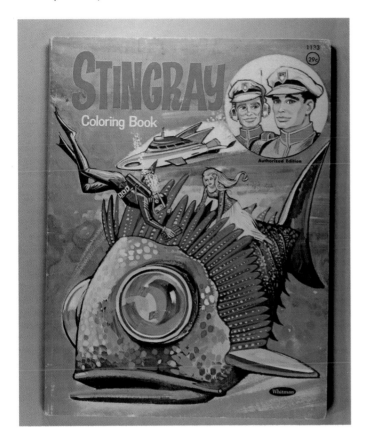

Stingray Coloring Book (#1133). © 1966. A.P. Films Ltd and ITC Ltd. Published by Whitman Publishing Company. $15-20.

Super Circus

"Super Circus" was an early children's program that aired on ABC from 1949 until 1956. It featured circus variety acts with Claude Kirchner and Jerry Colonna as ringmasters. Mary Hartline, called the "Queen of the Super Circus," was a regular on the show and acted as bandleader.

Tie-in products include Mary Hartline paper doll books made by Whitman (#2104 from 1952; #1175 from 1953; and #2044 from 1955) and Hartline dolls produced by the Ideal Toy Co. (1952). The Ideal dolls were made of hard plastic and came in sizes of 7 3/4", 15", and 22". The dolls came in red, white or green dresses and all had blonde wigs. Another small Hartline doll, marked Lingerie Lou on the back, was also made, probably by Duchess. The larger dolls came with batons. A puzzle was made by Whitman.

Mary Hartline doll, 15" tall, made by the Ideal Toy Company. The hard plastic doll dates from 1952. She has a blonde nylon wig and blue sleep eyes. She is marked on her back "Ideal Doll/P-91" and is wearing her original clothing. © Mary Hartline Enterprises. The doll originally came with an oversize baton. $175-250. ◆ Mary Hartline Cut-Out Dolls Coloring Book (#2104). © M.H.E. Published by Whitman Publishing Co., 1952. $30-40.

Super Circus by Helen Wing. Rand McNally and Company. © 1955 American Broadcasting Company. $5-10. ◆ Mary Hartline plastic doll, 8" tall. Back marked "This is an original / Lingerie Lou / Doll." The doll has sleep eyes and blonde hair. She is wearing her original outfit from "Super Circus." $25-30.

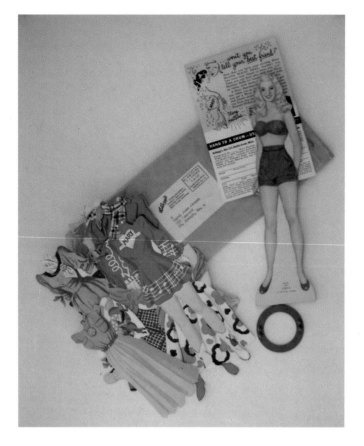

Mary Hartline paper dolls that were sold as a Kelloggs' premium. They cost 25 cents and a Sugar Frosted Flakes or Sugar Smacks box top in the early 1950s. There was only one doll in the set. $25-30.

S.W.A.T.

"S.W.A.T" was a police drama first telecast in 1975 on ABC. The series lasted until 1976. The show featured Steve Forrest as Lt. Dan "Hondo" Harrelson, Rod Perry as Sgt. David "Deacon" Kay, Robert Urich as Officer Jim Street, Mark Shera as Officer Dominic Luca, and James Coleman as Officer T.J. McCabe. The men were part of the Special Weapons and Tactics (S.W.A.T.) unit, which was called in when regular policemen couldn't handle a situation.

Figures representing the characters from the show were produced by L.J.N. Toys in 1975 and 1976. The all-vinyl jointed figures were 7 1/2" tall, and represented Deacon, Hondo, Luca, Street, and McCabe.

"The S.W.A.T. Game" by Milton Bradley. © 1976 Spelling-Goldberg Productions. $15-20.

Tales of the Texas Rangers

"Tales of the Texas Rangers" premiered on ABC in September 1957 and was discontinued in 1959 after fifty-two episodes. Stories for this western were based on early cases from the Texas Rangers, North America's oldest law enforcement organization. Willard Parker and Harry Lauter played the Rangers.

Related products include a game made in 1956 by All-Fair.

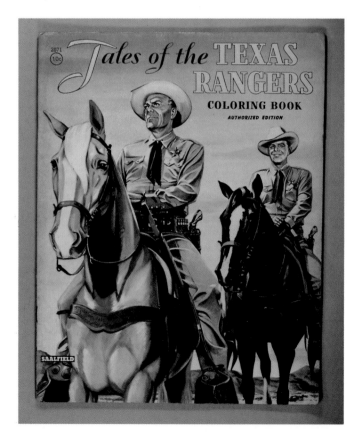

Tales of the Texas Rangers Coloring Book (#2071). Published by Saalfield Publishing Company, 1958. $20-25.

Tales of the Vikings

"Tales of the Vikings" was a syndicated program of thirty-nine episodes from 1960. It was an adventure series that took place in A.D. 1000. Leif Ericson (Jerome Courtland) and his sea raiders, the Vikings, were featured.

The Tales of Wells Fargo

"The Tales of Wells Fargo" began on NBC in 1957 as a thirty-minute show. From September 1961 through September 1962 it was a sixty-minute program. When the series first appeared, it was set in the West in the 1860s and starred Dale Robertson as Jim Hardie, a Wells Fargo agent. Later, the show expanded to include Hardie's home life as a rancher.

Tie-in products include a board game made by Milton Bradley in 1959; a guitar made by Rich Toys; and puzzles produced by Whitman in 1959.

Tales of the Vikings Coloring Book (#4566). Published by Saalfield Publishing Company. © Bryna Productions. S.A. United Artists Tel. Presentation. $20-30.

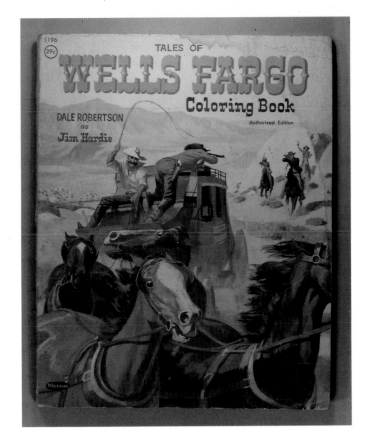

Tales of Wells Fargo Coloring Book. © 1957, Overland Productions, Inc. Published by Whitman Publishing Company. $20-30.

"Tales of Wells Fargo Frame-Tray Inlay Puzzle" by Whitman. © 1958 by Overland Productions, Inc. $15-20.

"Tales of Wells Fargo Game" by Milton Bradley Company. © 1959 by Overlord Productions., Inc. $40-50.

Tarzan

The Tarzan character, a man who had been raised by apes in Africa after his parents were killed, was created in stories by Edgar Rice Burroughs. Many successful motion pictures were made before NBC began the television series in 1966. The series lasted until September 13, 1968 and the fifty-seven episodes were put into syndication in 1969. The television series involved Tarzan's efforts to protect his country from those who had set out to harm it. Tarzan was played by Ron Ely.

Related products include a lunch box and thermos by Aladdin Industries (1966) and a Tarzan Aurora model kit (1967).

The Tennessee Ernie Ford Show

"The Tennessee Ernie Ford Show" aired on NBC from 1955 to 1960. Then ABC carried the show from 1961 to 1965. The show was a variety program that featured regulars Molly Bee, Doris Drew, Reginald Gardiner, Dick Noel, Anita Gordon, and Billy Strange through the years. Guest stars were also a part of the program.

Tarzan Coloring Book (#1157). © 1968, Edgar Rice Burroughs, Inc. Published by Whitman. $15-20.

"Tennessee Ernie Ford Spirituals" by Capitol Records. $5-8. ✦ Autographed picture of Ford from the late 1980s. $15-20. ✦ Molly Bee Cut-Out Doll (#2091). © 1962 Whitman Publishing Company. Molly was a regular on the Ford TV show at the time. $25-35.

That Girl

"That Girl" was broadcast over ABC from 1966 to 1971. The situation comedy was about a young woman leaving home not to get married, but to pursue a career as an actress. This series provided a new role model for young women, affirming that it was okay to be single and to seek a career. Would-be actress Ann Marie was played by Marlo Thomas. Ted Bessell was her boyfriend, and Lew Parker and Rosemary DeCamp played her parents.

One of the hardest "That Girl" collectibes to find is the doll called "That Girl–Marlo," made by the Madame Alexander Doll Co. in 1967. The vinyl doll has rooted brown hair and is 17" tall. She is usually dressed in a red velvet dress with clear glass beads around her neck. Remco also produced a game based on the series in 1968.

RCA 1950s small television pictured with several TV personality dolls. Included (from left to right) are a 17" Marlo Thomas "That Girl–Marlo" by Madame Alexander, 1967. All vinyl. Rooted hair, sleep eyes. Head marked "Alexander c 1966." Wearing original red velvet dress and glass beads. $350-450. ✦ Pinky Lee made by Juro (Eegee) in the early 1950s. The doll is 25" tall and has a vinyl head with a molded hat. The body is cloth. The head is marked "A Juro Celebrity Product." $175-250. ✦ Little Ricky (see listing under "I Love Lucy"). ✦ "I Dream of Jeannie" (see "I Dream of Jeannie"). ✦ Howdy Doody. Made by Effanbee Doll Company, with a composition head and a cloth body, circa 1950. $175-185.

That Girl Paper Dolls (#1379). © MCMLXVII (1967) Daisy Production, Inc. Based on the ABC TV Series. Published by Saalfield Publishing Company. $25-35. ✦ *That Girl Coloring Book* (#4510). "Based on the ABC TV Series Starring Marlo Thomas." © MCMLXVII, MCMLXIX (1967, 1969) Daisy Production, Inc. Published by Saalfield Publishing Company. $20-25.

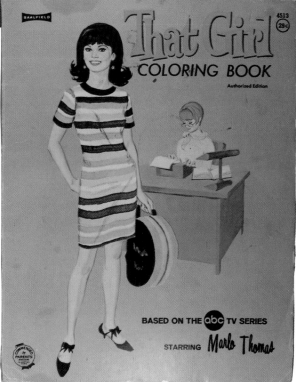

That Girl Coloring Book (#4513). "Based on the ABC TV Series Starring Marlo Thomas." © 1967 Daisy Production, Inc. Published by Saalfield Publishing Company. $20-25.

Three's Company

"Three's Company" aired on the CBS network from 1977 to 1984. The comedy was based on the funny situations that arose when two single girls took in a male as a roommate. The show starred John Ritter as Jack Tripper, Joyce De Witt as Janet Wood, and Suzanne Somers as Chrissy Snow (until 1981).

This series provided collectors with a doll representing one of its characters. The Suzanne Somers doll, 12 1/4" tall and vinyl, was made by Mego in 1978 to represent Somers in her role as Chrissy. The head is marked "C Three's Company." A puzzle based on the series was also produced in 1978 by American Pub. Corp.

Thunderbirds

"Thunderbirds," an English-produced television show syndicated in 1966, was an adventure series about an International Rescue Organization. The program was a marionette series. Gerry and Sylvia Anderson did the marionation process.

Tie-in products include the following items: "Lady Penelope's Fab 1" car J. Rosenthal Toys Ltd, 1966; game by Parker Brothers, 1967; and puzzles made by Whitman in 1966.

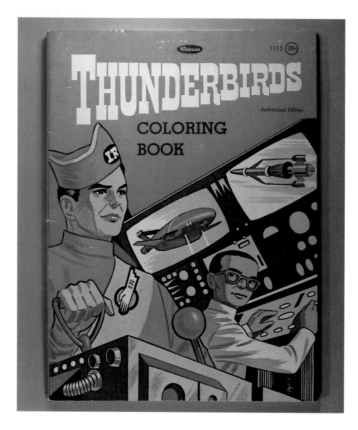

Thunderbirds Coloring Book (#1115). Published by Whitman Publishing Company, 1968. A.P. Films Ltd. $20-30.

The Time Tunnel comic #1. K.K. Publishing © 1966 by Kent Productions., Inc. and Twentieth Century-Fox, Inc. $8-10. ✦ Time Tunnel paperback book by Murray Leinster. Pyramid Publications, Inc. © 1967 by Kent Productions., Inc. and Twentieth Century-Fox Inc. $3-5.

Suzanne Somers as Chrissy of "Three's Company" doll, 12 1/4" tall, made of vinyl with rooted blonde hair and painted eyes. Head is marked "C Three's / Company." It was made by Mego in 1978. $20-25.

Time Tunnel

"Time Tunnel" was a science fiction series from the 1960s. The show aired on ABC as a sixty-minute show in 1966 and lasted for just one season, ending on September 1, 1967. Cast members included James Darren as Tony Newman, Robert Colbert as Doug Phillips, Whit Bisseel as General Heywood Kirk, and Lee Meriweather as Ann, an engineer. The plot deals with scientists' efforts to send man through time, and the adventures of Newman and Phillips as they travel from one time period to another.

Related products include View-Master reels (1966); "Time Tunnel Spin to win Game" by Pressman (1967); and board game by Ideal (1966).

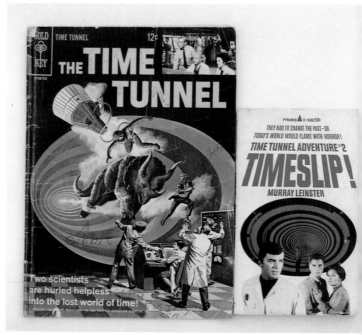

Tom Corbett, Space Cadet

"Tom Corbett, Space Cadet" was one of the early shows meant for kids. The program first aired on CBS in 1950; it moved to ABC in 1951, NBC in 1954 and 1955, and did a run on the Dumont network from 1953 to 1954. Tom Corbett was a Space Cadet at the Space Academy, U.S.A. (a space-age version of West Point). The cadets trained to be in a police force that would protect the planets in the Solar Alliance.

Related products include two lunch box and thermos sets by Aladdin (1952 and 1954); View-Master reels; a coloring book by Saalfield Publishing Co. (1953); and a punch-out book by Saalfield (1950).

Trouble With Father

"Trouble With Father" was an early situation comedy which aired on ABC in 1950 and remained on the air until 1955. In this typical family program, high school principal Stu Irwin tries to manage both his school and his family. Members of the family were June Collyer as his wife, Ann Todd as daughter Joyce, and Sheila James as daughter Jackie.

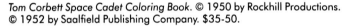

Tom Corbett Space Cadet Coloring Book. © 1950 by Rockhill Productions. © 1952 by Saalfield Publishing Company. $35-50.

June and Stu Erwin "Trouble With Father" Coloring Book (#125810). © 1954, Saalfield Publishing Company. $20-25. ✦ *June and Stu Erwin with Jackie and Joyce in Paper Dolls (#2735).* © Hal Roach Jr. and Roland Reid Television Productions, Inc. Published by Saalfield Publishing Company, 1954. $50-60.

Twenty-One

"Twenty-One" was a very popular game show that ran into trouble when it was found to be giving answers to contestants. The show aired on NBC from 1956 until 1958. Two isolation booths were used for the competing players while they answered selected questions. Jack Barry was the host.

"Twenty One TV Quiz Game." © California National Productions, Inc. Made by Lowell Toy Mfg. Company. $40-50.

The Twilight Zone

"The Twilight Zone" was an anthology of tales about regions of the "fifth dimension," an area unknown and beyond understanding. Host and narrator Rod Serling called this realm "The Twilight Zone." The show first aired on CBS in 1959 and continued until 1963, with rebroadcasts until 1965.

Besides many books and comic books, a board game was also made as a tie-in to this series. The game was made in 1964 by Ideal.

Twilight Zone comics from March 1967, March 1972 (K.K. Publishing Inc.), and August-October 1962 (Dell Pub.). © Cayuga Productions, Inc. $5-10 each.

Twin Peaks

"Twin Peaks" was an unusual television show that attracted a small but loyal following. The series first aired on ABC on April 8, 1990 and lasted only until April 18, 1991. The plot centered around the murder of high-school student Laura Palmer in Twin Peaks, a small lumber town in the Northwestern United States. FBI agent Dale Cooper was called in to help local sheriff Harry S. Truman investigate the case. The 1991 episodes became increasingly bizarre, and at the end of the series fans were left in a state of confusion. The program did generate a lot of publicity and gave viewers a totally different concept of a television drama. Characters included Sheryl Lee as Laura Palmer, Kyle MacLachlan as Agent Dale Cooper, Michael Ontkean as Sheriff Harry Truman, Peggy Lipton as Norma Jennings, Ray Wise as Leland Palmer, Piper Laurie as Kathryn Martell, and Joan Chen as Josie Packard.

"Twin Peaks" T-shirt. © 1990 Twin Peaks Productions, Inc. $3-5. ◆ The Secret Diary of Laura Palmer by Pocket Books. © 1990 by Twin Peaks Productions. Inc. ◆ Welcome To Twin Peaks; A Complete Guide to Who's Who and What's What by Scott Knickelbine. © 1990 Publications International, Ltd. Twin Peaks © 1989 by Lynch/Frost Productions., Inc. $3-5 each.

U

The Untouchables

Although "The Untouchables" was a crime drama, it took a different twist because it was set in Chicago during the Prohibition era, when gansters seemed to rule the city. The main character was Eliot Ness (played by Robert Stack), an agent of the U.S. Treasury Department in a special squad called the Untouchables. Ness and the other agents waged war against organized crime. The program was given a realistic feel with the addition of journalist Walter Winchell as narrator. The series aired on ABC from 1959 until 1963.

Product tie-ins include the "Untouchables Playset" by Marx (1961); an "Untouchables Mechanical Arcade Game" by Marx (circa 1960); and a board game called "Eliot Ness and the Untouchables" made by Transogram (1961).

"Eliot Ness and the Untouchables Game" manufactured by Transogram Company, Inc. © Desilu Productions Inc. © Langford Productions Inc. ABC TV. $50-60.

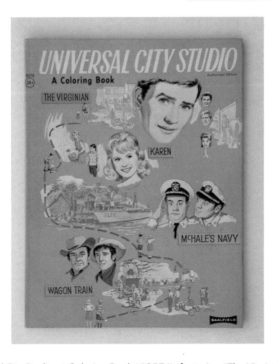

Universal City Studio: A Coloring Book (#9576), featuring "The Virginian," "Karen," "McHale's Navy," "Wagon Train." © 1964 by MCA Enterprises, Inc. Published by Saalfield Publishing Company. $20-30.

V

The Virginian

"The Virginian" was one of the westerns that took control of the networks during the late 1950s and into the 1960s. The show was unusual in that NBC allotted the program ninety minutes for each episode. The show aired from 1962 until 1970 (ending before the 1970-1971 season). The action centered on the Shiloh Ranch in Medicine Bow, Wyoming during the 1880s. Cast members included James Drury as The Virginian, Lee J. Cobb as Judge Henry Garth, and Doug McClure as Trampas. Related products include a game made by Transogram in 1962.

A new version of the show, called "The Men From Shiloh," was aired by NBC for the 1970-1971 season.

Voyage to the Bottom of the Sea

The "Voyage to the Bottom of the Sea" program was supposed to take place in 1983, even though it aired from 1964-1968. The sixty minute show from ABC dealt with an atomic powered submarine and scientific research.

Admiral Harriman Nelson was played by Richard Basehart, David Hedison was Crd. Lee Crane, and Henry Kulky was Chief Petty Officer Curley Jones.

Several related products were made to tie in to this series, including a board game made by Milton Bradley (1964); card game by Milton Bradley (1964); lunch box and thermos by Aladdin Industries (1967); View-Master reels; Flying Submarine model by Aurora (1968); and comic books by K. K. Publications (1967).

W

Wagon Train

"Wagon Train" was one of the first of many western shows to hit the airwaves when it premiered on September 18, 1957. It began as a sixty-minute program on NBC and remained with that network until 1962. It was then broadcast by ABC until 1965. ABC also rebroadcast the shows from January 1963 until September 1963 under the name "Major Adams, Trailmaster." The plots focused on the journey of the wagon train as it headed west, and on the individual people who were making the trip. Ward Bond played Seth Adams, the wagon master from 1957 to 1961. John McIntire took over the wagonmaster role from 1961 to 1965. Barbara Stanwyck also appeared in the series occasionally. This show ranked number one with viewers during the 1961-1962 television season according to the Nielsen rating service.

Several related products were produced for this long running show, including a board game by Milton Bradley (1960); gun and holster set by Leslie-Henry Co. (1958); a coloring book by Whitman (1959); and a lunch box and thermos by King-Seeley Thermos.

Voyage to the Bottom of the Sea comic (#3). © 1965 Cambridge Productions Inc. and Twentieth Century-Fox Television, Inc. Published by K.K. Publications. $8-10. ✦ *Voyage to the Bottom of the Sea Coloring Book* (#1851-B). © 1965 by Cambridge Productions, Inc. and Twentieth Century-Fox Television, Inc. Published by Western Publishing Company. $15-20.

"Wagon Train Game" by Milton Bradley Company. © 1960 by Revue Productions, Inc. $40-50.

"Wagon Train" lunch box, © 1964 Revue Studios. Made by Thermos. $75-100. ✦ "Wagon Train Frame Tray Puzzle" by Whitman Publishing Company. © 1961 Revue Prod Inc. $15-20.

The Waltons

The first glimpse television audiences had of the Walton family was in a television movie called *The Homecoming—A Christmas Story*. Earl Hamner, Jr. was the creator of the series, which was based on his childhood memories. The drama took place in Virginia in the 1930s, and the stories revolved around a poor rural family as they tried to cope with the hard times of the Depression. The adult family members were the father (played by Ralph Waite), the mother (Michael Learned), Grandpa (Will Geer), and Grandma (Ellen Corby). The children were John Boy (Richard Thomas), Mary Ellen (Judy Norton), Jim-Bob (David S. Harper), Elizabeth (Kami Cotler), Jason (Jon Warmsley), Erin (Mary Elizabeth McDonough), and Ben (Eric Scott). The television series began on CBS in 1972 and ended its run in 1981.

Because of the long run of this show, several products were made to tie in to this series. Mego made a set of dolls featuring Pop, Mom, John Boy, Ellen, Grandpa and Grandma, which are very much in demand by today's collectors. The same company also produced a truck that was 6" x 14" x 6" tall for these dolls. A house was also manufactured for the dolls to live in.

"The Waltons" books published by Whitman. © 1975 by Lorimar Productions, Inc. Set of six books. $3-5 each.

The Waltons: Paper Dolls of All 7 Walton Children (#1995). © 1975 by Lorimar Productions, Inc. Published by Whitman. $20-25. ◆ "The Waltons" lunch box by Aladdin Industries. © 1973 Lorimar Productions, Inc. $30-40.

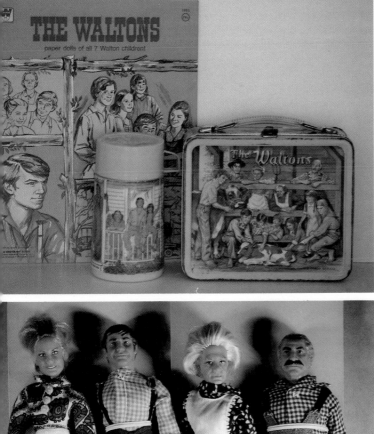

"The Waltons Game" by Milton Bradley. © 1974 Lorimar Productions., Inc. $15-20.

The other Mego dolls from 1975 include dolls representing Mom and Pop and Grandma and Grandpa. All the dolls are 8" tall. $25-30 each.

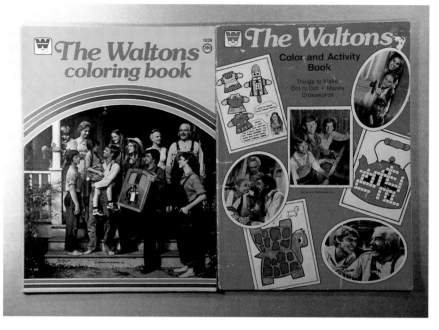

The Waltons Coloring Book (#1028). © MCMLXXV (1975) by Lorimar Productions, Inc. A Whitman Book by Western Publishing Company. ✦ *The Waltons Color and Activity Book* (#1254). © MCMLXXV (1975) by Lorimar Productions, Inc. A Whitman Book by Western Publishing. $10-15 each.

John Boy and Ellen dolls made by Mego in 1975. The vinyl dolls are 8" tall. $20-25 each.

"The Waltons Farmhouse" was produced by Mego in 1975 to be used with its 8" vinyl Walton dolls. © Lorimar Productions, Inc. The house is made of chipboard and measures 24" tall by 35" long. Several pieces of cardboard furniture also came with the house, along with a plastic radio. Pictured with the house are the Mego vinyl Mary Ellen and John Boy dolls. $100+.

Wanted: Dead or Alive

Steve McQueen starred as Josh Randall in the series "Wanted: Dead or Alive." The show aired on CBS from 1958 to 1961. This western used the 1870s frontier as its background. Randall's unique occupation as a bounty hunter provided the action.

Tie-in products include a game made by Lowell Toy Co. in the late 1950s, and the "Mare's Laig Western Rapid Fire Rifle" by Marx Toys. "Mare's Laig" was what Randall's rifle was called.

Welcome Back Kotter

Although Gabriel Kaplan played the leading role of high school teacher Gabe Kotter in the "Welcome back Kotter" series, it was John Travolta who became the most popular actor in the show. The show was set at a Brooklyn high school where Kotter—an alumnus—had returned to be a teacher. His pupils included Vinnie Barbarino (played by Travolta), Frederick "Boom Boom" Washington, Juan Epstein, Arnold Horshack, Rosalie "Hotsie" Totzi and Vernajean Williams. These "sweat hogs" were especially appealing to junior and senior high school students of the era. The show aired on ABC from 1975 to 1979.

Products associated with the show include the following: wind-up bank called "Sweathogs Action Bank" made by Fleetwood Toys (1975); Colorforms (1976); record carrying case by Peerless Vid-Tronic Corp (1976); lunch box by Aladdin Industries (1977); board game by Ideal (1976); and set of dolls by Mattel, Inc. (1976). The dolls were 9" tall and included John Travolta as Barbarino; Gabriel Kaplan as Kotter; Robert Hegyes as Juan Luis Pedro Phillipo de Huevos Epstein; Lawrence-Hilton Jacobs as Freddie "Boom Boom" Washington; and Ron Palillo as Arnold Horshack.

John Travolta doll, made by Chemtoy. The doll is 11 1/4" tall and is made of vinyl. The head is marked "43 / Hong Kong." © John Travolta T.M. Licenses by Meryl Corey Enterprises Ltd. $25-35.

"Welcome Back Kotter Card Game" by Milton Bradley. © 1976 The Wolper Organization, Inc. and the Komack Company, Inc. $10-15.

"Welcome Back, Kotter: The Up Your Nose With a Rubber Hose Game" made by Ideal. © 1976 the Wolper Organization, Inc. and the Komack Company, Inc. $15-20.

"Welcome Back Kotter: Barbarino" paper doll. Made by The Toy Factory. © 1976 The Wolper Organization and the Komack Company, Inc. ✦ *Welcome Back Kotter Coloring Book.* © 1977 the Wolper Organization and the Komack Co., Inc. Whitman Publishing Company. ✦ Kotter paper doll made by The Toy Factory. © 1976 by The Wolper Organization and the Komack Company, Inc. $12-15 each.

Wheel of Fortune

"Wheel of Fortune" was a long-running television game show that premiered on CBS in 1975. A large wheel turned to give directions to the three contestants. The players had to guess a mystery name to win the game. The host was Chuck Woolery. A game was produced to tie in to the game show.

"Wheel of Fortune Game" made by Pressman. © 1985 Pressman Toy Corp. Merve Griffin Enterprises. © Califon Productions Inc. $8-12.

Vanna White doll, approximately 12" tall and made of vinyl. © 1990 by Home Shopping Club, Inc. Twelve outfits were also made for the doll. The television personality gained fame because of her role "turning letters" on the "Wheel of Fortune" show. $20-25.

Wild Bill Hickok

The "Wild Bill Hickok" program first appeared as a syndicated show in 1952. In 1957 it was broadcast on ABC, on which network it continued until 1958 with a total of 113 episodes.

The program was a typical western, based on the adventures of U.S. Marshall Wild Bill Hickok and his partner, Jingles. Andy Devine made a memorable Jingles, and former movie star Guy Madison was a handsome Hickok.

Associated products include the following: lunch box and thermos by Aladdin Industries, Inc. (1955); puzzle by Built-Rite (1955); "Wild Bill Hickok and Jingles Pony Express Game" by Built-Rite (1956); and gun and holster by Leslie-Henry Co.

Wild Kingdom

Marlin Perkins was host of "Mutual of Omaha's Wild Kingdom." The program aired over NBC from 1963 to 1973 and then was continued in syndication. The shows documented the lives of wild animals from different parts of the world.

"Marlin Perkins Zoo Parade Game" was one of several products produced to tie in to this series. It was made by Cadaco.

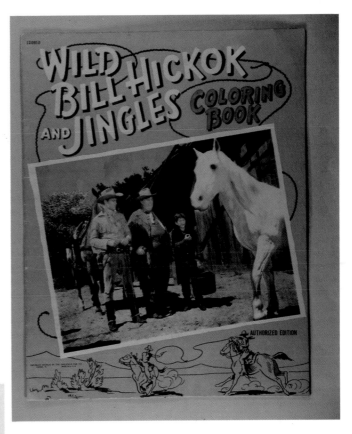

Wild Bill Hickok and Jingles Coloring Book (#1209). © 1953, Saalfield Publishing Company. $25-35.

"Marlin Perkins Wild Kingdom Game." A Teaching Concepts product. © 1977 Don Meier Productions. © 1977 Jeffrey D. Powell. $15-20.

"Marlin Perkins' Wild Kingdom Jigsaw Puzzle" by Whitman. © 1977 Don Meier Productions. $8-15. ✦ Mutual of Omaha's Wild Kingdom Coloring Book. © Don Meier Productions, 1976. A Whitman Book. Western Publishing Company. $10-15. ✦ Marlin Perkins' Wild Kingdom by Esta Meier. A Little Golden Book. Golden Press, Western Publishing Company, Inc. © 1976 by Don Meier Productions. $3-5.

The Wild, Wild West

"The Wild, Wild West" added to the overflow of westerns when CBS began airing the show in 1965. The series lasted until 1969. The interesting twist this show involved was the use of special scientific weapons to catch the bad guys. Robert Conrad as James T. West and Ross Martin as Artemus Gordon were the government intelligence agents who made the plot work.

Associated products include comic books and a lunch box and thermos by Aladdin Industries, Inc. (1969).

Wonder Woman

Trying to repeat the success of "Batman," ABC premiered a new series called "Wonder Woman" in December 1976. The network only carried the show until July of 1977. CBS had better luck when they picked up the program and aired it from 1977 until 1979. The show was based on the comic-book character of the same name. Lynda Carter played the role of Wonder Woman.

Associated products include a doll (pictured) and a vinyl lunch box by Aladdin Industries, Inc. (1977).

Wonder Woman Faces "The Menace of the Mole Men" (#1654-43). © 1975, D.C. Comics, Inc. Published by Western Publishing Company. $15-20. ◆ "Lynda Carter as Wonder Woman" doll, 12" tall and made of vinyl. It was made for Mego in 1976. © 1976 D. C. Comics Inc. The doll includes an extra outfit so the doll also could represent Diana Prince. $35-40.

"Lynda Carter is Wonder Woman Casse-tête Jigsaw Puzzle." Circa late 1970s. $8-12.

Wonderbug

"Wonderbug" was part of "The Krofft Super Show" aired on ABC in 1976. Wonderbug was a car that was a combination of several wrecked cars. Three teenagers–Susan (Anne Sefinger), Barry (David Levy), and C.C. (Anthony Bailey)–used the car to fight against evil.

Wonderbug Rock-A-Bye Buggy Coloring Book (#1006). © 1978 by Sid and Marty Krofft Productions, Inc. Published by Whitman, Western Publishing Company. $10-15.

Wyatt Earp

See "The Life and Legend of Wyatt Earp"

Y

Yogi Bear

"Yogi Bear" was an animated cartoon produced by Hanna-Barbera Productions. Yogi lived in Jellystone National Park and his adventures with the tourists provided some of the plots for the series. Other characters were Boo Boo Bear and the ranger, John Smith. The series was syndicated in 1958 and was also shown as "Yogi's Gang" on ABC from 1973 to 1975.

Related products include puzzles by Whitman (1963); 12" tall hand puppet with a vinyl head (1960s); "Yogi Bear Score-A-Matic Ball Toss Game," Transogram (early 1960s); and 19" tall plush stuffed doll by Knickerbocker (early 1960s).

You Bet Your Life

Although "You Bet Your Life" was primarily a game show, it was much more than that. The host of the series was Groucho Marx and the popularity of the program came from his interaction with the contestants. A secret word was selected for each show, and it was revealed to the audience with the help of a stuffed duck. The contestants were not shown the word, but if any of them accidently repeated the word during the regular question-and-answer game, they increased their winnings.

Two games were made to tie in to this show. They were "Groucho's You Bet Your Life" by Lowell Toy Corp. (1955) and "Groucho TV Quiz Game" by Pressman (1950s).

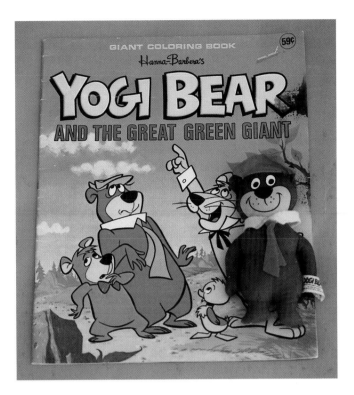

Yogi Bear and the Great Green Giant coloring book. Published by Modern Promotions, A Division of Unisystems, Inc. © 1976 Hanna-Barbera Productions, Inc. $8-12. ✦ Cloth Yogi Bear doll, made in 1972 by Knickerbocker. © Hanna-Barbera Productions, Inc. $8-15.

Groucho Marx ventriloquist doll made by Juro (Goldberger Doll Mfg. Company), dating from 1981. Back of neck reads "Groucho Marx C Eegee Co., Inc." Came with a cigar and glasses. The doll has a vinyl head and hands and a stuffed cloth body. $30-40.

You'll Never Get Rich (Sgt. Bilko)

Phil Silvers created one of television's all-time great characters when he was cast as Sgt. Ernie Bilko in the series "You'll Never Get Rich." The program aired on CBS from 1955 to 1959. The 138 episodes were put into syndication and continued to be popular in this form as well. The show was a situation comedy about an army camp in Roseville, Kansas. Bilko was in charge of the motor pool and he spent every waking hour trying to make money the easy way–without working for it. Paul Ford played his commanding officer.

"Phil Silvers / Sgt. Bilko / CBS Television's You'll Never Get Rich" game. Produced by Gardner Games, © CBS Television Enterprises. Circa 1950s. $50-60.

TV Guide featuring a Phil Silvers cover, dated May 19-25, 1956. Published by Triangle Publications. Also pictured is Elizabeth Fraser. $4-6. ✦ *Sgt. Bilko Coloring Book* (#330). © 1959 Columbia Broadcasting Sys., Inc. Published by Treasure Books, Inc. $25-35.

Z

Zorro

"Zorro" was a Walt Disney Production aired on ABC from 1957 to 1959. The plot involved Don Diego de la Vega, who became Zorro when wearing a mask. He assumed this dual role in order to overcome the evil ruler in power in Monterey, California in 1820. Guy Williams played the dual role in the series.

Because this was a Walt Disney Production, many products were made to tie in to this series. Included were a trace-and-color book by Whitman (1958); a View-Master set from 1958; sheet music with the theme of the show; lunch box and thermos by Aladdin Industries, Inc. (1958); Derringer gun by Marx; puzzles by Jaymar (1958); wristwatch; board game by Whitman (1965); target and dart shooting gun by T. Cohn; paint by number set by Hasbro (1958); and a playset by Marx Toys.

Walt Disney's Zorro comic from December-February 1961. © 1960 Walt Disney Productions. Published by Dell Publishing. $8-10. ✦ A Zorro handkerchief, © Walt Disney Productions. $15-20. ✦ A gum card, © Walt Disney Productions. © T.C.G. PRTD. USA. $2-3.

Walt Disney's Zorro Coloring Book (#1158). From "Zorro" television series based on famous characters created by Johnston McCulley, MCMLVIII (1963), Walt Disney Productions. Published by Whitman Publishing Company. $20-25. ✦ *Walt Disney Presents Zorro* comic. © 1959 Walt Disney Productions. March 1967. $8-10.

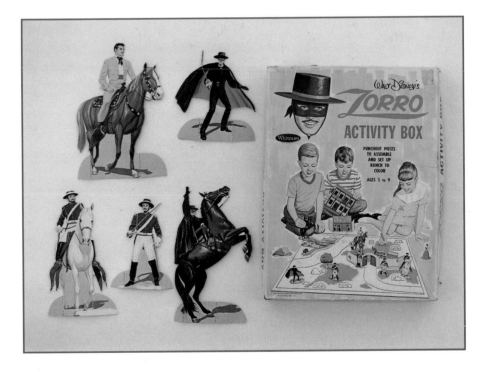

"Walt Disney's Zorro Activity Box" by Whitman. Includes punchout pieces to assemble and set up, and a ranch to color. © 1965 Walt Disney Productions. $30-40.

Bibliography

Axe, John. *The Encyclopedia of Celebrity Dolls.* Cumberland, MD: Hobby House Press, Inc., 1983.

Brooks, Tim; Marsh, Earle. *The Complete Directory to Prime Time Network TV Shows 1946- Present.* New York: Ballantine books, 1988.

Brown, Les. *Les Brown's Encyclopedia of Television 3rd Edition.* Detroit: Gale Research Inc., 1992.

Brown, Les. *The New York Times Encyclopedia of Television.* Times Books, 1977.

Buxton, Frank; Owen, Bill. *The Big Broadcast 1920-1950.* New York: Avon Books, 1973.

Campbell, Robert. *The Golden Years of Broadcasting.* New York: Charles Scribner's Sons. Rutledge Book, 1976.

"Christmas Morning" catalogs. 1850 Crown Rd., Suite1 1 1 1, Dallas, TX, 75234-9414.

"52 Girls Collectibles" catalogs. P.O. Box 36, Morral, OH. 43337.

Fischer, Stuart. *Kids' TV: The First 25 Years.* New York: Fact on File Publications, 1983.

Foulke, Jan. *11th Blue Book Dolls and Values.* Cumberland, Maryland: Hobby House Press, 1993.

Gaylesworth, Thomas G. *Television in America: A Pictorial History.* New York: Exeter Books, 1986.

Gianakos, Larry James. *Television Drama Series A Comprehensive Chronical Programming 1980-1982.* Metuchen, N.J.: The Scarecrow Press, Inc., 1983.

Gianakos, Larry James. *Television Drama Series A Comprehensive Chronical Programming 1982-1984.* Metuchen, N.J.: The Scarecrow Press, Inc., 1987.

Hake, Ted. *Hake's Guide to TV Collectibles.* Radnor, PA: Wallace-Homestead, 1990.

"Hake's Americana" catalogs. P.O. Box 1444, York, Pa 17405.

"Hi-De-Ho Collectibles" catalogs. P. O. Box 2841, Gaithersburg, Maryland. 20886-2841.

Longest, David. *Character Toys and Collectibles Second Series.* Paducah, KY: Collector Books, 1987.

Shulman, Arthur; Youman, Roger. *How Sweet It Was.* New York: Bonanza Books, 1966.

Smith, Patricia. *Doll Values: Antique to Modern Tenth Edition.* Paducah, KY: Collector Books, 1994.

Terrace, Vincent. *The Complete Encyclopedia of Television Programs 1947-1979 Vol. I, Vol. II.* New York: A.S. Barnes and Co., 1979.

Terrace, Vincent. *Television Character and Story Facts.* Jefferson, North Carolina: McFarland and Company, Inc., 1993.

Woodcock, Jean. *Paper Dolls of Famous Faces.* Binghamton, New York: Printed by Niles and Phippe, 1974.

Young, Mary. *A Collector's Guide to Paper Dolls.* Paducah, KY: Collector Books, 1980.

Young, Mary. *A Collector's Guide to Paper Dolls Second Series.* Paducah, KY: Collector Books, 1984.

Zillner, Dian. *Collectible Coloring Books.* West Chester, Pennsylvania: Schiffer Publishing Ltd., 1992.

Hoppy milk carton made by Producers. © Wm Boyd. $10-15. ✦ Hopalong Cassidy thermos made by Aladdin Industries, Inc. in 1950. $30-35. ✦ Hopalong Cassidy china cup, circa early 1950s. By W.S. George. At least four different styles were produced. $15-20.

Sources For Television Memorabilia

The Antique Trader
P.O. Box 1050
Dubuque, Iowa 52004
Weekly Publication $32

Baby Boomer Collectibles
922 Churchill St. Suite #1
Waupaca, Wisconsin 54981
One year for $18.95, $4.95 for sample.

Collectors United
P.O. Box 1160
Chataworth, GA. 30705
$24 for 12 issues

52 Girls Collectibles
P.O. Box 36
Morral, Ohio 43337
Mail Order Catalog
$10 per year, single issue $2

Frasher's Doll Auctions, Inc.
Rt. 1–Box 142
Oak Grove, Missouri 64075
$25 for doll auction catalogs

Hake's Americana and Collectibles
P.O. Box 1444
York, PA 17405
Sample catalog $7.50; five issues
one year subscription $30

Hi-De-Ho Collectibles
P.O. Box 2841
Gaithersburg, Maryland 20886
Sales catalogs

Paper Collector's Marketplace
P.O. Box 12857
Scandinavia, WI 54977-0128
Monthly magazine $17.95

Toy Collector and Price Guide
700 E. State St.
Iola, Wisconsin 54990
$16.95 for 6 issues

Toy Shop
700 E. State St.
Iola, Wisconsin 54990
$23.95 for 26 issues